SMALL FIRMS

NATIONAL SMALL FIRMS'
POLICY AND RESEARCH CONFERENCES

Available from:
Paul Chapman Publishing
144 Liverpool Road
London
N1 1LA

Telephone 0171 609 5315/6
Fax 0171 700 1057

Towards the Twenty-First Century: *The Challenge for Small Business*
edited by
Martyn Robertson, Elizabeth Chell and Colin Mason
(ISBN 0 9519230 0 5)
Selected papers from the 13th National Small Firms' Policy and
Research Conference 1990.

Small Enterprise Development: *Policy and Practice in Action*
edited by
Kevin Caley, Elizabeth Chell, Francis Chittenden and Colin Mason
(ISBN 1 85396 215 5).
Selected papers from the 14th National Small Firms' Policy and
Research Conference 1991.

Small Firms: *Recession and Recovery*
edited by
Francis Chittenden, Martyn Robertson and David Watkins
(ISBN 1 85396 249 X).
Selected papers from the 15th National Small Firms' Policy and
Research Conference 1992.

Small Firms: *Partnership for Growth*
edited by
Francis Chittenden, Martyn Robertson and Ian Marshall
(ISBN 1 85396 288 0).
Selected papers from the 16th National Small Firms' Policy and
Research Conference 1993.

SMALL FIRMS

Contributions to Economic Regeneration

edited by
Robert Blackburn
and Peter Jennings

Published on behalf of
The Institute for Small Business Affairs
by
Paul Chapman Publishing

P·C·P

Paul Chapman
Publishing Ltd

Copyright © 1996, ISBA

Paul Chapman Publishing Ltd
144 Liverpool Road
London
N1 1LA

British Library Cataloguing in Publication Data

Small firms: contributions to economic regeneration.–
    (National Small Firms' Policy and Research Conferences)
    1. Small business
    I. Blackburn, Robert A., 1957– II. Jennings, P.
    338.6'42

    ISBN 1 85396 339 9

Typeset by Dorwyn Ltd, Rowlands Castle, Hants.
Printed and bound in Great Britain

A B C D E F G H   9 8 7 6

CONTENTS

FOREWORD

The success of small business is vital to the UK economy. A strong SME sector is vital to a flexible and buoyant economy, creating jobs, providing the foundations for large companies of the future and contributing to the UK's long term growth and international competitiveness.

The most fundamental distinction for small firms is between those seeking to grow and other small firms. Many small business owners are in business to earn a comfortable living and are unwilling, or unable, to take on the risks and responsibilities of growth. There is a gap, however, between those wishing to grow, and those able to achieve it. Closing this gap between expectation and reality, even by only a fraction, would have a major effect on employment and output.

In recent years it has been recognised that small businesses need to improve their business skills to help them survive and grow. Possession of a qualification or attendance on a training programme, however, does not ensure economic survival and nor does it imply that those who do not undertake training are doomed to fail. Running a business is unlike any other job. It requires a high level of skills in a variety of disciplines, from accountancy and sales to production and personnel. Small business owners frequently lack a broad range of skills, particularly in the case of technology industries, where entrepreneurs have often left large companies to establish their own firms with their specialist skills, but lack the all-round knowledge necessary to compete effectively.

The challenge facing small businesses is related to the environment in which they have to operate and survive. A key factor in achieving economic progress is long-term stability of the economy. Instability makes it difficult to plan, and the inability of small businesses to forecast accordingly is often their downfall. The current economic environment provides an ideal platform for sustainable growth. Small businesses are now operating in the most benign economic conditions for thirty years. In a low inflation economy, however, a small business cannot afford to makes mistakes, as their losses will not be eroded by rising prices, as was often the case in the past.

Banks must also play their part. The ability of small businesses to raise appropriate finance is vital to the interests of the national economy. We have moved away from minimum lending rates to base rate-linked finance. More businesses are seeing the advantages of term lending, rather than relying on overdraft finance. We will continue to look for innovative financing options to suit a growing range of businesses, including equity finance, factoring, invoice discounting, hire purchase, leasing and vehicle hire and trade finance as well as the more traditional loans and overdrafts.

At Midland, we believe in the philosophy of community banking. Our local managers and staff have an important role to play in social and economic activity. Many act as school governors, directors of Training and Enterprise Councils, or are involved with their local Chamber of Commerce or Business Link. We have recognised the desire of business owners to have bank managers with business expertise and the authority to take decisions based in their local High Street branches. By returning our senior managers to branch positions, decisions are made quickly at local level, by experienced banks with a knowledge of the local trading environment.

All of us, including researchers and policy makers, as well as central and local government, have a common interest in finding ways to improve the position of SMEs. Partnership is the key. By working in partnership at national, regional and local levels, we can provide the clear focus and concentrated effort that will facilitate the growth, employment and regeneration prospects small businesses can provide.

Midland is delighted to support the 17th ISBA National Small Firms' Policy and Research Conference.

Mike Conroy
Small Business Services
Midland Bank plc

Contributors

Brian Abbott, School of Human Resource Management, Kingston Business School, Kingston University, Kingston upon Thames, Surrey KT2 7LB.

Richard Barkham, Department of Land Management and Development, University of Reading, Whitenights, PO Box 219, Reading RG6 6AW.

Robert A Blackburn, Small Business Research Centre, Kingston University, Kingston Hill, Kingston upon Thames, Surrey KT2 7LB.

Francis Chittenden, Business Development Centre, Manchester Business School, University of Manchester, Booth Street West, Manchester M15 6PB.

Patrick Coveney, New College/Templeton College, Oxford University, Oxford OX1 3BN.

James Curran, Small Business Research Centre, Kingston University, Kingston Hill, Kingston upon Thames, Surrey KT2 7LB.

Margaret Fletcher, Scottish Enterprise Foundation, University of Stirling, Stirling FK9 4LA.

Ted Fuller, Knowledge Systems Research Centre, Durham University Business School, Mill Hill Lane, Durham DH1 3LB.

Suzan Gunn, Hertfordshire Training and Enterprise Council, Business Link Hertfordshire, 45 Grosvenor Road, St Albans, Hertfordshire AL1 3AW.

Eric Hanvey, Northern Ireland Economic Research Centre, Belfast, 46–48 University Road, Belfast BT7 1NJ.

Simon Harris, Department of Management and Organisation, University of Stirling, Stirling FK9 4LA.

Mark Hart, School of Public Policy Economics and Law, University of Ulster, Shore Road, Newtownabbey, County Antrim BT37 OQB.

Peter L Jennings, Business School, Southampton Institute, East Park Terrace, Southampton SO14 0YN.

Paul Joyce, Business School, University of North London, 166–220 Holloway Road, London N7 8DB.

Syeda Masooda Mukhtar, Business Development Centre, Manchester Business School, University of Manchester, Booth Street West, Manchester M15 6PB.

David North, Centre for Enterprise and Economic Development Research, Middlesex University, Queensway, Enfield, Middx EN3 4SF.

Panikkos Poutziouris, Business Development Centre, Manchester Business School, University of Manchester, Booth Street West, Manchester M15 6PB.

Martyn Robertson, Leeds Business School, Leeds Metropolitan University, 80 Woodhouse Lane, Leeds LS2 8AB.

Christine Seaman, Central London Training and Enterprise Council, 12 Grosvenor Crescent, London SW1X 7EE.

David Smallbone, Centre for Enterprise and Economic Development Research, Middlesex University, Queensway, Enfield, Middx EN3 4SF.

Hamish Stevenson, Venture Capital Report Ltd, Boston Road, Henley on Thames, Oxfordshire RG9 1DY.

Adrian Woods, Department of Management Studies, Brunel University, Uxbridge, Middlesex UB8 3PH.

1.

INTRODUCTION: THE CONTRIBUTION OF SMALL FIRMS TO ECONOMIC REGENERATION

Robert Blackburn and Peter Jennings

BACKGROUND

It is now recognised universally that the contribution of small and medium enterprises (SMEs) to employment and output in the economy has expanded over the last two decades.[1] The most recent aggregate data show that this trend has continued unabated, despite the general recessionary conditions of the early 1990s, and illuminate even more strongly the role of SMEs in the economy (Table 1).

Table 1: Businesses Employment and Turnover By Size of Business, end 1993%

Size band	Businesses	Employment ('000)	Turnover (£m ex VAT)
0	72.3	14.6	2.3
1–9	22.0	13.5	6.7
10–49	4.6	15.9	10.9
50–99	0.5	6.3	9.1
100–199	0.2	5.8	15.8
200+	0.2	43.8	55.0
N=	3,581,469	20,607	3,593,132

Source: Department of Trade and Industry (1995a)

These aggregate patterns indicating the growth in the economic contribution of SMEs continue to provide researchers with a multitude of areas for investigation and policy makers with an agenda for intervention. The importance of research on SMEs is crucial, not only as a means of understanding SMEs but as a basis for sound policy formulation.

The 17th National Small Firms' Policy and Research Conference, hosted by Sheffield Hallam University's Business School, had as a central theme the contribution of small business to economic generation. The Conference attracted a variety of contributions, and this book provides a selection of papers deemed significant in terms of raising our knowledge, level of theorising and contribution to policy.

Small business research derives from a number of sources and the contributions to this volume are no exception. It is this breadth of research and the seemingly unlimited avenues for investigation which make study of the small business both academically interesting and challenging. Earlier contributions studying the role of small businesses to economic regeneration have emphasised their importance in the innovation process and the contribution of entrepreneurs to generating a swarm of innovations as an economy comes out of recession (Schumpeter, 1934). More recently some writers have suggested that small businesses have become part of a post-Fordist economy, in which the old industrial order has been dismantled, to be replaced by a more flexible production and distribution methods (eg Murray, 1989; Pyke, 1992). Indeed, some authors have argued strongly that specific variations of this newer form of production, in the form of 'industrial districts', provide ways in which industrial societies can regenerate their economies (Hirst and Zeitlin, 1989). This theme of smaller businesses contributing to economic development has also been discussed from a spatial perspective where some recent evidence suggests that even in unfavourable regional environments, small business growth is possible (Vaessen and Keeble, 1995).

Alternatively, in relation to small firms and economic regeneration some have cautioned against high expectations of small firms (Binks and Jennings, 1986). Also attempts to replicate the science park model of local economic regeneration in the USA have been viewed as a failure in the UK, particularly in their inability to develop strong local linkages with academic institutions (Massey et al., 1992). More pessimistically, some authors have gone so far as to question the more fashionable depictions of the new economic order, instead arguing that there remains an uneven power relationship between small firms and large, multinational conglomerates (Harrison, 1994). Whether or not small businesses are emerging in the UK in the spatial and network configurations proposed by some authors, however, remains to be confirmed by empirical evidence. The problem gap between our level of empirical knowledge and general theories, however, remains wide and much more research and ingenuity are required to test the many assertions in the literature and expectations of policy makers.

Critics of government policy have pointed out its incoherent and piecemeal approach during the last two decades (eg Storey, 1994). The most recent White Paper *Competitiveness: Forging Ahead* (Department of Trade and Industry, 1995b) has, however, positioned smaller businesses as the keystone in the Government's economic regeneration policy. This White Paper has been supplemented with *Competitiveness: Helping Smaller Firms* (Department of Trade and Industry, 1995c), which illustrates the significance of small businesses to overall Government economic policy. In practical terms, this continued interest from a policy perspective has been manifested in the newly created Business Links.

For researchers these policy initiatives and sustained, if not heightened, interest in small businesses at a national, European and international level provide ample opportunities for an expansion in research.[2] These opportunities arise not merely from straightforward evaluation exercises of specific policies, but from the opportunity to contribute to the debates, for example, regarding job generation and the desirability and efficacy of selectivity in policy. The recently completed ESRC initiative on small firms (see for example Storey, 1994) illustrates the high level of interest in, and government support of, research in this field. This pluralism in both the background of the research and issues for investigation is reflected in the themes of this book. These chapters are written by experts in their field, from the academic or practitioners' standpoint, and represent a major contribution to contemporary debates.

OVERVIEW OF CHAPTERS

The financing of small firms is among the most researched subject in the literature and one of the most controversial, frequently cited by owner-managers as an obstacle to growth and expansion (Keasey and Watson, 1993). This volume provides three contributions to this literature, each with a particular new angle. In Chapter 2, Fletcher focuses on the bank-business relationship and the process of how bank managers make lending decisions to business propositions. Fletcher's chapter is important, not only in terms of the actual results and their implications, but as a means of illustrating how we can build on existing literature and develop research methodologies. Thus, Fletcher seeks to go beyond the realms of official bank policies and actually to provide different bankers with the same business proposition, to allow a detailed investigation of decision making. By focusing on the processes of decision making, rather than just outcomes, Fletcher provides an interesting insight to the real world of lending and its complexities. Some interesting comparisons between her study in Scotland and that of bank managers in England by Deakins and Hussain (1991) are also provided including the relative importance of different criteria in the lending decision. This chapter provides a significant contribution to our knowledge of how banks make lending decisions and provides some recommendations on how these processes may be improved. Ultimately, this research will contribute to a strengthening of the bank-business relationship as well as to overcoming fundamental problems such as poor information asymmetries discussed in other studies (Binks, 1991).

Access to venture capital, that is the provision of equity finance and business skills for business, continues to attract research and policy interest. This is no surprise since the rise in venture capital investments in the United Kingdom has been dramatic, one estimate indicating a rise from £66m in 1980 to £989m in 1991 (Storey, 1994, p221). This book provides evidence on two different aspects of the venture capital market: from a survey of the suppliers of institutional venture capital, and a survey of those involved in providing 'informal' venture capital or 'business angels'. In Chapter 3, using face-to-face methods, Harris examines the management approach of six directors of venture capital organisations. His study reveals a more sympathetic approach to assessing business propositions by venture capitalists than many outsiders or business owners often perceive. Harris points out the very strong proactive approach by venture capitalists, injecting a wide range of resources into the business, rather than merely selecting businesses for investment passively. As a result, Harris argues that it is not only the financial support which benefits the business but the range of other support which accompanies the investment.

Amongst the more recently discussed forms of equity investment is that deriving from 'business angels'. This form of investor comprises '. . . private individuals who provide risk capital directly to new and growing businesses in which they have no prior connection' (Mason and Harrison, 1994, p68). In the USA this market is relatively well developed and has been the subject of extensive research, with some reporting that this is the largest form of external equity for small businesses (Gaston, 1989). Mason and Harrison estimate that SMEs have raised about £2 billion from the informal venture capital market, which is approximately twice the amount by the institutional investors. Apart from the research in the UK by Mason and Harrison (1994) our knowledge of informal venture capital is currently rather limited.

In Chapter 4, Stevenson and Coveney provide evidence from a mail survey of business angels and develop a typology of angels. One of their key findings is that the angels report a lack of suitable business proposals, rather than of funds for investment, echoing those researchers who suggest that the finance gap, in the sense of market failure in the supply of available finance, may be overstated (for discussion see Storey, 1994, pp239–252). Their typology of business angels provides a breakthrough in our thinking on informal equity. Business angels have different motivations, experiences and funding levels available. This typology not only raises our awareness but may also assist policy-makers and businesses to target particular types of angels thus improving the informal equity process. Stevenson and Coveney conclude with a strong argument for a national network of angels.

Section Two focuses on the broader issue of the strategic performance of small business. Of course, many scholars of small business would argue that 'business strategy' is something of an oxymoron depicting owner-managers as essentially non-strategic thinking. Yet, the changing nature of the small business population, especially the move towards professional, service sector businesses (Keeble et al., 1992) and the continued high death rates of small business (see Storey, 1994, Ch 4) place business strategy among the forefront of research.

In Chapter 5, Joyce, Woods and Seaman focus on identifying different kinds of strategic management in small businesses and their benefits. The development and applications of strategic management models to small businesses are significant in the finding that there is some correlation between strategic planning and business performance. Planning in a generic sense is often regarded as irrelevant or inappropriate to the small business, especially by owner-managers themselves, and the very antithesis of the dynamic flexible firm operating in rapidly changing business environment. Joyce, Woods and Seaman, however, find the opposite to be the case. Those businesses with a formal or written business plan, that is the more strategic planning orientated firms, were more likely to be engaged in process and product innovations. This finding gives rise to the authors concluding that more strategic planning should be undertaken in smaller businesses, including more attention to a self assessment of the overall performance of the business.

In any planning exercise, consideration of all known factors is essential for the best possible outcome. However, the business environment facing smaller firms is often difficult to assess let alone predict with any level of accuracy. In the first part of his chapter, Robertson points out the variation in the contribution to GDP by SMEs between countries. For example, Japanese SMEs contributed 60% of total GDP compared with 32% in the UK. In other words, while the contribution of the small business to employment in the UK has expanded in the 1980s and 1990s, this has not been matched by similar increases in output. While the causes of these differences are debatable Robertson focuses on the vulnerability of SMEs in the UK. Businesses are subject to a variety of external factors which are beyond the business owners' control including late payment and high compliance costs involved with government regulation. Internally also, Robertson suggests that constraints on business derive from the owners and their *modus operandi* themselves. The final part of Robertson's polemical contribution looks at the future for SMEs. He points out the increasing internationalisation of business, although among smaller firms there is a lower propensity to export, and suggests that this may pose a threat to smaller businesses. A recent trend in the 1990s has been the outsourcing of activities especially by corporate organisations, and Robertson suggests that this may pave the way for new economic networks which may be conducive to small business activity. However, there is a price to be paid to access these networks and Robertson implores small businesses to become much more proactive in training and quality management. After considering these and other factors influencing the future of small businesses, Robertson exercises caution in delivering a definitive view. Yet, overall this chapter offers an alternative approach and view to other exercises which have endeavoured to understand the future for SMEs (Curran and Blackburn, 1990 and 1991; Ragab, 1992).

This theme of the relationship between small firms in their wider environment is continued in Section Three, which provides different perspectives on small firms in the economy. Obviously, a major determinant of small business performance is the condition of the wider macro economic environment in which they operate. In Chapter 7, Fuller focuses on the changes in the number of VAT registered businesses, with a view to analysing their contribution to economic regeneration during a recession. A central point made by Fuller is the heterogeneity of small businesses, and this leads him to undertake a sector analysis of changes in business VAT registrations having turnovers between £51,000 and £5m. Overall, the analysis shows huge variations in the stock of businesses by main sector and more importantly four digit Standard Industrial Classification level. While the chapter provides some useful findings, what is more significant is that the data help to illustrate the variety of factors influencing the continued rise in small scale capital. For example, the sector with the largest percentage rise in businesses in the period studied was 'Opticians', a finding which is largely a result of deregulation of services and recent inclusion under VAT. Thus, changes in government policies undoubtedly influence the recorded number of small businesses and this instance represents mainly a transfer of economic activities rather than a genuine reflection of an upsurge in entrepreneurial energies. Other transfers in economic activity, resulting from organisational restructuring within the private sector, are reflected in the rise in dairymen (Boyle, 1994).[3] In contrast, the rise in computer services, for example (Keeble et al., 1992), illustrates the opportunities deriving from changes in technology and represents a genuine expansion in economic activity where smaller businesses can compete with the corporate sector. In the second part of his analysis, Fuller provides evidence on the trends in businesses by turnover size. The analysis reveals an increase in the percentage of larger small firms, although again there are vast sector differences. While analysis of VAT data has its limitations (Bannock and Ganguly, 1985), this chapter is illustrative of how much aggregate data may be used to provide an important background to small business trends.

A major weakness in small business research is its tendency to rely on snapshot surveys of samples which, although providing useful cross-sectional data, do not raise our level of understanding of how businesses change over time. Such a weakness inhibits both the ability to theorise on small businesses and the development of appropriately tailored policies for different types of business. As a result, models of business development often suffer from a reliance on information from different businesses at different stages of development (Stanworth and Curran, 1976) despite the continued popularity of some models using this method (eg Churchill and Lewis, 1983). Building models of business development is much more complex than has hitherto been acknowledged, and we should refrain from making leaps towards building models until our knowledge base is adequate. This involves, at least, longitudinal studies of businesses.

North and Smallbone, in Chapter 8, use evidence from a longitudinal study of small businesses to follow their experience over a period of four years to address the contribution small businesses can make to the economic base of their region. A major perceived advantage of smaller businesses in an economy is their level of economic embeddedness within their locality. North and Smallbone focus attention on the role of established enterprises towards employment, their 'export' orientation and innovativeness thus providing a major contribution to knowledge on small business development. Between 1990 and 1994, their survey found on average a relatively high survival rate of businesses of over 8 out of 10. This is partly explained by the relative maturity of these businesses, compared with, for example, data on business start-ups which estimate that over a third deregister during the first three years of operation (Department of Trade and Industry, 1995d). In terms of job generation, the authors seek to contribute to the debate on whether a large number of jobs are created by a few firms or spread across a wider number of firms. Their evidence tends to support the latter, although they do emphasise the importance of variations according to the sector context of the businesses. The notion of a few jobs being generated by many businesses has support elsewhere from the service sector (Curran et al., 1995). This finding is significant for our thinking on policy and especially for debate regarding selectivity. Alternatively, the pattern of job generation identified in these latest surveys may be a reflection of a response to slow increases in output as the economy emerges from recession. Similarly, the latest policy fashion is to support already established businesses[4] yet these authors find the greatest contribution to jobs coming from younger businesses. Finally, the theme of an increased sensitivity to sector consideration in our theorising and policy receives a further fillip in this chapter. On all aspects of their research results, North and Smallbone find significant variations in business performance. Clearly, policy requires a balanced approach and the advocates of targeting need to take these findings into consideration. The chapter illustrates the strength of a longitudinal element in research design and can act as a model for further studies.

The ability of public policy to affect small business economic activity levels occurs in a variety of ways. A major development in the last decade has been the privatisation of many government activities, including the rise in the contracting out of some local authority services notably through compulsory competitive tendering (CCT). While contract relations between private businesses and small firms have received some attention, and are often attributed as one of the factors behind the revival of smaller firms (eg Shutt and Whittington, 1987), the effect of contracting-out of local authority services has hitherto received no research attention. In Chapter 9, Abbott, Blackburn and Curran report results from a pioneering investigation of the effect of the contracting-out of services on SMEs in four London local authorities. At a national level this market is estimated to be over £2 billion. However, their research finds a poor level of involvement in CCT contracts by

SMEs, despite their 'snowball' research design and attempt to track any subcontracting activities. However, on a more positive note for small firms the authors anticipate a greater degree of involvement once this market stabilises. For example, they find that although small businesses struggle to meet the tendering requirements and contract sizes issued, in practice their advantages of flexibility and close knowledge of specific local market conditions help win contracts. Looking to the future, the authors conclude that the opening of professional services to CCT may provide better opportunities because of the strength and growth of small firms in these sectors. Clearly further research is required in this field before we can move towards a satisfactory level of theorising and policy prescription.

The final section of the book examines growth and development issues facing small businesses. One feature of small firms research is the variety of methodologies and disciplines it attracts. In Chapter 10, Barkham, Hart and Hanvey report findings on a quantitative study of growth in small manufacturing firms. One weakness of research on small firms is an absence of multivariate statistical approaches which can take into account the relative weight of different factors in the growth process, reflecting Storey's overview (Storey, 1994). Understanding growth in the small firm involves considering a variety of phenomena and it is because of this sheer complexity that our knowledge and level of theorising on business growth is weak. Of course, growth in the small firm beyond the 'micro' size (0–9) is an exceptional rather than a common occurrence, but this should not deter us from attempting to understand this concept. Barkham, Hart and Hanvey classify the influences on growth into three groups: company characteristics, entrepreneur characteristics and business strategy. What is important about their modelling process is that it illustrates the difficulties of attempting to unpack the influences on growth. Their model produces a respectable R^2 of 0.51, thus taking into account at least a half of the variation in business growth within their sample. However, the predictive power of such statistical models is currently limited and further development of such techniques is necessary to increase their ability to model the real world. Whether this will ever improve our modelling capabilities is questionable, because of the multifaceted nature of the influences on business performance. However, what the statistical models do provide is a useful overview of factors related to business performance thus acting as guidance for qualitative research, for example being interested in the internal processes of the firm and seeking to understand the causes of certain outcomes. Modelling small business growth is also important from a policy perspective and in its crudest terms academics are often pushed to answer the question where should support service resources be deployed to make the maximum impact? Isolating the individual components of business performance would certainly help target policy towards these aspects of business.

Of late, one factor receiving increasing attention in the performance of business is the issue of quality within that business. Nobody would disagree that the quality of the businesses' services or products is central to business survival. Yet, the more recent fashion in quality has been an emphasis on control over the processes within the business rather than merely inspection procedures of final goods and services. Formal quality standards (namely BS5750, ISO9000 and EN29000) are regarded by many as routes to success for business (Ashton and Jackson, 1994; Department of Trade and Industry, 1992) although this view has been received somewhat sceptically in relation to smaller firms (North et al., 1995).[5] In Chapter 11, Chittenden, Mukhtar and Poutziouris provide valuable further evidence on quality and small firms from a multi-staged postal and telephone survey of businesses. Their results show a lack of adoption of BS5750 in SMEs, with around 10% using the standard. However, within their sample they found a higher incidence of registration or implementation among larger small firms. What is significant in their results is that formal quality standards are acknowledged by some business owners as important but not necessarily in the same spirit as the origins of the standards. Owner-managers cited marketing and competitive reasons for adoption of the standard as well as internal efficiency. However, it is the judgement of Chittenden, Mukhtar and Poutziouris that BS5750 and other quality standards should not be imposed on small firms and need not necessarily lead to improvements in the performance of such businesses. This resistance by small business owners to formalities and government regulation has been a theme running throughout research ever since the Bolton Report. Business owners tend to be resistant to outside regulation and seek external advice on matters only in rare circumstances (Curran and Blackburn, 1994).

Changes in the framework and content of small business support, culminating most recently in the establishment of Business Links, have been plentiful during the past decade or so. The DTI has described the Business Link concept as a revolution in the delivery of support services (Department of Trade and Industry, 1995c; 1995d). Certainly, providing businesses with a single point of access to a range of services remained a notion until the establishment of the Business Links. It is too early to provide a balanced assessment of these new bodies, and indeed there are some to still be established. Yet, if the Business Links are to be a success one of the key ingredients will be their credibility in the minds of other business advisers or intermediaries including bankers, accountants and solicitors. Failure to convince these network brokers may lead to a serious weakness in the application of the 'one-stop-shop' notion and a breakdown in the referral system. In Chapter 12, Gunn provides an analysis of information from the operation of a business support network in Hertfordshire. Her research style, as a manager in a Business Link, is very much action learning oriented. She argues strongly for a proactive approach to forge connections with other intermediaries and a regular programme of updating to explain, for example to bank managers, changes in the support infrastructure. Her contribution provides a useful insight into the operation of the emerging support network offering views on a TEC and Business Link from both intermediaries and business owners themselves. Whether the emerging new infrastructure arrangements will help overcome some of the 'fortress enterprise' attitudes of small business owners (Curran and Blackburn, 1994) remains to be seen. Yet the latest initiatives in small business support have provided an impetus not seen since the Bolton Report.

MAJOR THEMES AND RECOMMENDATIONS FOR FURTHER RESEARCH

The 11 very different contributions to this text illustrate the wide variety of alternative perspectives and sources of small business research. Each contribution has concentrated upon one specific area and has drawn detailed conclusions and presented detailed recommendations applicable to that area. However, there are a number of general conclusions and recommendations which can be found underpinning and intricately interwoven within each separate contribution. These conclusions and recommendations have a much wider applicability and, in many ways, establish the agenda for future research within the small business sector.

Researching the small business sector is an extremely complex and difficult task given the paucity of available, published secondary data. Whilst VAT statistics are considered to be a good proxy for UK small firms it must be remembered that a significant proportion of very small (micro) businesses do not necessarily need to register for VAT and are therefore excluded from such analyses. This is particularly significant given that young, very small (micro) firms show greatest relative growth potential although older, larger firms grow less spectacularly but in a more sustained and therefore less risky manner.

The SME sector holds the key to future growth and prosperity for the UK economy as older, traditional industries die. There remains considerable uncertainty concerning which types of small firms offer the best job generation potential although it is known that new small firms are a relatively unstable source of job creation. During the financial year 1993/94 about 50% of all small firms experienced a fall in turnover with about 30% reporting growth. At the beginning of 1994 business start-ups exceeded closures, leading to an increase in the stock of UK small firms for the first time since the late 1980s.

The SME market cannot be considered to be homogeneous and, therefore, a generic, universal support policy may satisfy no individual segment. At the same time, current support service provision is in need of rationalisation to improve coordination and specialisation. There is broad support for current efforts to rationalise and simplify support services and this may be achieved through the concept of Business Links. However, with regard to this initiative, there are a number of reservations concerning:

- the success of asking 'competing' organisations to collaborate and act cooperatively in sharing contacts and avoiding service duplication;
- the reactions of organisations whose markets are threatened by local Business Links;
- the quality and training of personal business advisers (PBAs);
- the level of support for marketing Business Link services both from central government and from within Business Links themselves;
- the criteria for and methods of assessment of performance in the short, medium and long term.

If these developments are to be successful in raising owner-manager awareness and take-up of the available services it is vital that Business Links do not become just another layer in the support system hierarchy. Equally, support services must not be targeted solely upon start-ups. Established medium sized enterprises which have growth potential are in just as much need of help and support. Indeed, as already mentioned, the 1995 Government White Papers (DTI, 1995b and c) concerning competitiveness have emphasised the desirability of targeting scarce resources upon those small firms with maximum growth potential. This has led to highly polarised opinions of the concept of targeting support or making support widely available for all.

Of course, survival, growth and success amongst small firms, however these may be defined, are not solely dependent upon the availability of high quality, relevant support services. SME development and growth is a complex, multi-faceted phenomenon. However, it appears that the characteristics of the owner-manager, and especially their level of competence in strategic management, are an important influence. Owner-managers therefore have a responsibility to develop basic strategic management skills which will enable them to manage their business without continuous recourse to consultants or PBAs. It must be recognised, however, that strategic management in SMEs is a very different process from strategic planning often found in larger organisations.

The problems and difficulties encountered both in researching SMEs and by entrepreneurs and owner-managers themselves, highlight a number of areas which require further, substantial research. An obvious area for future research concerns the effectiveness of training and development programmes. As yet there is no clear evidence of a positive correlation between management education and skills and growth in small firms. The general received wisdom would suggest that this is the case and a whole industry has been created based upon this assumption. Notwithstanding the methodological difficulties of establishing a link, future research must continue to evaluate the effectiveness of the myriad of interventions aimed at raising managerial skills and competencies. Certainly the challenges and opportunities brought to business by newer technologies, including telematics, have implications for the training needs of owner-managers, not merely from a technical point of view but more importantly for shifting to knowledge based business development.[6]

Access to suitable finance remains an obstacle to growth and development for many small firms. However, representatives of many financial institutions argue that there is no shortage of funds but instead only a shortage of high quality business proposals presented in an effective manner. New small businesses in particular tend to suffer from adverse selection problems when seeking to raise finance through banks. This can impose additional financial constraints which increase pressure on management. Improving risk assessment and decision-making techniques for bank managers may help to overcome adverse selection problems. Accordingly, banks and other financial institutions should be more proactive in helping new small firms develop quality business plans and in facilitating better financial management in the longer term. Interestingly, Scottish banks appear to adopt more consistent policies towards assisting start-ups than their English counterparts.

As an alternative source of external finance business angels can make an effective contribution to start-ups via Business Links. Naturally, business angels adopt a rigorous approach to evaluating proposals and again restrictions on further investment are more likely to be due to a lack of high quality proposals than a lack of available funding. Nevertheless, external venture capital providers can provide much more than simply finance. This includes access to a network which may assist the entrepreneur.

Given the difficulties of adverse selection and generally obtaining access to suitable funding there is a need to redress the problem of bank/SME information asymmetry by researching and generating an accurate sector database. Whilst such a database would be particularly useful in assisting financial institutions to make investment decisions there would be many other uses offering substantial benefits to all support agencies. Such a database could also include a longitudinal study of SMEs using a 'business barometer' approach to generate information reflecting the temporal development of SMEs.

Current Government policy of targeting scarce resources upon those small firms considered to offer the greatest growth potential demands further research to assist in the process of 'picking winners' or the desirability of such a policy. Success must be defined from a pluralistic perspective and criteria must be established which reflect the wide ranging and sometimes mutually exclusive hopes, aspirations and expectations of the host of stakeholders who affect and are affected by small firm activity. A corollary of such further research would be the development of more effective guidelines for targeting support services by enabling specific packages of services, designed to meet particular needs, to be offered.

Of course the effects of wider government policies require constant evaluation. For example, in this volume the effects of compulsory competitive tendering and the promotion of formal quality standards have received some attention from a smaller business perspective. In other words, future research on SMEs must not ignore the effects of policies not merely targeted at SMEs, since these policies can be swamped by other general policies. Research on the effects of non-SME policies on SMEs would certainly be welcomed not only as a means of enhancing our knowledge base but as a way of influencing broader government economic and social policies.

Overall, this text illustrates that small firms are unique in both their operation and their position within the economy. Effective economic regeneration policies can be enhanced if the particular limitations, needs and potential contributions of SMEs are recognised.

NOTES

1. This is not to be confused with the productivity of smaller businesses compared with larger businesses. Productivity in SMEs, in aggregate, is lower than larger firms. All aggregate data on small and medium enterprises should be treated with caution (see Bannock and Daly, 1994). The latest data from the Department of Trade and Industry on SMEs are not comparable with earlier data because the new definitions for inclusion as a business have raised the number of businesses by 540,000 (Department of Trade and Industry, 1995a, p4). This problem aside, there are no readily published time-series data available on the contribution to output by size of businesses.
2. The Labour Party in opposition has also realised the significance of smaller businesses and produced a recent discussion document on its policies towards smaller businesses (see The Labour Party, 1994).
3. Other examples include the rise in freelance teleworkers in book publishing (Stanworth et al., 1993; Granger et al., 1995).
4. For example, the Business Link's initiative has literature which implies a focus of attention on established businesses and those with 'growth potential' rather than start-ups per se (Department of Trade and Industry, 1995c).
5. More recently, government itself has encouraged ISO 9000 accreditation for Business Links with high standards in customer service (Department of Trade and Industry, 1995c, p4).

6. Telematics includes computer networks and their applications: for example, the use of electronic data interchange and databases.

REFERENCES

Ashton D and Jackson P (1993) Implementing Quality Through BS 5750, Kogan Page, London.

Bannock G and Daly M (1994) (eds) Small Business Statistics, Paul Chapman, London.

Bannock G and Ganguly P (1985) UK Small Business Statistics and International Comparisons, Paul Chapman, London.

Binks M and Jennings A (1986) 'Small Firms as a Source of Economic Rejuvenation', in Curran J, Stanworth J and Watkins D (eds) The Survival of the Small Firm, Vol 1, Gower, Aldershot.

Binks M (1991) 'Banks and the Provision of Finance to Small Businesses', in Stanworth J and Gray C (eds) Bolton 20 Years On: The Small Firm in the 1990s, Paul Chapman, London.

Boyle E (1994) 'The Rise of the Reluctant Entrepreneurs', International Small Business Journal, 12, 2, pp63–69.

Churchill N C and Lewis V L (1983) 'The Five Stages of Small Business Growth', Harvard Business Review, 6, 3, pp43–54.

Curran J and Blackburn R A (1990) Small Business 2000, Small Business Research Trust, Open University.

Curran J and Blackburn R A (1991) (eds) Paths of Enterprise, The Future of the Small Business, Routledge, London.

Curran J and Blackburn R A (1994) Small Firms and Local Economic Networks: The Death of the Local Economy?, Paul Chapman, London.

Curran J, Blackburn R, Kitching J, North J and Blizzard D (1995) 'Small Firms in Services – the 1995 Survey', Small Business Research Centre, Kingston University, November.

Deakins D and Hussain G (1991) Risk Assessment by Bank Managers, Small Business Research Centre, University of Central England, December.

Department of Trade and Industry (1992) BS 5750/ISO 9000/ EN 29000: A positive contribution to better business, DTI, London.

Department of Trade and Industry (1995a) Small and Medium Sized Enterprise Statistics for the United Kingdom, 1993, DTI, London, June.

Department of Trade and Industry (1995b) Competitiveness: Forging Ahead, White Paper, HMSO, London Cmnd 2867.

Department of Trade and Industry (1995c) Competitiveness: Helping Smaller Firms, DTI, London, May.

Department of Trade and Industry (1995d) Small Firms in Britain 1995, DTI, London.

Gaston R J (1989) 'The Scale of Informal Capital Markets', Small Business Economics, 1, pp223–230.

Granger B, Stanworth J and Stanworth C (1995) 'Self Employment Career Dynamics: The Case of 'Unemployment Push' in UK Book Publishing', Work, Employment and Society, 9, 3, pp499–516.

Harrison B (1994) Lean and Mean: The Changing Landscape of Corporate Power in the Age of Flexibility, Basic Books, New York.

Hirst P and Zeitlin J (1989) Reversing Industrial Decline? Industrial Structure and Policy in Britain and her Competitors, Berg, Oxford.

Keasey K and Watson R (1993) Small Firm Management: Ownership, Finance and Performance, Blackwell, Oxford.

Keeble D, Bryson R and Wood P (1992) 'The Rise and Role of Small Business Service Firms in the United Kingdom', International Small Business Journal, 11, 1, pp11–22.

The Labour Party (1994) 'Winning for Britain, Labour's strategy for industrial success', Labour Party, London.

Mason C M and Harrison R (1994) 'Informal Venture Capital in the UK', in Hughes A and Storey D J (eds) Finance and the Small Firm, Routledge, London.

Massey D, Quintas P and Wield D (1992) High Tech Fantasies: Science Parks in Society, Science and Space, Routledge, London.

Murray R (1989) 'Fordism and Post Fordism', in Hall S and Jacques M (eds) New Times, The Changing Face of Politics in the 1990s, Lawrence and Wishart, London.

North J, Curran J and Blackburn R A (1995) 'Small Firms and BS5750: A Preliminary Investigation', in Chittenden F, Robertson M and Marshall I (eds) Small Firms Partnerships for Growth, Paul Chapman, London.

Pyke F (1992) Industrial Development Through Small Firm Co-operation, International Labour Office, Geneva.

Ragab M (1992) 'The Business Environment of the 1990s: Implications for Entrepreneurship', Proceedings of International Council for Small Business 37th World Conference, Toronto, June 18–21.

Schumpeter J (1934) The Theory of Economic Development, Harvard University Press, Cambridge, Mass.

Shutt J and Whittington R (1987) 'Fragmentation Strategies and the Rise of Small Units: Cases From the North West', Regional Studies, 21, 1, pp13–24.

Stanworth J and Curran J (1976) 'Growth and the Small Firm – An Alternative View', Journal of Management Studies, 13, pp95–100.

Stanworth C, Stanworth J and Purdy D (1993) 'Self Employment and Labour Market Restructuring: The Case of Freelance Tele-workers in Book Publishing', Future of Work Research Group, University of Westminster, London.

Storey D (1994) Understanding the Small Business Sector, Routledge, London.

Vaessen P and Keeble D (1995) 'Growth-Oriented SMEs in Unfavourable Regional Environments', Regional Studies, 29, 6, pp489–505.

2.

How Bank Managers Make Lending Decisions to Small Firms

Margaret Fletcher

INTRODUCTION

Research shows that banks are the most important source of external finance for small firms in the UK (Hall, 1989; Cambridge University, 1992). Thus of those borrowing money, small firms rely on short term debt, in particular bank overdrafts (Burns et al., 1992). Inadequacies of banks' appraisal processes in applications under the Small Firms Loan Guarantee Scheme were highlighted in the Robson Rhodes Report (1984). The National Economic Development Council (Doran and Hoyle, 1986) called for improvements in banks' appraisal methods. As discussed by Berry et al. (1993) banks are making small firm lending decisions under conditions of uncertainty and asymmetry of information. Binks et al. (1992) point out banks face the problems of moral hazard (monitoring entrepreneurial behaviour) and adverse selection (making errors in lending decisions). Banks will find it difficult to overcome moral hazard because it is not economical to devote resources to closely monitor ventures where lending is for relatively small amounts of finance.

Altman (1971) identifies two types of adverse selection. Reversing the Altman classification and following Deakins and Hussain (1991), we define these as Type I errors, where the banker turns down a good proposal which turns out to be a success, and Type II errors, where the bank manager accepts a proposal which later turns out to be a business failure. We can hypothesise that bank managers will be more concerned with avoiding Type II errors, as Type I errors will not be discovered, nor affect the career of the banker unless the branch fails to meet profitability targets.

Banks have instructions which regulate their lending. Although there is delegated decision making, bank managers make their lending decisions against a background of rules and head office instructions. There are many variables which influence the rules and the work environment, and affect the lending decision (for example, training, internal guidelines, upward referral system and discretionary limits, specific head office directives). We can hypothesise that the decision is a process of interface between the rules and a manager's experience. The extent of variability is affected by the interpretation of the rules and accountability in interpreting these. One extreme is the strict interpretation of the rules, which is a product of their rigour and detail. Where they lack detail or are imprecise then the decision will depend on their interpretation, accountability and level of ambiguity. At the other extreme, the decision is made on experience and attitude, and depends on the conviction of the value of the bank manager's own experience. Furthermore, because of the high amount of variables in commercial lending, eg heterogeneous nature of loan applicants, quality of information, presentation of the proposal, Altman (1971) argues some element of qualitative, intuitive analysis is required in decision making. Thus credit scoring for business loans is limited especially to businesses with a history. As a result it can be manipulated by experienced bankers to reach the decision they want and inexperienced bankers may turn down good proposals. Further, as mentioned above, the banker will be assessing the proposal with limited and imperfect information.

Traditionally, banks in the UK see themselves purely as lenders against security and aim to minimise risks, whereas entrepreneurs usually incur risk in starting ventures. This results in a mismatch between the objectives and orientations of banks and the objectives and orientations of entrepreneurs. Banks' relationship with small firms has been widely criticised in the press (eg Batchelor, 1993). It has been suggested the relationship problems are a result of: mutual misunderstanding, technical problems (bank charges, interest rates and levels of security) and mutual fear (Bradford, 1992). Binks et al. (1988) revealed these mismatches between banks and small firms. The mismatches result in liquidity constraints, which combined with moral hazard and adverse selection contribute to the finance gaps which have been well documented (Stanworth and Gray, 1991). Where asymmetries of information exist banks can adopt a capital gearing approach to loan evaluation where asset backed security is required. The provision of personal security or collateral can be seen as a signal of commitment by the business owner, as offered to increase gearing.

Government concerns over the availability of finance for small firms are highlighted by the Nelson review of the financing of business by the Treasury (*Sunday Times*, 1993). The Bank of England (1994) has noted a withdrawal of credit by banks to small firms, both during and since the recent recession. It concluded not only that banks have become more cautious in their lending decisions, but also that small firms have sought to repay loans and reduce overdrafts. Also, the banks are committed to small firms and continue to seek out viable propositions. The small firms sector is important to banks in terms of profitability. Although there are high risks associated with small business lending, banks are compensated in terms of fees, interest margins and deposit balances held in the banks (Churchill and Lewis, 1985).

The Bank of England (1994) reports a move away from 'character lending'. For example, banks are increasingly taking the view that lending decisions should be based on the cash flow, business plan and prospects. Good banking practice suggests that a proposition is evaluated on underlying viability (Rouse, 1989, p53), security is taken only as a 'comfort factor'. However, assuming bankers are risk adverse, lack of security may result in the proposition being turned down.

English and Scottish banks

There are over 400 banks in the UK, the majority are members of the British Bankers Association. There are 9 main banks known as the 'Major British Banking Groups'. This consists of 6 banks based in London: the 'Big 4' main banks (Barclays, Lloyds, Midland and National Westminster), the Trustees Savings Bank (TSB) and the Standard Chartered Bank; and 2 in Scotland (the Bank of Scotland and the Royal Bank of Scotland); plus the Abbey National. There are 4 main Scottish banks which make up the Committee of Scottish Clearing Bankers: the Bank of Scotland, the Royal Bank of Scotland, the Clydesdale Bank, and the TSB Scotland.

Over the years the banks have changed their way of conducting business (Dewhurst and Burns, 1993). There has been restructuring and the main clearers have adopted a policy of closing their high street branches. In the 1980s there was a move away from a hierarchical structure to a specialised approach splitting corporate and retail (personal and very small business) customers. More recently the English banks have moved towards a 'clustering' or similar structure where a senior manager looks after some 6 to 8 branches which include corporate, retail and small business. The major banks have small business departments, many of which have decentralised units, the services of the staff can be called on by the branch manager. The officer undertaking the risk assessment of small firms may be a branch manager or a specialist enterprise or small business manager.

In Scotland the Royal Bank of Scotland and the Clydesdale Bank are reorganising their management into cluster style structures for business lending. The Royal Bank has introduced a system of group offices where a relationship manager operates within a corporate group, and the Clydesdale has recently introduced a similar structure (Baird, 1994). The Bank of Scotland, on the other hand, has retained the system whereby the branch manager is responsible for small firms lending (Paton, 1993), but there is some specialisation through the introduction of business banking managers. The banks have general guidelines for risk assessment of small business proposition by their officers.

Research in the UK (Binks et al., 1993) into the relationship between banks and small firms found differences exist between Scottish and English banks in the perceptions held by small firms. Scottish firms perceive better service and relations with their banks. The causes of the differences are not clearly apparent, but Binks and Ennew (1993) suggest that they may be due to differences in internal policies, systems and cultures, the Scottish banks are generally smaller than the 4 clearing banks which dominate the English market. It may be argued Scottish banks have more experience in dealing with the needs of smaller firms under depressed economic conditions. Binks and Ennew (1993) conclude that Scottish firms may either be receiving a better banking service, or the service is no different but only appears so, as Scottish business managers have lower expectations of the quality of service they should expect from their bank.

A recent enquiry into Scotland's low business birth rate by Scottish Enterprise (1993a), however, has found that raising finance is perceived as a significant constraint in new firm formation in Scotland. Lower levels of security are available in Scotland than England, but take up of the Loan Guarantee Scheme has also been lower than in the rest of the UK.

AIM OF THE STUDY AND METHODOLOGY

This study was carried out to investigate how Scottish bank managers make lending decisions to small firms and the importance of criteria used to evaluate lending propositions. In order to understand the importance of different factors in bank managers' risk assessment practices, it is desirable to observe the process of real decision making. Central issues were considered to be important in the design of this research. The first was reliability. It was felt necessary to structure the research in order to establish bank managers' true beliefs and bases of their decisions. It was felt insufficient to rely on official bank policy and public relations material given by head office. For example, many banks downplay the role of security, but it is not known to what extent it is an important factor. Second, it was necessary to create a situation where bank managers were required to make a realistic assessment of lending proposals, in order to frame lending decisions and processes in a consistent and realistic context.

Recent studies carried out on risk assessment by bank managers recognise the need for qualitative research. Berry et al. (1991a; 1993b) researched the views of bank managers of business plans and the importance of accounting ratios. As part of a further study, Berry et al. (1993) took a small sub-sample of bank managers from a bank and presented case studies, recognising that the managers' analysis of the case studies provided details of the processes which could not be generated in interview. Berry et al. (1991a, 1993b) investigated the information used by bank managers. They recognised the need for a qualitative approach to give in-depth insight to the decision making process and for the situation to be as near as possible to the actual lending conditions. The bank managers were allowed, however, to choose their own case studies and talked through lending cases. No comparative analysis was made on the importance of different criteria.

Deakins and Hussain (1991, 1994) carried out a study in the West Midlands of England. The co-operation of the main commercial banks was secured. A cross section of 30 bank managers from 7 banks took part, the majority (23) were from the Midland and Barclays, so that the sample was representative of different banks and branches. This chapter reports the findings of a comparative study carried out in Scotland to investigate regional differences in bank officers' risk assessment practices of small firm lending propositions. It was the first study of this type to be carried out in Scotland. Access to 38 bank managers was obtained in the 3 main Scottish banks active in small business lending (Bank of Scotland, Royal Bank of Scotland and Clydesdale Bank). A sample of bank managers was taken, with a regional spread from urban, rural, small and large branches and centres, and a spread of ages and experience of bank managers.

The interviews were in two parts. The first part involved the bank managers in evaluating a business proposition under as near conditions as possible to an actual lending situation. The bank managers were sent in advance a standard business plan for a new business based on a real lending proposal. The case study used by Deakins et al. (1991) was adapted for use in the Scottish study. Although the studies were carried out in different time periods, the economy generally was in recession for both studies. The proposition was based on the construction industry (quantity surveying) which was in severe recession in 1991, and still in recession in 1993 (a sector which is notorious for being first into and last to come out of recession). The proprietors were seeking to raise £60,000 (the amount was slightly less in Scotland due to a drop in interest rates in 1993). There was an equity stake of £30,000 and a consequent gearing ratio of 2:1. The researcher took on the role of an entrepreneur and was interviewed as a potential client. The interviews were recorded and transcribed, except where staff preferred not to be recorded and in the case of one bank which would not allow it, in these cases notes were taken. Most of the interviews lasted between 60 and 90 minutes. The process of decision making was recorded through the questions asked by the bank managers, their responses to the answers given and the funding decision which resulted. This enabled the analysis of the importance of different criteria actually used and consistency of decision making.

The second part of the interview consisted of questions on the importance of different criteria generally used to assess all lending propositions. The bank managers ranked the importance of 18 criteria identified by Deakins et al. (eg ratios, equity stake, security, track record) on a 6 point scale, from 0, indicating not at all important, to 5, being of substantive importance. Two further criteria, source of referral and presentation of the business plan, were included. The managers were asked to choose the three most and three least important criteria to establish if and why they differ, and most important reasons for accepting and rejecting propositions. Further questions were asked on other aspects which influence the decision, the bank managers' views of the Small Firms Loan Guarantee Scheme, the banks' commitment to small firms, and their level of autonomy. Details of bank managers' background, experience and training were obtained.

FINDINGS

Bank managers' lending decisions
The lending decisions are shown in Table 1. The bank managers' attitudes to the proposition were scored on a 10 point scale, with 5 or greater being a positive decision and less than 5 being a negative decision. Those that turned the proposition down were scored according to how they treated the proposition, for example, a score of 4 indicated the bank manager would lend if there was more capital, whereas a score of 1 was more negative, the banker was not prepared to help even with changes. Twenty six (68%) of the 38 Scottish bank managers agreed to support the lending proposition, this is significantly higher than the 50% split found by Deakins et al. This suggests more favourable treatment by the Scottish banks. Only 13% (5) of the Scottish bankers scored less than 3 out of 10, compared with 30% (9) of the English bankers. Further, Deakins et al. reported there was no significant association between the decision and the bank, there was a remarkably even split between banks and amongst managers of the same bank. However, Table 2 shows this is not the case in Scotland with 2 banks accounting for the more favourable attitudes (due to reasons of confidentiality the banks cannot be named).

Table 1: Scoring of Bank Managers Decisions on the Proposition By Bank

Number of bank managers
Scottish

Score	Bank 1	Bank 2	Bank3	Total	English*
0	1	0	0	1	1
1	2	1	0	3	4
2	1	0	0	1	4
3	1	0	1	2	3
4	2	2	1	5	3
5	0	0	1	1	1
6	1	2	1	4	3
7	4	6	3	13	10
8	1	1	5	7	1
9	1	0	0	1	0
10	0	0	0	0	0
Total	14	12	12	38	30

*(Deakins and Hussain 1991)

Note: Based on a 10 point scoring system, with 5 or more being a positive decision and less than 5 a negative decision.

Table 2: Comparison of Yes/No Decisions

Number and % of bank managers by bank

	NO <5	YES ≥5
Bank 1	7 (50%)	7 (50%)
Bank 2	3 (25%)	9 (75%)
Bank 3	2 (17%)	10 (83%)
TOTAL	12 (32%)	26 (68%)
(Average %)		

Deakins et al. show a wide range of scores reflecting a divergence of opinions of the English bankers, and considerable variations in approaches of the bankers. This variation exists despite attempts by banks to provide general guidelines (mnemonic guides were mentioned by the English bankers). In Scotland each of the banks provided a variety of different lending guidelines in different forms for use by the managers (internal guidelines, industry information and norms, manuals, checklists, *aides mémoire*, computer programmes, published books, mnemonics). Comparing the mean scores shows a higher average score for Scottish bank managers shown in Table 3. There was high degree of variability in both Scotland and England as indicated by the relative size of the standard deviations of the total groups. However, this masks the observation above that in Scotland much of the variation is by one bank (Bank 1). Only one bank manager in either of the other two banks rated the proposition very unfavourably (scoring 1) and was not prepared to help.

Table 3: Scottish and English Bankers' Decisions

	Mean	Standard Deviation
Scottish bankers	5.68	2.39
English Bankers	4.47	2.52

Why Banks rejected or accepted the proposition

There was some consistency in the reasons behind the decisions by the Scottish bankers. For example, 8 bankers scored between 2 and 4. Although the proposition was rejected, they were willing to help, but were concerned with the financial aspects. Six were concerned with gearing levels and would support if there was more capital and the other 2 required more financial information. The bankers were impressed with the credentials of the proprietors and had taken the equity injection (and security) as showing commitment, but were concerned with the effect of high gearing on costs and financial viability. Five who accepted the proposition but scored 5 to 6 were prepared to lend due to qualities of the individuals, but were concerned with gearing, 3 also requested more information.

Of the 4 bankers who scored 0 to 1, all were concerned with the gearing of the proposition. Three were also concerned with the commitment and credibility of the individuals, the owners' contribution of £30,000 was considered too low in relation to the bank's required input of £60,000, and did not show commitment. However, those managers who did support the proposal interpreted the level of owners' contribution as showing commitment. Other reasons given in support of the negative lending decision were: the plans were not firm enough, they contained unsubstantiated assumptions, not professional, director lacked experience to run a business. One banker who rejected the proposition (scoring 1) was highly impressed by the individuals and business plan but applied a strict capital adequacy approach and would not lend as he considered this fundamental to the viability.

It was not clear to what extent the guidelines were used by all managers, some managers specifically referred to the aid(s) they had used, others did not. It was suggested earlier that the extent of variability will be affected by whether the manager uses the guidelines and their interpretation. We observed that they were used inconsistently in some cases. For example, one bank provided a comprehensive manual with information on over 200 business sectors. Taking 3 cases for illustration one manager at the end of the interview, volunteered that he had used the manual under a section on surveyors. The proposal had applied to the expected financial ratios indicated and had given the banker the confidence to lend, scoring 7. A second bank manager did not appear to use guidelines; when questioned he answered that he had looked at the manual but did not see a relevant section (the proposition was quantity surveying, the guidelines referred to surveying only) the decision in this case was negative, scoring 4. In the third case the manager had used the manual but the decision was very negative, he had no confidence in the individuals, scoring 1.

Criteria used by bankers to assess the proposition
The Deakins et al. study found that the English bank managers placed emphasis on financial information, gearing and security. Further, the bankers adopted a non-specialist approach, relying on information such as balance sheet ratios and income forecast, which could be generally interpreted across different types of industries. Lack of experience with similar propositions or knowledge of the industry sector was not regarded as important.

Table 4 shows an extract of the criteria used or sought by the Scottish bankers. In Scotland the bank managers were less concerned with higher gearing levels than in England, only 45% of the Scottish managers were concerned with the gearing level of 2:1, compared with 86% of English bankers. As noted earlier gearing tended to be the main reason why the proposal was turned down for those managers who were still prepared to help, ie they were happy with the other aspects of the proposal (the proprietors, markets etc.). There is a dependency on financial information in risk assessment in both Scotland and England, though perhaps less so in Scotland. For example, 47% of the Scottish bankers and 66% of the English bankers requested balance sheet and profit and loss information. We would expect that assessing the abilities, qualities and experience of the entrepreneurs would be of more importance in risk assessment in a start up situation where there is no track record. Of the Scottish managers 76% questioned various capabilities. However, of particular concern is that only 21% of the bankers questioned the entrepreneurs' small business management abilities or training (15% in England). Only 16% of the bankers questioned their qualifications, reflecting the detail contained in the entrepreneurs' CVs.

In particular the bankers were interested in the financial management of the business, 42% asked specifically if a chartered accountant would be employed, 55% questioned if other sources of finance and grants had been considered. Location of the business was questioned by over half, they were interested in availability of local business support (eg grants, premises) and suitability of location for the business.

The Scottish bankers were more prepared to back the proposition without security. Twenty-nine per cent would have accepted the proposition either with reduced security requirements, charged a lower interest rate because of the level of security available, or reviewed the security requirements in time (Deakins et al. reported that all the English bank managers required security). This greater willingness in Scotland to avoid reliance on security corroborates other evidence (Binks and Ennew, 1993) and may reflect the regional environment in Scotland where the level of house ownership is lower and banks have developed risk assessment strategies which do not rely on security (Scottish Enterprise, 1993b).

Although all the bankers were generalists (only a small proportion had a working knowledge of the industry), there was some evidence in Scotland that there were attempts to access sectoral information. This involved phoning contacts, head offices, other branches and using sectoral information provided in internal documents such as manuals and industry study guides (29% questioned the industry sector). A quarter of the Scottish bankers (compared with only one of the English bankers) questioned the role of an IT consultant in the proposition whose role was important to the success and growth strategy of the business. Three bankers asked for a demonstration of the software. Almost nine out of ten bank managers had been on training courses within the last year. However, only one manager had been on an industry sector specific (farming) training course, two managers had been on a small business course. The most frequently attended training courses were on communication and negotiation, 42% had attended such courses; only two managers had been on a small business course. Improving communication skills with clients would help the small firms/bankers relationship.

Table 4: Criteria Used or Sought By the Bankers

	Per cent
Management capabilities	76
Location	58
Forecasted balance sheet and P&L	47
Gearing	45
Role of IT	45
Motivation of directors	32
Role of IT consultant	24
Industry sector	29
Small business experience	21
Employing a Chartered Accountant	42
Qualifications	16
Sources of finance/grants	55
Connection with bank	29

Importance of criteria used to assess all lending propositions

The second part of the investigation was concerned with the importance of criteria used by the bankers to assess all propositions, from both established and start up businesses. Table 5 presents the importance of criteria which might be used. The relatively high values for the standard deviations indicated that there was a high variance across the sample in rating each criterion (this was also the case in England).

Trading experience was ranked as most important followed by equity and gearing. However, the bankers often remarked that all were important and their importance may depend on the situation. This is consistent with the bankers' view of our proposition: for example in our start up proposition where there was no trading experience, the high gearing was a cause for concern, particularly amongst those who rejected it. The importance of trading experience and equity stake suggests that the people involved and their track record are critical, that they have the ability to do what they say they will do. Equity stake is important from the point of view of gearing and showing commitment by the owner. This is confirmed by Table 6 which shows the most frequently identified as the three least important and three most important criteria (ranked). However, this shows that for a significant proportion of the bankers (29%) the people involved are the most important criteria ie their experience, enthusiasm, drive and ability to work with the bank manager.

Table 5: Rank Order and Mean Scores of Criteria used on All Propositions

Criteria	Rank order	*	Mean score	Standard deviation
Trading experience	1	(1)	4.29	0.69
Equity stake	2	(4)	4.11	0.83
Gearing	3	(6)	3.95	0.84
Existing profitability	4	(3)	3.87	0.88
Debtors	5	(12)	3.68	0.78
Net profit to sales	6	(8)	3.53	0.92
Liquidity ratios	7	(=13)	3.45	0.92
Fixed charge on business	8	(17)	3.42	1.03
Creditors	9	(15)	3.37	0.79
Gross profit to sales	10	(=13)	3.34	1.10
Repayment of previous loans	11	(5)	3.26	1.11
Projected income	12	(2)	3.24	0.97
Presentation of business plan	13	NA	3.21	0.94
Cvs of clients	=14	(11)	3.18	0.96
Floating charges	=14	(18)	3.18	1.21
Personal guarantees	16	(=9)	3.03	1.08
Previous loans	17	(=9)	2.82	1.14
Charge on personal assets	18	(16)	2.79	1.04
Client an existing customer	19	(7)	2.29	1.29
Source of referral	20	NA	2.21	1.19

Note: 6 point scale used from 0 to 5
* Deakins and Hussain 1991, English bank managers' ranking

Although there is some consistency when comparing rank order between the Scottish and English bankers, e.g. trading experience is rated as the most important by both sets of bankers, there are considerable differences in rank order of some criteria. However, the most important are relatively consistent: trading experience, existing profitability and equity stake are in the top 4 for each set. Gearing is rated 3rd by the Scottish bankers and 6th by the English, though Deakins et al. have argued that gearing (and security) may have been understated and be more important for particular propositions eg start-ups.

The relative disparity in rank order of the other criteria suggests there are regional differences in the importance of different criteria which are used in risk assessment practices between Scottish and English bank managers. For example, one criterion, that of 'client is an existing customer', is ranked as the 2nd least important criterion by the Scottish bankers compared with 7th in ranking by the English bankers. This may indicate that the Scottish bankers are more proactive in seeking new customers. The importance of previous loans is also rated significantly lower by Scottish bankers. Table 6 collaborates this where 'client is an existing customer' and 'existence of previous loans' are identified as least important criteria.

Table 6: Importance of Criteria

Most important criteria	People	29%
Second important criteria	Owners' equity stake	26%
Third important criteria	Security/exit routes	26%
Least important criteria	Source of referral	34%
Second least criteria	Client an existing customer	13%
Third least criteria	Previous loan	10%

We were interested in the influence on the decision on a proposition of a client being an existing customer (either personal or business) and how this has implications for the banks' relationship with their small business customers. Thirty three bankers (87%) responded it would make a difference if the proposition came from an existing customer. The main reason given was that the banker will have access to information, but this may have a positive or negative influence. In rank order reasons given were: will know client's background (42%), will have track record with bank (39%), why did other bankers decline or come to us if not existing customer (13%). Two indicated it may help in a borderline case and 1 that more time might be given to an existing client.

The Scottish bankers appear to have high levels of autonomy to make small firms lending decisions without referring upwards (though there were indications that this may be changing in one bank). At least 82% indicated they have sufficient autonomy, 77% of the bankers referred less than 30% of propositions upwards and 81% indicated a 70% plus success rate.

Small Firms Loan Guarantee Scheme

Scotland has a low uptake of the Small Firms Loan Guarantee Scheme (Scottish Enterprise, 1993a). We were interested to establish if the bank managers had used it in the past and what were their views. The majority of the sample favoured the scheme, 84% had used it. However, it was used fairly infrequently, on average two or three times. Three-quarters made positive comments on the scheme for example: 'useful tool', 'serves a purpose', 'not used enough'. Eighteen per cent had negative views; some felt a lack of security affected fundamental viability of the proposition. One manager commented 'something is wrong if you have to use it'. Others had bad experiences trying to arrange it for clients, commenting, 'it was too bureaucratic, 'was too rigid'.

CONCLUSIONS AND POLICY DISCUSSION

Improving risk assessment and bank manager decision making can help reduce the adverse selection problem and resultant liquidity constraints that are faced by entrepreneurs and new small businesses. There was more favourable treatment of the proposition by the Scottish bankers than by the English sample. Two of the Scottish banks appeared to be more consistent in decision making than the third. However, there was variability among all banks in the way managers assessed the proposition. There was still an emphasis on financial information, gearing and security, which reflects a capital based approach to risk assessment in the UK.

Security was important but there was a willingness with a minority of Scottish bankers to back the proposition with less security, placing greater emphasis on the abilities of the entrepreneur in risk assessment. As a result Scottish bankers were less concerned with the relatively high gearing level of the proposition. This significant minority approach in Scotland may reflect a closer relationship with the small business customer and the traditions of the banking sector in Scotland where the small business customer has been an important customer, whereas in England it is only in recent years that commercial banks have raised the profile of the relationship with the small business customer (Storey, 1994). Lower levels of security may have contributed to this difference in Scottish banker risk assessment practices. Deakins and Philpott (1993) have argued that lower levels of house owner occupation in Germany than in England resulted in German bank managers being more reliant on risk assessment when assessing the abilities, qualities and experience of the entrepreneur, than on surrogate criteria such as security.

Improved risk assessment and greater uniformity of decision making have implications for bank manager training and support. Overcoming information asymmetries can be aided with the provision of good sectoral analysis information. Training of personnel to understand the problems peculiar to small firm ownership and management and in interpersonal skills, eg communication and negotiation skills, may go some way to overcoming problems in the banking/small firms relationship. Finally we suggest the banker/ accountant relationship could be an important link, as use of the accountant was in some cases an important criterion in the lending decision. This collaborates findings by Chaston

(1994) and suggests that the accountant is an important source of advice to the small firm owner-manager, and can have a vital role acting as an informed mediator between the banker and the manager.

ACKNOWLEDGEMENTS

The author would like to acknowledge with thanks the research grant received from Carnegie Trust for the Universities of Scotland and the co-operation of Deakins and Hussain in carrying out the study.

REFERENCES

Altman E I (1971) Corporate Bankruptcy in America, Heath Lexington, Massachusetts.

Batchelor C (1993) Calling lenders to account, *Financial Times*, 9/1/1993, p11.

Baird A (1994) Brave New World, Business and Finance in Scotland, Scottish County Press Ltd, 20, 12, June.

Bank of England (1994) Finance for Small Firms, Note by the Bank of England, January.

Berry R H, Crum R E and Waring A (1991a) Corporate Appraisal by Banks, University of East Anglia, Norwich.

Berry R H, Crum R E and Waring A (1993b) Corporate Performance Evaluation in Bank Lending Decisions, Research Studies CIMA, London.

Berry A J, Faulkner S, Hughes M and Jarvis R (1991a) 'Financial Information, The Banker and The Small Business', Occasional Paper No 14, University of Brighton Business School.

Berry A J, Faulkner S, Hughes M and Jarvis R (1993a) 'Financial Information, the Banker and the Small Business', British Accounting Review, 25, pp131–150.

Binks M R, Ennew C and Reed G (1992) 'Information asymmetries and the provision of finance to small firms', International Small Business Journal, 11, 1, pp35–46.

Binks M, Ennew C and Reed G (1988) Small Businesses and Banks: A Two Nation Perspective, Forum of Private Business, Knutsford.

Binks M R, Ennew C T and Reed G V (1993) Small Businesses and Their Banks 1993, Report to the Forum of Private Business, Knutsford.

Binks M and Ennew C (1993) Regional Financial Segmentation: Small Businesses and their Banks in England and Scotland, University of Nottingham Discussion Paper, Nottingham.

Bradford J (1992) 'Business Ethics – The Role of Banking Codes for SMEs', 15th Small Firms Policy and Research Conference, Southampton.

Burns P, Burnett A, Myers A, and Cain D (1992) Financing Enterprise in Europe, Special Report 5, Cranfield Business School, Cranfield.

Cambridge University Small Business Research Centre (1992), The State of British Enterprise, Cambridge Small Business Research Centre, University of Cambridge.

Chaston I (1994), Banker/Accountant interrelationship management and financial advice provision in the UK SME Sector, Small Business and Enterprise Development, 1, 2, Summer.

Churchill N C and Lewis V L (1985) Profitability of Small Business Lending, Journal of Bank Research, Summer, pp63–71.

Deakins D and Hussain G (1991) Risk Assessment by Bank Managers, University of Central England, Birmingham.

Deakins D and Hussain G (1994) Risk Assessment with Asymmetric Information, International Journal of Bank Marketing, 12, 1, pp 24–31.

Deakins D and Philpott T (1993) Comparative European Practices in the Finance of Small Firms: UK, Germany and Holland, University of Central England Business School, Birmingham.

Dewhurst J and Burns P (1993) Small Business Management, 3rd ed, Macmillan, Basingstoke.

Doran A and Hoyle M (1986) Lending to Small Firms: A study of Appraisal and Monitoring Methods, report by Economist Advisory Group, NEDC, London.

Hall G (1989) 'Lack of Finance as a constraint on the expansion of innovatory small firms', in Barber J, Metcalfe J S, and Portious M, (eds) Barriers to Growth in Small Firms, Routledge, London.

Paton S (1993) Getting the Relationship Right, Partners in Business, Bank of Scotland, Edinburgh.

Robson Rhodes (1984) A Study of Businesses Financed Under the Small Firms Loan Guarantee Scheme, DTI, London.

Rouse C N (1989) Bankers' Lending Techniques, The Chartered Institute of Bankers, London.

Scottish Enterprise (1993a) A National Enquiry, Scotland's Business Birth Rate, Scottish Enterprise, Glasgow.

Scottish Enterprise, (1993b) Improving the Business Birth Rate: A Strategy for Scotland, Scottish Enterprise, Glasgow.

Stanworth J and Gray C (1991) (eds) Bolton 20 Years On: the Small Firm in the 1990s, Paul Chapman, London.

Storey D J (1994) Understanding the Small Business Sector, Routledge, London.

Sunday Times (1993) Treasury aims to bridge finance gap, 19 September, p11.

3.

MANAGING PUBLIC SECTOR VENTURE CAPITAL ORGANISATIONS

Simon Harris

INTRODUCTION: VENTURE CAPITAL AND ENTERPRISE

Concern that an absence of appropriate finance has been hindering the birth and development of embryonic, young and small businesses has been long standing. The Macmillan Committee report (HM Government, 1931) concluded that a 'gap' existed in the availability of finance for small businesses, in amounts of less than £200,000. Both the 1971 Bolton and 1979 Wilson reports (HM Government, 1971; 1979) investigated the availability of finance to young and small businesses, seen to be fundamental for sustained long term economic growth. The Bolton report concluded that the gap had, broadly, been filled by a variety of institutions, but recognised an 'information' gap for entrepreneurs which could be met with appropriate agencies. The Wilson report saw both a loan gap (which could be met with a government loan guarantee scheme), and an equity gap. The latter could be met with a range of measures, including the creation of small business investment companies of the type then established in the United States, as well as a range of fiscal measures to encourage private investment in small companies.

For example, the late 1970s and early 1980s witnessed considerable economic growth in California and Massachusetts, derived largely from rapid expansion of new enterprises in some new high-technology industries, associated with considerable growth of the venture capital finance. Venture capital organisations were recognised as having played a key role in fostering this process (Hambrecht, 1984; Florida and Kenney, 1988). The Bank of England shared an optimistic view of the potential of the rapidly growing venture capital industry both to meet any 'equity gap' in the UK and to foster new business growth (Bank of England, 1982). Rapid growth in the venture capital industry seemed to show that this was happening (Shilson, 1984; Tyebjee and Vickery, 1988). More recently, a Department of Trade and Industry (1991) report concluded that 'small firms in Great Britain currently face few difficulties in raising finance for their innovation and investment proposals in the private sector'. It asserted 'results suggest, as many commentators since the time of Bolton have argued, that the institutional framework for investment in small firms is broadly adequate and not in need of supplementation by public sector institutions'(p75).

A number of studies have indicated that the contribution of new firms to employment generation, over a period of up to five years, in comparison with the growth of established businesses, is relatively low (Armington and Odle, 1982; Binks and Jennings, 1986; Storey 1986). This, combined with indications of an absence of a major finance gap, provided little support for direct involvement of the public sector in providing capital to young businesses. A study of the economic contribution of the Massachusetts Technology Development Corporation (Fisher, 1988) concluded that the benefits were so low in relation to the costs that the operation failed to meet public welfare criteria.

Concerns persist over finance

A number of doubts have remained concerning small firm finance, and there has been a political if not a rigorous economic rationale for the establishment of subsidised venture capital operations, usually at a regional level. First, studies which question established companies to enquire whether or not there is a 'gap' do not establish if companies are failing to be created because of its presence. Second, there may be wider political objectives beyond the creation of jobs, such as regional economic restructuring towards different types of companies and industries, with growth and jobs payoffs of a very long term nature (Gallagher and Miller, 1991). Rothwell (1985), for example, emphasised the importance of young and technologically dynamic firms in regional economies, and argued in favour of government encouragement of venture capital vehicles which would encourage their presence.

Third, since the mid 1980s, UK private sector venture capital companies have not been active in providing long term (including equity) finance for small and young businesses (Murray, 1992), in the way that many earlier commentators had hoped. In addition, fiscal measures to encourage this type of finance have largely failed (Rhodes, 1984; Mason et al., 1988).

The involvement of private sector venture capital in seed, start-up, or early stage finance, finance in amounts of less than £250,000, finance more patient than about five years, and finance for starting innovatory high-technology ventures, is now trivial (Rhodes, 1984; Boocock, 1990; Pratt, 1990; Murray and Lott, 1992). In 1991 fewer than 300 companies received seed, start-up or expansion finance from venture capital companies, and even these investments' average size was over £200,000 (BVCA, 1991). A cabinet office advisory committee report (ACOST, 1990) noted, 'the contribution of the venture capital industry to overcoming barriers to growth in smaller firms remains limited'(p35).

The reason for this departure appears to be that this market segment has been found unprofitable. The risks involved with funding these types of businesses are high in relation to re-financing or funding the expansion of larger established businesses, necessitating very high internal rate of return (IRR) hurdle rates, typically of between 60 and 80% per annum (Murray, 1991). Venture capitalists' rewards are largely linked to the amount of funds invested, but their monitoring and managing costs for investing in larger established businesses may be lower (BVCA, 1989; Cary, 1991; McMeekin, 1991; Stanworth and Gray, 1991).

Capital for young businesses

A wide range of studies have examined the sources of investment finance for young enterprises in the United Kingdom (HM Government, 1979; Lloyd and Dicken, 1982; Storey, 1982; Binks and Vale, 1984; Peterson and Shulman, 1987; Mason, 1989; Thorne, 1989; Walker, 1989). Internal sources dominate, and owner's own resources provide over half business start-up costs. The principal form of external capital is from banks, normally in the form of bank overdraft loans, repayable on demand, secured on assets, and relatively cheap to administer. Other sources include family and friends of the business owner, and private informal equity, or business angels, which comprise the principal external source of equity finance in young businesses.

There remains a widespread view that capital finance, from institutions or individuals outside the businesses needing it, on terms which include a long period before required repayment and an acceptance of much of the risk of the business, whether long term debt or equity, is inadequately available. The 1990 ACOST report concluded that 'there is a clear need . . . for the ready availability of smaller amounts of risk capital if the rate of business formation and small firm growth – a vital element in economic development – is to be increased'(p87). One effect of reliance on own equity and overdraft finance by UK small businesses may be a pattern of undercapitalisation and over gearing, which for vulnerable young businesses may result in a high rate of failure of such businesses (Hall and Young,

1991). It must be recognised, however, that entrepreneurs themselves often shy away from many forms of such capital, particularly equity capital, not wishing to risk their control over the business. As Rhodes (1984) notes, entrepreneurs often regard equity capital as a source of last resort.

Recent research by Mason and Harrison has shown how facilitation of links between entrepreneurs and business angels may provide one effective way of closing the 'equity gap' (Mason and Harrison, 1991). There have also been calls for a range of other measures. Reports by the National Economic Development Office (NEDC, 1986; ACOST, 1990) have advocated an expansion of venturing by the corporate sector. Over a decade ago, Local Investment Companies were proposed by the CBI (CBI, 1983). The British Venture Capital Association proposed that its members could manage seed capital funds if the government would subsidise the management costs. An idea based on low cost or subsidised 'due diligence' investigations was rejected by venture fund managers, who regard this as a fundamental aspect of their investment decision process. The European Union's seed capital initiative subsidises the operating and capital costs of such funds, and a Business in the Community initiative has attempted to establish a network of regional development capital funds. None of these calls or initiatives has yet had significant effect.

One of the more significant developments since the late 1970s, however, has been the establishment of venture capital bodies specifically to meet these needs, with local government, regional government, or charitable support. Local enterprise boards and councils expanded into this business in the 1980s, until legislation at the end of the decade limited their ability to offer these services (Hayton, 1989).

A number of organisations remain in the UK and overseas which are active in supplying long term seed, start-up and early stage capital in small amounts. Some have grown out of local and regional government operations, others have been established by large businesses as part of redundancy amelioration programmes, others are charities, and some remain within the public sector. As commercially based venture capital companies have withdrawn, these organisations have become, relatively, more important in seed, start-up and early stage finance. Some have been in existence for some years, and some have developed records of successful investment. These organisations, with the common feature of having business development amongst their objectives, their approaches and experiences of their managers, are the subject of this study.

A NEW STUDY OF VENTURE CAPITAL ORGANISATIONS

This study investigates the management approach of venture capital organisations (VCOs) which continue to supply seed, start-up, and early stage long term risk finance (debt or equity) in amounts of less than £150,000. Only VCOs active in this process were investigated, for which evidence of an ongoing deal flow in young and small businesses was sought. Evidence that the organisation was being managed with some investment effectiveness was also sought, as it was hoped to identify processes that lead to successful investment in young businesses, rather than loss making investment in businesses which tend to fail. The measures of investment success were twofold: evidence of a likely positive return on investment before management expenses, and survival in the venture capital business of more than ten years. While the exact form of finance provided by the organisations was not a criterion, only suppliers of 'patient capital' were included, requiring minimum target investment realisation periods of five years or more.

Guides to venture capital sources in the UK, the US, and Canada were used to identify twenty VCOs likely to meet the criteria for the study. Following telephone contact, five were found to have stopped supplying early stage finance in small amounts, and the track records of three others were too short to be able to make an assessment of the success of the operation. The directors of twelve VCOs were interviewed for the study, but six were found not to fulfil all the criteria for eligibility. Two had clearly adopted investment exit periods of less than five years, and another had made no small deals in the previous eighteen months. The investment performance of three could not be regarded as successful.

Six organisations in the United Kingdom and the United States provided data for analysis for this study. Directors of each agreed to three-hour structured interviews, and to supply extensive data concerning investment policies, management philosophies and arrangements, and their investments. Their characteristics are outlined in Table 1.

Organisations A and B were formerly owned by county and regional authorities, and have since been privatised. C is a charity with a goal of helping entrepreneurs successfully to establish their own businesses. D has public sector owners, but uses public and private sector finance, and is required to be self financing. E's parent is the subsidiary of a large multinational, established to help restore employment prospects in an area it had left. F is a regional development authority. The fund sizes ranges from £2m to £10m, and the number of financings per annum from 2 to 30.

The investment focus of the different organisations were very different, as Table 2 shows. Two are specialist technology firms, and while one specifically avoided technology based businesses, two others would avoid it in practice. It was felt from the interviews, however, that investment biases within each firm were inevitable, based on the particular backgrounds and experiences of the VCO managers.

Interview questions were standardised for each interviewee, and were oriented to gain data which would help identify similarities and differences in:

- how prospective investees were found
- behaviour towards applicants for finance
- the investment decision processes
- the structuring and types of finance supplied
- the closeness and nature of the relationship with investees
- the added value, other than finance, that the VCO thought it was supplying.

The data was triangulated with other sources whenever possible, and then analysed. The absence of methodological rigour behind this approach inevitably limits the conclusiveness of the findings, which are derived only from the attitudes and perceptions of the managers of the VCOs, and not their customers. Nonetheless, a number of interesting themes emerged, in the VCOs' approach to:

Table 1: Characteristics of the VCOs Studied

VCO	Form of Ownership	.. £'000 .. Minimum Investment	Average Investment	Investment Type Equity/Loan	Fund size (£m)
A	PLC	100	180	E	10
B	PLC	10	100	E / L	8
C	Charity	1½	3	L	9
D	Private	150	175	E	2
E	Subsidiary	50	100	E / L	2
F	Public	50	150	E	10

Table 2: Different Approaches to Businesses Financed

VCO	Industry focus	Seed	Start-up	Early stage
A	No high tech	no	no	yes
B	No property	yes	yes	yes
C	All industries	yes	yes	yes
D	Only technology	no	yes	yes
E	None	no	yes	yes
F	Only technology	yes	yes	yes

- supplying finance
- financial control
- fostering of appropriate business 'networks', and

- supplying appropriate skills, counsel, and practical support.

These approaches are considered in the rest of this chapter.

The approach to the supply of finance

A number of common features of all the funds towards the businesses they supplied with finance are set out in Table 3. Finance supplied on a commercial basis was used only for a proportion of early-stage development financing by some of the organisations, one used some for some start-up financing and none was available for use in seed financing, even though the management costs were charged to the supplier only by two VCOs.

Despite the wide variety of sources of this finance, and the different types of business it supported, the approach adopted by the VCOs was highly consistent between each other. The most important criteria expressed were the realism of the sales forecasts (and being able to believe that there would be customers), the ability to see cash flow from the businesses, and the perceived capabilities of the management teams. These criteria appear similar to the normal practice of both commercially based venture capital organisations (Dixon, 1989) and business angels (Mason and Harrison, 1994). The calculations made on prospective deals, involving cash flow forecasts and internal rate of return (IRR) calculations, also mirror commercial practice. While the unreliability of these forecasts was widely recognised, so was their value in identifying potential problem areas. Three VCO managers reflected on earlier years when a less rigorous approach was made to the assessment of investment propositions: the waste involved, not only of finance, but also of the fruitful development of entrepreneurial potential, was regretted.

The VCO managers' approaches to business plans were both very similar, and worthy of note. All the VCOs interviewed were keen to engage with applicants with whom they believed an investment opportunity may lie, even if the business plan presented (if any) was, in their view, seriously flawed. All would, if the prospective investee were willing, be prepared to employ the time and expertise not only of the VCO staff, but also, if available, of consultants, specialist development staff and networked experienced individuals who might both refine the business idea and help in its implementation. In this way, a viable investment prospect, and a more probable business success, would emerge, but at considerable cost to the VCO. On occasion, but rarely, some of these 'consultancy costs' were charged to the business.

Table 3: Resourcing and Managing Finance: Common Features

Sources of finance:	seed:	Non-commercial
	start-up:	Mainly non-commercial
	early stage:	Commercial and non-commercial
Dominant investment criteria:	Visibility of sales	
	Cash flow forecasts	
	Individuals involved	
Calculations undertaken:	Equity invs:	Cash flow; IRR
	Loans:	Cash flow
IRR Hurdles for equity (range):	seed:	30% – 60%
	start-up:	20% – 40%
	early stage:	20% – 40%
Attitude to business plan:	The plan developed with the VCO may support an investment decision	
Maximum travelling times from VCO office:	2 – 2½hrs	

All the venture capital operations limited their operations to their local area. In practice, this was noted to be a two to two and a half hour driving distance from the investment office. While many noted how this restricted their overall scope, all felt that a greater distance would effectively prohibit a closeness of contact with investees which was necessary to do their job effectively. It is aspects of this closeness which are examined next.

The approach to financial control

Successive studies over the past 10 years have shown the importance of strict financial control in the infant business development process (Ray and Hutchinson, 1983; Ritchie et al., 1984; Milne and Thompson, 1986). Studies have also shown that one of the principal activities of venture capitalists with investee businesses is in financial aspects, including the financial control (Gorman and Sahlman, 1986; Macmillan et al., 1988; Sapienza and Timmons, 1989; Harrison and Mason, 1992). These studies have also shown that this control is mainly exercised through exercising roles as non-executive directors, and by reviewing management accounts.

Like venture capitalists with a pure commercial orientation, all the VCOs examined pay close attention to financial control within their investee businesses. All regard the inclusion of financial skills to be imperative within the management team before an investment is made.

As Table 4 shows, this is undertaken in ways which differ greatly, but two broad approaches can be identified. The first, adopted by three VCOs (B, E and F) involves delegation of a large part of the financial control process to NEDs or other outsiders. The other approach (adopted by VCOs A, C and D) involves close involvement of VCO staff themselves in the financial control process, including the provision of training in financial control skills for investee managers.

Though the approaches to ensuring financial control within the investee businesses varied considerably, it was rigorous in all the VCOs examined. More significant, more rigorous approaches were adopted by five of the six organisations only as a result of poor investment and business development experience under more 'relaxed' management approaches.

The use of business networks

The role and importance of networks in the enterprise formation and development process has been widely recognised and studied (Birley, 1985; Aldrich et al., 1987; Larson and Starr, 1993), particularly in new technology based ventures (Oakey et al., 1988). Studies in the United States have highlighted the importance of venture capitalists in those linkages in areas such as Silicon Valley and Massachusetts (Florida and Kenney, 1988b). Venture capitalists in the UK often advertise their networking capabilities, though rarely specify what they are.

Table 4: Approaches to Financial Control

VCO	Approach
A	Ensure financial expertise; weekly visits; regular review of management accounts.
B	Appoint NEDs with remit to help management team keep tight control.
C	Close and active involvement of financial adviser with financial expertise; training and development of managers where necessary.
D	Construction/reconstruction of management teams; appointment of NEDs with remit to help keep financial control; on-hand financial counsel and advice; appropriate training.
E	Appoint part-time consultants and NEDs with financial expertise; appropriate training.
F	Reconstruction of management teams; ensure appropriate NEDs.

If the main orientations of the venture capitalists are financial rather than industrial or technological in nature, those linkages may be strong with other finance organisations (Gorman and Sahlman, 1986; Bygrave, 1988; MacMillan et al., 1988; Sapienza and Timmons, 1989), but may be weak in other areas, particularly in ways concerning their strategic, operational, personnel, product or market development.

The six VCOs studied, however, were all actively involved in network fostering, both before investment (at the business planning stage) and as part of a 'hands-on' management process. The specific networking activities are listed in Table 5. In four organisations, the networking role is publicised; in two, A and E, it is more discreet. While the processes differ, they are viewed as highly important within all the organisations studied, and are an aspect of the management of the VCOs to which most have given increased attention as a result of experience.

Like commercially focused VCOs, these organisations network with other financial institutions in order to put financial packages and deals together. The specific activities, though they vary greatly, also indicate an attention to networks of a commercial and technical nature as well. The networking is therefore also oriented towards finding customers, suppliers, partners, technical solutions, collaborators, and specific skills which may be needed by the business.

For these activities, VCO staff backgrounds in industry, particularly the industries of the investee businesses, tend to be of greatest value. Table 6, below, shows how the backgrounds of the investment staff tend to be either in industry or in a mix of finance and industry. In no organisation is the background of the investment staff exclusively financial.

Resourcing additional skills and counsel

While a number of studies undertaken in recent years have examined the financial needs of young businesses, relatively few have examined the other needs of such businesses, though many have identified 'management' as a prime requirement for both venture capital

Table 5: Network Fostering Activities

VCO	Activities
A	Focus on businesses in which VCO staff have business experience; use is then made of their networks.
B	Active use of the organisation's local and overseas networks gained through its various activities; events to foster networking amongst investees.
C	Local and national network formation fundamental to the operation; specific events organised to encourage networks between investees and to others.
D	VCO buildings designed to foster networks between investees; relationship development with individuals and businesses locally and internationally.
E	Network for and through team development and the use of consultants or appropriately experienced NEDs.
F	Events and programmes to link with other entrepreneurs; strong linkages with other VCOs to ensure access to other finance.

Table 6: Backgrounds of VCO Managers

VCO	Backgrounds
A	Industrial, mainly marketing and planning.
B	Broad including finance, marketing and production.
C	Broad range, bias towards big business and banking.
D	Technology: marketing, production and finance.
E	Industrial, mainly marketing and planning.
F	Even mix of finance and industry.

investment and business success. Too little precision has been offered to the definition of 'management', however, to make it a useful categorisation of these other needs.

In addition, while many studies have examined how newly established businesses have met their external financial needs, few have identified other external needs, and how these were resourced. Gibb and Scott (1986) investigated the external assistance needs of owner-managed firms, and found them to be information (as can be resourced through networking), counselling, and education and training (ie the acquisition of skills).

While the need for financial skills and control has already been noted, marketing is another area which has been highlighted. Joyce et al. (1990) have identified marketing knowledge, to be as important as finance to the development of small firms, and Smallbone (1990) found the need to establish a customer base to be the most serious problem facing new start-up businesses.

A number of studies have examined the role of venture capitalists in supplying other resources (Gorman and Sahlman, 1986; MacMillan et al., 1989; Rosenstein et al., 1989; Sapienza and Timmons, 1989; Harrison and Mason, 1992). MacMillan et al. (1989) surveyed venture firm managers, who felt their principal roles to be a source of counsel on strategic issues, networks for additional finance, and monitoring of financial and operating performance.

Rosenstein et al (1989) surveyed investee businesses, and found that US venture capitalists' actual contributions to the development of the businesses they invest in are of less value than many commentators on the industry claim. Harrison and Mason's (1992) survey of investee firms compared the contribution of venture capitalists with that of business angels. Venture capital funds were weakest in the development of actual products and services, in providing contacts with customers, and in motivating personnel, three areas where business angels performed much better.

Table 7 outlines the specific activities of each of the organisations studied in providing active, skill based support for the operational development of investee businesses.

Like commercial venture capital firms, the VCOs surveyed also contribute a role of 'strategic counsel', or acting as a sounding board to the managements of the investee businesses concerning their ideas, problems, and developments. In this role they also bring perspectives gained from backgrounds in the investee sectors or industries, and from a variety of different disciplines.

Typically, they also contribute, in a number of ways, the availability of a broader range of skills at times when they may be required for (and may be critical for) the development of

Table 7: Resourcing Additional Skills and Counsel

VCO	Activity
A	Supply company secretarial and legal skills; training offered and encouraged; weekly meetings with staff with relevant industrial experience.
B	Strong linkages to the rest of the organisation, offering training and consultancy support; 'incubator' type arrangements for seed and start-up businesses; NEDs and advisers organised to give active support.
C	All investees receive intensive adviser and training support; joint marketing programmes organised.
D	Active involvement in constructing balanced management teams; skilled finance, marketing and production support on hand, in-house; help and experience of other investees facilitated; training offered.
E	Intensive help at pre-finance planning stage; well established business support office on-hand; training organised where required.
F	Networking both for team development and thereafter to encourage learning; advisory services on-hand.

investee businesses in their early years. While the range and scope of their offerings in this respect vary greatly, as are the ways in which they are offered, there appears to be a high level of attention to this aspect of helping their businesses to grow in comparison with other financial institutions.

DISCUSSION

A significant finding of this study is that the venture capital organisations surveyed do not feel that they now face institutional competition in sourcing businesses to finance. Three of the 6 organisations noted that their competitors, which had previously come from both the private and public sectors, had all departed, and 2 of the others had never had any competitors.

Murray (1992), in a review of the industry, noted the departure of many private sector venture capitalists from the provision of risk finance to young enterprises, but expressed a hope that new niche suppliers would enter the business. This study indicates that such a development has not yet taken place, and that the process of departure is almost complete. The study also found a lack of profitability of these venture capital organisations as a whole, even if the funds themselves achieved a reasonable return. Only one fund's management costs were not subsidised, and this fund's managers were facing intense pressure to increase the minimum deal size to £200,000.

As a result, these organisations were usually the only source of institutional finance available to their investees, though, as Mason and Harrison (1991) note, business angels may represent an alternative source of finance for many of these investees. Table 8 notes the managers' own unprompted impressions of their most important contributions to the local economy.

Fully commercial suppliers of finance clearly provide more than finance to their investee businesses. The range of resources supplied by the organisations in this study to further the business development process, however, is much wider, and is characterised in Figure 1.

In their approach to supplying finance, the critical issue for investees concerns its patience and flexibility, and not whether it is debt or equity finance. The appropriate form of finance for a particular business depends on its characteristics and entrepreneurial preference: the gap is for appropriate finance, not necessarily for equity finance. Long term debt (with appropriately structured interest holidays), preference shares (straightforward or convertible) and equity are all viable early stage finance vehicles used by the organisations

Table 8: Managers' Own Perceptions of their VCO's Particular Contributions

VCO	Contributions
A	The only organisation locally left in the small deal niche, yet are making a commercial success of it.
B	The only investors who work with and build a business around prospective entrepreneurs, using the whole organisation (of which the VCO is part), yet have achieved profitable investment performance.
C	Releases energy, creativity and talent in individuals who would not otherwise have a chance, yet experiences few bad debts by commercial standards.
D	The organisation is unique: it develops successful and resilient businesses which otherwise would not exist.
E	One of only two funds locally in small, early stage finance and in patient finance (the other is public sector); the only fund which works with the individuals to develop an investible plan; able to offer flexible equity:debt mixes.
F	Competency in managing early stage deals profitably: its management represents 70% of the success, selection only 30%.

examined. The institutional finance 'gap' is for all and any of these forms of finance for seed, start-up and early stage businesses, in amounts under £200,000, and capable of waiting five years or more before realisation, whether debt or equity.

The venture capital managers examined, who appear to achieve positive returns on their funds, are equally as selective about the individuals whom they are prepared to support as their fully commercial counterparts, and appear to seek the same kinds of characteristics. Their approach to the financial monitoring and control of investee businesses is also similarly rigorous. Here, however, the approach may reflect a closer involvement with the managements of the businesses than would be typical for managers of a purely commercial orientation, who for reasons of cost, tend to rely on more formal mechanisms of financial reporting.

In fulfilling their business development objectives, these organisations do very much more than provide finance. If encouraged by an entrepreneur or management team, for example, but concerned about the business idea, the plan, or the management team, they can afford to work with the team over an extensive period. The idea might be refined or changed, the plan redeveloped, or the management team reconstructed. A wide range of additional skills and perspectives is engaged, using a wide range of resources, and a lot of time. Some might be held in-house, others accessed through participation in appropriate networks. The process starts before investment, and continues throughout the investment period.

One manager noted, 'We make money not so much through the selection of winning businesses, but through the growth of the managers we invest in, and though them, the growth of their businesses'. Another declared 'Venture capitalists usually succeed through good deal selection. Thirty % of our success comes from this, the other 70% comes from managing the deal afterwards.'

It is noteworthy how this pattern of intensive 'hands-on' activity reflects that identified in studies of other environments where the institutional provision of capital has promoted business development. Studies of the role of venture capitalists in the growth of technology based businesses in Silicon Valley (Timmons et al., 1983; Hambrecht, 1984; Amit et al., 1990) note the wide range of help and assistance they supply to investee businesses. Business angels, in the United States at least, have also been found to inject close and experienced management support (Wetzel, 1983; Haar et al., 1988).

Figure 1: The External Resources for Enterprise Development

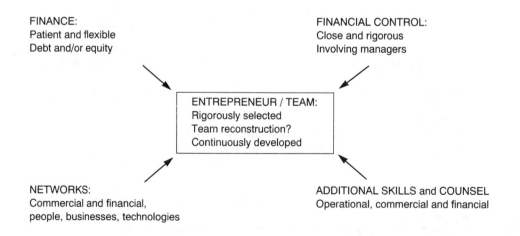

FINANCE:
Patient and flexible
Debt and/or equity

FINANCIAL CONTROL:
Close and rigorous
Involving managers

ENTREPRENEUR / TEAM:
Rigorously selected
Team reconstruction?
Continuously developed

NETWORKS:
Commercial and financial,
people, businesses, technologies

ADDITIONAL SKILLS and COUNSEL
Operational, commercial and financial

CONCLUSION

Enquiry into the barriers to young firm growth and development has tended to seek to identify particular resource gaps (such as in finance, market, property, skills or motivations), or particular 'provision' gaps (such as education/training, advice or information). Government policy initiatives have been devised to address these 'gaps'. The creation of national, regional or local public sector venture capital organisations has been one manifestation of this approach. The remit of these organisations has been, in the main, to address a perceived finance gap.

Few, if any, of these organisations remain in their original form. Nearly all have either died following poor investment records, or have repositioned themselves to financing only larger, established businesses. This study has found that those which survive, and invest successfully in young businesses, do so only by widening their remit to supplying not only finance, but also a range of other resources essential for young firm development. Their evidence confirms much small business research that the availability of a variety of (less tangible) human resources is at least as important for the young business development process as the availability of appropriate finance. Critically, however, the two issues are closely interlinked. Just as studies of one independent of the other are likely to be deficient, so policy measures, such as the provision of public sector venture capital, which address one independently of the other, are also likely to be inadequate and ineffective.

Recognition of the importance of these 'other' resources in young business birth and development is reflected in the array of support services available to young businesses. The experience of the organisations in this study is that by closely linking the provision of finance to the provision of a range of identified 'other' resources, rather than regarding them as discrete unrelated resource packages, both sides of the transaction (the supplier and recipient) retain an interest in successful exchange. Successful investment is seen only to result from rigorous financial control, network development, and access to additional skills and counsel. Successful young business development requires all of these, as well as finance.

If the possibility of public sector involvement in the venture capital business is once again to be considered, for reasons of industrial regeneration or simply for job creation, the evidence that the objectives of young business development and responsible financial stewardship are not contradictory is particularly relevant. Not only does successful business development appear to require a rigorous approach to financial stewardship, but achieving a satisfactory level of investment success amongst young businesses also requires a range of supportive business development activities. Organisations able to perform this task require a range of skills which embrace and extend beyond rigorous venture capital management and business development.

REFERENCES

Advisory Committee on Science and Technology (ACOST) (1990) The Enterprise Challenge: Overcoming barriers to growth in small firms, HMSO, London.

Aldrich H, Rosen B and Woodward W (1987) 'The impact of social networks on business foundings and profit: a longitudinal study', in Churchill et al. (eds) Frontiers of Entrepreneurship Research 1987, Babson College, Wellesley, MA. pp154–168.

Amit R, Glosten L and Muller E (1990) 'Does venture capital foster the most promising entrepreneurial firms?' California Management Review, 32, 1, pp102–11.

Armington C and Odle M (1982) 'Small business – How many jobs?' Brookings Review, 4, pp14–17.

Bank of England (1982) 'Venture Capital', Bank of England Quarterly Bulletin, 22, 4, pp511–3.

Binks M and Vale P (1984) 'Finance and the Small Firm', Nottingham University Small Firms Unit, Discussion Paper No.2.

Binks M and Jennings A (1986) 'New firms as a source of Industrial Regeneration', in M Scott et al. (eds) Small Firms Growth and Development, Gower, London.

Birley S (1985) 'The role of networks in the entrepreneurial process', Journal of Business Venturing, 1, pp167–84.

Boocock, J G (1990) 'An examination of non-bank funding for small and medium sized enterprises in the UK', Services Industries Journal, 10, 1, pp124–46.

British Venture Capital Association (1989) The Need to Stimulate Seed Capital, BVCA, London.

British Venture Capital Association (1991) Report on Investment Activity, BVCA, London.

Bygrave W D (1988) 'The structure of the investment networks of venture capital firms', Journal of Business Venturing, 3, 3, pp137–57.

Cary L (1991) The Venture Capital Report guide to venture capital in Europe (5th ed) Pitman, London.

CBI (1983) Smaller Firms in the Economy, Confederation of British Industry, London.

Department of Trade and Industry (1991) 'Constraints on the growth of small firms: A report of a survey of small firms' Aston Business School, HMSO, London.

Dixon R (1989) 'Venture Capitalists and Investment Appraisal', National Westminster Bank Review, November, pp2–21.

Fisher P S (1988) 'State venture capital funds as an economic development strategy', Journal of the American Planning Association, 54, 2, pp166–77.

Florida R L and Kenney M (1988a) 'Venture capital, high technology and regional development', Regional Studies, 22, 1, pp33–48.

Florida R L and Kenney M (1988b) 'Venture capital financed innovation and technological change in the US', Research Policy, 17, pp119–37.

Gallagher C and Miller P (1991) 'The performance of new firms in Scotland and the south east 1980–87', The Royal Bank of Scotland Review, No.170.

Gibb A and Scott M (1986) 'Understanding small firms growth', in M Scott, A Gibb, J Lewis and T Faulkner (eds) Small Firms Growth and Development, Gower, London.

Gorman M and Sahlman W A (1986) 'What do venture capitalists do?' in C Vesper (ed) Frontiers of Entrepreneurship Research, Babson College, Wellesley, MA. pp414–36.

Haar N E, Starr J and MacMillan I C (1988) 'Informal risk capital: Investment patterns on the East Coast of the USA', Journal of Business Venturing, 3, 3, pp11–29.

Hambrecht W R (1984) 'Venture Capital and the growth of Silicon Valley', California Management Review, 26, 2, pp74–82.

Hall G and Young B (1991) 'Factors associated with insolvency amongst small firms', International Small Business Journal, 9, 2, pp54–63.

Harrison R and Mason C (1992) 'The roles of investors in entrepreneurial companies: A comparison of informal investors and venture capitalists', Venture Finance Research Project Working Paper No.5, University of Southampton / University of Ulster.

Hayton K (1989) 'The implications of the Local Government and Housing Bill for Local Economic Development', Local Economy, 4, pp3–16

HM Government (1931) Report of the Committee on Finance and Industry (Macmillan Report) Cmnd 3897, HMSO, London.

HM Government (1971) Report of the Committee of Inquiry on Small Firms (Bolton Report) Cmnd 4811, HMSO, London.

HM Government (1979) Interim Report on the Financing of Small Firms (Wilson Report) Cmnd 7503, HMSO, London.

Joyce P, Woods A, McNulty T and Corrigan P (1990) 'Barriers to change in small business: some cases from an inner city area', International Small Business Journal, 8, 4, pp49–58.

Larson A and Starr J A (1993) 'A network model of organization formation', Entrepreneurship Theory and Practice, 17, 2, pp5–16.

Lloyd P and Dicken P (1982) Industrial change: Local manufacturing firms in Manchester and Merseyside, Department of the Environment Inner Cities Directorate, London.

MacMillan I C, Kulow D M and Khoylian R (1988) 'Venture capitalists' involvement in their investments: extent and performance', in B A Kirchhoff et al. (eds) Frontiers of Entrepreneurship Research, 1988, Babson College, Wellesley, MA. pp202–23.

Mason C M (1989) 'Explaining recent trends in new firm formation in the UK: some evidence from South Hampshire', Regional Studies, 23, pp331–46.

Mason C M, Harrison J and Harrison R T (1988) Closing the Equity gap? An assessment of the Business Expansion Scheme, Small Business Research Trust, London.

Mason C and Harrison R (1991) 'A strategy for closing the small firms' finance gap', Venture Finance Research Project Working Paper No.3, University of Southampton / University of Ulster.

Mason C and Harrison R (1994) 'Why 'business angels' say no: A case study of opportunities rejected by an informal investor syndicate', Venture Finance Research Project Working Paper No.7 University of Southampton / University of Ulster.

McMeekin D (1991) 'Finance for enterprise: closing the equity gap', 14th Small Firms Policy and Research Conference, Manchester.

Milne T and Thompson M (1986) 'Patterns of successful business start up', in T Faulkner et al. Readings in Small Business, Gower, London

Murray G C (1991) 'The changing nature of competition in the UK venture capital industry', National Westminster Quarterly Review, November, pp65–80.

Murray G C (1992) 'A challenging marketplace for venture capital', Long Range Planning, 25, 6, pp79-86.

Murray G C and Lott J (1992) 'Have UK venture capital firms a bias against investment in technology-related companies?' Babson Entrepreneurship Research Conference, INSEAD, Fontainbleu.

National Economic Development Office (NEDO) Committee for Finance and Industry (1986) External Capital for Small Firms . . . a Review of Recent Developments, NEDO, London.

Oakey R, Rothwell R and Cooper S (1988) Management of Innovation in High Technology Small Firms, Pinter, London.

Peterson R and Shulman J (1987) 'Capital structure of growing small firms: a 12 country study on becoming bankable', International Small Business Journal, 5, 4, pp10–22.

Pratt G (1990) 'Venture Capital in the United Kingdom', Bank of England Quarterly Bulletin, 30, 1, pp78-83.

Ray G H and Hutchinson P J (1983) The Financing and Financial Control of Small Enterprise Development, Gower, London.

Rhodes R (1984) A Study of Businesses Financed under the Small Firms Loan Guarantee Scheme, DTI, London.

Ritchie D, Asch D and Weir A (1984) 'The provision of assistance to small firms', International Small Business Journal, 3, 1, pp62–65.

Rosenstein J, Bruno A V, Bygrave W D and Taylor N T (1989) 'Do venture capitalists on boards of portfolio companies add value besides money?', in R H Brockhous et al. (eds) Frontiers of Entrepreneurship Research (1989) Babson College, Wellesley, MA. pp216–9.

Rothwell R (1985) 'Venture finance, small firms and public policy in the UK', Research Policy, 14, 5, pp253–65.

Sapienza H J and Timmons J A (1989) 'Launching and building entrepreneurial companies: do the venture capitalists add value?' in R.H. Brockhous et al. (eds) Frontiers of Entrepreneurship Research (1989) Babson College, Wellesley, MA. pp245–57.

Shilson D (1984) 'Venture capital in the United Kingdom', Bank of England Quarterly Bulletin, 24, 2, pp207–11.

Smallbone, D (1990) 'Success and failure in new business start-ups' International Small Business Journal, 8, 2, pp34–47.

Stanworth J and Gray C (1991) (eds) Bolton 20 years On: The small firm in the 1990s, Paul Chapman, London.

Storey D J (1982) Entrepreneurship and the Small Firm, Croom Helm, Beckenham.

Storey D (1986) 'New Firm Formation, Employment Change and the Small Firm: the Case of Cleveland County', in J. Curran et al. (eds) The survival of the small firm, Gower London.

Thorne J R (1989) 'Alternative sources of financing for entrepreneurial ventures Entrepreneurship', Theory and Practice, 13, 3, pp67–76.

Tyebjee T and Vickery I (1988) 'Venture capital in Western Europe', Journal of Business Venturing, 3, 2, pp123–36.

Timmons J A, Fast N D and Bygrave D (1983) 'The flow of venture capital to highly innovative technological ventures' in J A Hornaday et al. Frontiers of Entrepreneurship Research, Babson College, MA.

Walker D A (1989) 'Financing the small firm', Small Business Economics, 1, pp285–96.

Wetzel W E (1983) 'Angels and Informal Risk Capital', Sloan Management Review, 24, Summer, pp23-34.

4.

A Survey of Business Angels: Fallacies Corrected and Six Distinct Types of Angel Identified

Hamish Stevenson and Patrick Coveney

INTRODUCTION

The term Business Angels, or simply Angels, is now commonly used to describe predominantly rich individuals who make equity investments in small unquoted businesses, often at an early stage, and who frequently play an active part in the management of these businesses. The Chancellor used the term in his 1993 Budget, which resulted in a *Financial Times* headline proclaiming it as a 'Business Angels Budget'. Even *The Archers* on BBC radio has recently featured Business Angels! However, current research on Angels is not supported by sufficient empirical evidence and this new survey covers a more typical cross section of Angels.

A few well-publicised, exceptionally successful investments in Britain have helped to raise public awareness of the potential rewards of becoming an Angel. For instance, Ian McGlinn invested £4,000 in 1978 for a 50% equity stake in the Body Shop and in 1994 his remaining 28% stake is worth £120 million. However, despite media interest about the economic importance of Angels helping to bridge the equity gap (and in management journals such as *Harvard Business Review*, 1993; *Management Today* 1993; and *The Director* 1994) the level of empirical research to date is very limited.

METHODOLOGY

Large scale quantitative research was carried out in March 1994 for this project using a postal questionnaire as the primary research instrument. A targeted sample population of 7,123 possible Angels was identified, predominantly through the support of Business Introduction Services but also through contacts in the venture capital industry. In all, 484 responses were received, a response rate of 7% overall. A third (33%) of the respondents were current Business Introduction Service subscribers, 33.5% former users of this type of service, and 33.5% were Angels or potential Angels who had not used introduction services in making their investments (Table 1).

The 484 respondents whose replies have been analysed for these preliminary findings show that the surveyed Angels represented a broad range of different types of Angel. These Angels were grouped into a typology of six Angel types using statistical differences (at either the 1% or 5% confidence level) between various groupings of Angels. Throughout the analysis, the chi-square test of significance was considered most appropriate.

Table 1: Sources of Sample of Business Angels

Target Angel population	Total sample	Response rate	Percentage of total sample
Current subscribers to BIS			
VCR subscribers	583	18.4%	22.1%
LINC subscribers	200	22.0%	9.1%
TEChINVEST subscribers	50	12.0%	1.2%
Bedford Investment Exchange Subscribers	40	7.5%	0.6%
Former subscribers to BIS			
Former VCR subscribers	2500	6.5%	33.5%
Other Business Angels			
VCR subscriber enquiries	1000	9.2%	19.0%
3i MBI program managers	50	2.0%	0.2%
General speculative group (i.e. venture capital executives etc)	2700	2.6%	14.3%
Total	**7123**	**6.8%**	**100%**

RESULTS OF A SURVEY OF BUSINESS ANGELS

This new survey of 484 Angels in Britain is about five times the size of previous surveys conducted in Britain and the United States of America (USA). The most frequently quoted studies in Britain are two surveys conducted by Mason and Harrison (1993a and b) whose results have influenced government policy significantly. These surveys had very small sample sizes and the Angels they researched had invested £3–5 million over three years. Preliminary findings from this new study show that a total figure of over £60 million was invested over the last three years by the Angels surveyed. The 484 respondents who have been analysed for these preliminary findings show that the surveyed Angels represented a broad range of different types of Angels from a cross section of established Business Introduction Agencies.

The Angel market in Britain is relatively untapped but may be much larger than previously estimated
The results reveal that, although the recent coining of the term 'Business Angel' has helped to raise their profile, they remain a largely untapped source of capital for small businesses. Although the survey targeted Angels associated with established Business Introduction Agencies, over one third of the respondents (37%) were Virgin Angels, who were looking to make Angel type investments but had not yet done so. Over half (55%) were active Angels who had made investments over the past three years, while 9% were Latent Angels who had made Angel investments but not in the last three years. The survey highlights that those Angels who do invest are actually much richer and make much larger, and more frequent investments, than portrayed by previous surveys.

These survey findings suggest that the total funds invested by Angels in Britain may be significantly more than the previous estimate of £2 billion, if the calculation adopted by Mason and Harrison to arrive at this figure is valid. This is because one of the key figures used to calculate this figure was an average investment per Angel of £20,000, as opposed to an average investment of £120,000 or a median of £40,000, identified by this new survey (Table 2). Another important finding, which is also supported by previous surveys, was that the large majority (70%) of Angels would have liked to have made more investments had they come across suitable opportunities, and that no less than 76% expected to increase their Angel investment activities over the next 5 years.

Table 2: A Comparison Between New and Previous Surveys

	New Survey	Previous Survey Informal Investors	Previous Survey LINC Agency Investors
Survey size	484	86	55
Wealth			
Number of businesses founded	1.6 (turnover >£1m >5 staff)	67% >1 business (any size)	71% >1 business (any size)
% of Angels with net worth >£500k	53%	37%	30%
% of Angels with net worth >£1m	30%	19%	18%
% of Angels with income >£50k	75%	43%	66%
% of Angels with income >£100k	30%	15%	20%
Funds still available for Angel investment	47% >£100k	Avge £50k	Avge £100k
Investment activity over 3 yrs			
Average investments per Angel	2.34	1.5	1.5
Average total Angel investment	£226k	£52k	£152k
Median total Angel investment	£85k	£22k	£100k
Average amount invested by Angels per investment	£120k	£18k	£66k
Median amount invested by Angels per investment	£40k	£10k	£30k
% of Angels with >2 investments	65%	48%	37%
% of Angels with >£100k invested	39%	14%	33%
Preference of Angels			
Investment motive	financial/fun	financial	financial
Importance of location	not very important	very important	very important
Minimum rate of return pa	21%	20–50%	20–50%
Minimum growth rate pa	22%	na	na
Time frame before exit	6 yrs	3 yrs	5 yrs

Notes:
1. Preliminary results are incomplete and an additional 50 late questionnaires have still to be analysed.
2. The new survey classified active Angels as those Angels who had made one or more investments in the past three years. The previous surveys conducted by Mason and Harrison also incorporated Angels who were actively seeking to make investments, and others who had made investments over three years ago into their category of active Angels.
3. For the new survey, a detailed preliminary analysis is only available for 506 reported investments made by 231 Angels totalling £61m, and not for all the 262 Angels who reportedly made over 600 investments, totalling over £61m.

British Angels are richer, invest more, and are more like their entrepreneurial American counterparts, than depicted in previous surveys

This new study reveals that Angels in Britain are more similar to their American counterparts in terms of wealth, income and investment activities than depicted by previous surveys, although they are probably considerably fewer in number and exhibit several other differences. This study helps to correct a number of common fallacies about Angels in Britain. However, the new survey is of such a different magnitude to previous surveys that comparisons are not particularly illuminating, other than to emphasise this study's important new empirical contribution. The major finding, that there are Angels in Britain who are much richer and make more regular investments on a much larger scale than portrayed by previous researchers, should help redress the prevalent image implied by previous, smaller surveys. These new findings suggest that the image of Angels as typically making small, local investments, is a fallacy. However, one similarity between the surveys is that they all confirm that Agencies attract some of the richest and most active Angels.

Angels have definite investment criteria and location is less important than government initiatives assume

The survey shows that almost all (92%) Angels saw themselves as 'business partners', as opposed to 'altruistic benefactors' (3%) or 'ruthless financiers' (5%). The majority of Angels (86%) reported that they contributed more than just capital. This contribution can either be advice or hands-on involvement in the management of the business. Despite the popular image that Angels' investment decisions are ruled by their heart, this research showed that the majority of Angels (86%) felt that their investment decisions were ruled by their head.

The principal investment motive for about half the Angels (51%) surveyed was their expectation of greater financial rewards than from the stock market (Table 3). Other Angels (34%) were most attracted to the opportunity to create a job/income for themselves and interestingly, a significant number of Angels (29%) were most attracted to the fun and satisfaction of investing.

Table 3: Principal Attraction for Making Angel Investments
(Respondents could rank jointly)

Greater financial return than stock market	51%
To create a job/income	34%
Fun and satisfaction	29%
Sense of social responsibility	3%
Other	7%

However, the survey also highlighted that Angels' financial expectations varied considerably. Whilst on average Angels were looking for projected growth rates of 22% pa and expected annual rates of return of 21% pa, many expected higher returns. The time frame in which Angels expected to exit their investments was found to be a little more than six years, which is longer than identified by previous surveys.

Table 4: Principal Criteria When Assessing a Proposal
(Respondents could rank jointly)

Impression of the founder/manager	59%
Experience/understanding of the sector	29%
Projected profitability	9%
Content and presentation of business plan	8%
Attractive margins	7%
Location of the venture	5%

When assessing investment proposals, the principal concern of the majority of Angels (59%) was their impression of the founder/management of the business (Table 4). Most Angels (45%) and Virgin Angels (51%) therefore preferred to receive initially a detailed four to five page summary of the business plan, including full curriculum vitae and direct contact numbers, which enables them to gauge an impression of the management before assessing proposals at length. Investors' personal experience and understanding of an industry sector was also an important criterion for a significant number of Angels (29%).

Contrary to previous research findings, the location of the business was identified as the most important criterion by only 5% of Angels. The majority (58%) did not think that location was very important. Nearly half the Angels (45%) were prepared to invest in businesses more than 200 miles – or a three hour drive – from their main place of work. This challenges the popular belief that most Angels will only invest locally, which has been a major conclusion of previous research and has become a fundamental pillar of current government policy. For example, the *DTI Guide To Increasing the Supply of Informal Equity Capital* (DTI, 1993) emphasises that 'most informal investors have a strong preference to investing locally, the majority of their investments being made in firms located within 100 miles of the investor's home or office'. This survey shows that this belief is a fallacy and that Angels are far more concerned about the quality of the management and their understanding of the industry sector than location of the business.

A TYPOLOGY OF BUSINESS ANGELS

Angels are not a homogeneous group and could be better targeted using a typology based on their entrepreneurial backgrounds and levels of investment. In general, the survey supported previous survey findings that the majority of Angels in Britain are male (98%), middle aged (average age 48), university educated (74%), and highly entrepreneurial. Half the Angels surveyed had founded two or more of their own substantial businesses (with sales of more than £1m or more than five staff) and the principal source of wealth for the majority of Angels (48%) was their own business. Only 12% were found to have inherited their current wealth. The survey identified the following six different types of Angels with distinct characteristics and investment strategies.

Virgin Angels

Virgin Angels have funds available and are looking to invest but have yet to find a business (Table 5). Their available funds for Angel investment are slightly less than half that of active Angels. Although they are generally less rich than active Angels they do not cite lack of funds as restricting their investment behaviour, but rather an absence of suitable proposals. Their motive for investing is to gain better financial returns than the stock market or to gain a job/income. When assessing proposals they are less concerned about their impression of the management and more concerned about the business plan and a closer location. They are more interested in tranquil sports and less interested in competitive sports than the other types of Angels!

Table 5: Virgin Angel

% of total respondents		37%
Wealth		
Average No of businesses founded		
(sales >£1m or >5 staff)		
Financial net worth	>£1m	23%
	>£500k	34%
Income pa	>£200k	6%
	>£100k	19%
Investment portfolio over 3 yrs		
Total (quoted and	>£500k	14%
unquoted)	>£200k	32%
Funds still available for Angel investment		
	>£200k	10%
	>£100k	29%
Angel investment activity over 3 yrs		
No of Angel investments		0
Preferences		
Principal investment motive		income/financial
Importance of location		
(% willing to invest >200 miles away)		22%

Virgin Angels made up 37% of the total survey. They come from a distinctly less entrepreneurial background and, as a result, are probably more risk averse. They are less likely to be encouraged to take the plunge by tax incentives than by the provision of better support services.

Latent Angels

Latent Angels are rich individuals who have made Angel investments but not in the past three years, principally because of a lack of suitable locally based proposals (Table 6). They tend to be significantly wealthier and more entrepreneurial than Virgin Angels and have more funds available to invest.

Their financial and business backgrounds are very similar to that of Wealth Maximising Angels. Latent Angels are much more concerned with venture location than any other Angel type and focus on local ventures. They could be encouraged to invest more by gaining a better knowledge of the management of prospective businesses and by the availability of clear exit routes.

Table 6: Latent Angel

% of total respondents		9%
Wealth		
Average No of businesses founded		
(sales >£1m or >5 staff)		
Financial net worth	>£1m	40%
	>£500k	55%
Income pa	>£200k	13%
	>£100k	27%
Investment portfolio over 3 yrs		
Total (quoted and	>£500k	29%
unquoted)	>£200k	43%
Funds still available for Angel investment		
	>£200k	14%
	>£100k	45%
Angel investment activity over 3 yrs		
No of Angel investments		0
Preferences		
Principal investment motive		financial/income
Importance of location		
(% willing to invest >200 miles away)		16%

Wealth Maximising Angels

Wealth Maximising Angels are rich and experienced businessmen who make investments in several businesses for financial gain (Table 7). They are not as rich as Entrepreneurial Angels, but they tend to make as many investments by investing slightly smaller amounts in each investment. They have marginally higher expected rates of return, and they are much more inclined to co-invest with other Angels. They are the least concerned about the proximity of the businesses they back.

Table 7: Wealth Maximising Angel

% of total respondents		20%
% of *active* Angels		37%
Wealth		
Average No of businesses founded		
(sales >£1m or >5 staff)		1.5
Financial net worth	>£1m	30%
	>£500k	58%
Income pa	>£200k	5%
	>£100k	24%
Investment portfolio over 3 yrs		
Total (quoted and	>£500k	21%
unquoted)	>£200k	46%
Funds still available for Angel investment		
	>£200k	26%
	>£100k	43%
Angel investment activity over 3 yrs		
No of Angel investments		2
Average total investment per Angel		£125k
Median total investment per Angel		£80k
Average per Angel per investment		£60k
Median per Angel per investment		£40k
Total funds invested	>£200k	11%
	>£100k	28%
Preferences		
Principal investment motive		financial
Importance of location		
(% willing to invest >200 miles away)		47%

Wealth Maximising Angels represented the largest group of active Angels surveyed (37%) which suggests that they may typify the largest number of existing Angels in Britain. They appear to adopt a portfolio approach to investing and often provide hands-on support to the businesses in which they invest. They are probably the most likely to use Business Introduction Agencies as a source of business proposals.

Entrepreneurial Angels

Entrepreneurial Angels are very rich individuals who invest for both the fun of it and as a better option than the City (Table 8). They are older than other Angels, less inclined to co-invest, and they take majority stake holdings more often than others. They enjoy the 'buzz' of being involved and are not too concerned about the proximity of businesses.

Entrepreneurial Angels often have the highest profile, and serve as useful role models. They represented 18% of the Angels surveyed and can be difficult to gain direct access to. However, Sir John Aird, who was recently featured in the *Financial Times* and on the BBC *Money Programme,* has used a Business Introduction Agency to find a number of his investments. He was introduced through Venture Capital Report (VCR) to Ivan Semenenko's one-man engineering company, Matcon, in 1981. He invested £23,000 for 50% of the equity in the company which had grown to sales of over £14 million in 1993 and has plans to go public. Sir John was also introduced to a company promoting trade to China, Chance China Ltd, in which he invested £200,000.

Table 8: Entrepreneurial Angel

% of total respondents		10%
% of *active* Angels		18%
Wealth		
Average No of businesses founded		
(sales >£1m or >5 staff)		4.1
Financial net worth	>£1m	61%
	>£500k	79%
Income pa	>£200k	26%
	>£100k	49%
Investment portfolio over 3 yrs		
Total (quoted and	>£500k	50%
unquoted)	>£200k	71%
Funds still available for Angel investment		
	>£200k	49%
	>£100k	75%
Angel investment activity over 3 yrs		
No of Angel investments		3
Average total investment per Angel		£750k
Median total investment per Angel		£250k
Average per Angel per investment		£250k
Median per Angel per investment		£60k
Total funds invested	>£200k	53%
	>£100k	69%
Preferences		
Principal investment motive	fun/financial	
Importance of location		
(% willing to invest >200 miles away)		40%

Income Seeking Angels

Income Seeking Angels are less affluent individuals who invest some funds in a business, often to generate an income or even a job for themselves (Table 9). They typically make significantly fewer investments, are less entrepreneurial and have founded the least number of businesses. They also have a particularly strong preference for co-investing with other Angels and are the most concerned of Angels about the proximity of the businesses in which they invest.

Table 9: Income seeking Angel

% of total respondents		16%
% of *active* Angels		29%
Wealth		
Average No of businesses founded		
(sales >£1m or >5 staff)		0
Financial net worth	>£1m	20%
	>£500k	31%
Income pa	>£200k	9%
	>£100k	24%
Investment portfolio over 3 yrs		
Total (quoted and	>£500k	14%
unquoted)	>£200k	37%
Funds still available for Angel investment		
	>£200k	10%
	>£100k	26%
Angel investment activity over 3 yrs		
No of Angel investments		2
Average total investment per Angel		£95k
Median total investment per Angel		£35k
Average per Angel per investment		£50k
Median per Angel per investment		>£20k
Total funds invested	>£200k	4%
	>£100k	16%
Preferences		
Principal investment motive		income/financial
Importance of location		
(% willing to invest >200 miles away)		41%

Table 10: Corporate Angel

% of total respondents		9%
% of *active* Angels		16%
Wealth		
Average No of businesses founded		
(sales >£1m or >5 staff)		na
Financial net worth	>£1m	na
	>£500k	na
Income pa	>£200k	na
	>£100k	na
Investment portfolio over 3 yrs		
Total (quoted and	>£500k	45%
unquoted)	>£200k	71%
Funds still available for Angel investment		
	>£200k	63%
	>£100k	81%
Angel investment activity over 3 yrs		
No of Angel investments		3
Average total investment per Angel		£600k
Median total investment per Angel		£165k
Average per Angel per investment		£200k
Median per Angel per investment		£100k
Total funds invested		
	>£200k	50%
	>£100k	75%
Preferences		
Principal investment motive		financial/social responsibility
Importance of location		
(% willing to invest >200 miles away)		53%

Income Seeking Angels represented 29% of the Angels in this new study but in many respects most closely resemble the majority of Angels depicted by the previous surveys, which appear to have predominantly focused on this one type of Angel, and are therefore less representative. They are very much the smaller players and less likely to subject their limited resources to very high risks. However, they can play a particularly useful role in local small businesses if they take an active, or full-time, role in them.

Corporate Angels

Corporate Angels are companies which make numerous large Angel type investments and often for majority stakes (Table 10). They have corporate resources at their disposal which enable them to make more frequent investments and consistently invest significantly higher levels of funds in each investment and are more concerned with the expected financial returns than individual Angels. They are the only group to consider 'a sense of social responsibility' to be an important investment motive. They rarely choose to co-invest and tend to take majority stakes. The proximity of the businesses is not an important investment criterion.

This important group of Angels has been overlooked in the current debate. They only represented 16% of the active Angels in the survey, although there are over 20,000 private companies in Britain making profits of more than £250,000, which could make suitable investors. As well as making the largest and most frequent investments, Corporate Angels will usually also have additional resources to contribute.

INVESTMENT BEHAVIOUR OF ANGELS

The typology of Angels can be used to target distinct types and to predict their investment strategies. To enable small businesses, business introduction agencies and policy makers to successfully target active Business Angels a matrix detailing the most prominent characteristics of each active Angel type was developed.

Table 11: Reasons Restricting Investment

	Per cent	
	Angels	Virgin Angels
Lack of suitable proposals	70	66
Lack of faith/trust in management	42	30
Lack of reliable information	32	22
Lack of available funds	32	20

Note: Respondents can offer more than one answer.

The principal factor restricting further investment by Angels and Virgin Angels is the lack of suitable business proposals, and not the lack of funds (Table 11). The survey identified similar factors restricting investment by both Angels and Virgin Angels to those highlighted by previous surveys. The most common reason cited by Angels (70%) and Virgin Angels (66%) for not making investments is the lack of suitable business proposals. Only a minority identified the lack of funds as restricting them, and this actually limited Angels more than Virgin Angels.

The survey also revealed that similar factors would stimulate both Angels and Virgin Angels to make more investments. The most common factor which would encourage the majority to invest more would be better knowledge of, or trust in, the management (Table 12). This important factor is difficult to facilitate and is also identified by entrepreneurs as a major restriction to them in seeking Angel investors.

However, nearly half of both Angels and Virgin Angels would be encouraged to invest more if more suitable exit routes were made available. The establishment of an unlisted market has been called for by a number of key players in the venture capital industry, and the Stock Exchange has recently published its plans for the Unlisted Security Market in 1995, the Alternative Investment Market (AIM).

Table 12: Factors Stimulating More Investment

	Per cent	
	Angels	Virgin Angels
Better knowledge/trust of management	63	57
Available exit routes	44	45
Co-investment with experienced Angels	38	42
Better tax incentives	45	34
Knowledge of successful Angel investments	25	23
Corporate finance advice	16	19
Other	24	21

Interestingly, better tax incentives would stimulate Angels more than Virgin Angels and the survey highlights the fact that tax benefits are only an incentive for a minority of Angels. This is further supported by the survey finding that 25% of Angels and Virgin Angels expect to invest more under the new Enterprise Investment Scheme (EIS) than under the old BES. As one would perhaps expect, given the opportunity to co-invest with experienced Angels, more Virgin Angels than Angels would be encouraged to invest.

Business Introduction Agencies

Business Introduction Agencies attract some of the richest and most active Angels and although the track record of a select few rival those of their US counterparts, there is still significant room for improvement. This survey highlights that Angels who use Agencies appear to be much bigger investors than those who do not. It also exposes how these Agencies are hardly making any impression on the huge potential available market. In addition, the survey reveals the preferences Angels have about how Agencies should operate. Agencies are not intended to replace other informal mechanisms, such as golf club and old school tie networks and personal contacts, which account for the vast majority of Angel investment. Experience has shown, however, that they do provide one solution to overcoming some of the factors restricting Angels identified by the survey and they also address the inefficiencies in the market for businesses seeking investment. However, as this survey confirms, Agencies are by no means a panacea.

Past experience has shown that Agencies which do not vet proposals (with the costs and expertise this involves) are less likely to succeed. For example, the Institute of Directors *Business Opportunities Digest* and the computer-based Information Resource Exchange failed, despite the support of some of 'the establishment'. There are a few notable exceptions amongst Agencies in Britain whose track record appears, perhaps surprisingly, to rival those of their US counterparts.

The much heralded Venture Capital Network (VCN) pioneered by Professor Wetzel in the US had only 407 Angels and raised investment for an average of 5 businesses pa, before moving to MIT in 1992 after it failed to attract continued sponsorship (and was renamed the Technology Capital Network Inc). In contrast, since VCR was founded in Britain by Lucius Cary in 1978, it has operated on a commercial basis. VCR currently has 625 Angels and has raised investment for an average of 15 identifiable businesses pa. The newly championed Texas Capital Network has only about 200 registered Angels. This is slightly fewer than Britain's national not-for-profit Agency, Local Investment Networking Company, which has operated since 1987 and has raised investment, typically at the smaller end, for about 10 businesses pa. At a regional level, Pennsylvania Private Investors Group (PPIG) has a total of 33 Angels and has raised investment for an average of about 4 businesses pa. This better success ratio relative to the number of Angels is because PPIG pay particular attention to vetting its proposals, unlike the other networks in the USA. The leading regional DTI Angel pilot scheme in Britain, TEChINVEST, which has established links with the two aforementioned national Agencies, has 80 Angels and has raised investment for 10 businesses since it was started at the beginning of 1993. However, a fundamental difference between Agencies in America and Britain is that, despite raising investment for fewer businesses, these US Agencies have raised investments from more Angels. In the case of VCN, the 31 businesses raised a total of $12 million from 55 different Angels, which highlights the prevalence of co-investment in the US. However, it is important to note that all Agencies have difficulty tracking their successful investments, and may not learn about many of them, particularly if they charge a success commission!

Despite these relatively favourable comparisons for the performance of some Agencies in Britain, the survey highlights that there is still significant room for improvement if Agencies are to begin to meet the demand of their existing Angels and if they are to attract more Angels. The survey findings identify a number of Angels' preferences about how they would best like Agencies to operate.

The majority of Angels (62%) and Virgin Angels (64%) would like to see the formation of a single national Angel network. This preference for a network, run on a national basis, and the relative low importance of location to most Angels, challenges the existing DTI policy of distinctly regional initiatives. The survey findings also challenge the desirability of the government operating such schemes. Of those surveyed who expressed a preference about the type of organisation which best operates an Agency, only 4% of Angels preferred the government, a minority (32%) preferred not-for-profit organisations, and the majority (64%) preferred a commercial organisation. This preference for the commercial running of Agencies is also confirmed by previous surveys.

Angels expressed a variety of preferences about the format in which they like to receive their proposals. However, the largest number of Angels (45%) preferred initially to receive a detailed 4–5 page appraisal of the business plan (including detailed curriculum vitae and financial information, and direct contact details) written by experienced Agency staff. Preference for this format is perhaps not surprising given that it is used by VCR and about half (55%) of the respondents were either current or former VCR subscribers.

CONCLUSIONS AND IMPLICATIONS

These preliminary findings show that there are Angels in Britain who are actually much richer and make much larger and more frequent investments than previous smaller surveys have identified. Past surveys' limited focus on one type of Angel is the main reason for this difference. This new survey has identified a typology of six distinct types of Angels that can be used by businesses, Agencies and policy makers to target distinct types of Angels and encourage them to invest more.

The survey confirms that the availability of, and access to, good investment opportunities is the main factor restricting Angel investment. However, the survey also highlights that most types of Angel are prepared to invest outside of their local area. Therefore, if a more enterprising culture is to be encouraged in Britain a mechanism should be created which would give Angels access to a greater number of suitable proposals. Such a mechanism could be achieved by the setting up of a national network which links existing Agencies, as opposed to the current fragmented and inefficient marketplace. Member Agencies would maintain their own distinct regional identities but would offer standard quality service at a standard price. Agencies would subcontract an organisation to run the national network to ensure quality control of each investment proposal circulated within the scheme. Most Angels surveyed, who expressed a preference about who should run such an organisation, would prefer it to be a commercial organisation, as opposed to not-for-profit.

With the establishment of a national network, Angels would only need to register with one member Agency and thereby gain access to all proposals, which as this survey shows, must be suitably vetted. Businesses seeking capital would only need to register with one Agency and, once they had been suitably vetted, gain access to all Angels. Unfortunately the current government policy of small regionally focused initiatives is ineffective because it does not give Angels sufficient access to all business proposals, and vice versa.

Although some leading Agencies and Business Links currently support the concept of such a network, they cannot agree on the operational principles, such as the costs, processes of vetting proposals, and quality standards. However, by highlighting the untapped potential Angel funds, and clearly identifying Angels' distinct preferences, these survey findings will hopefully facilitate the debate about the necessary operational principles behind the establishment of an effective National Business Angel Network.

There have been several calls supporting the establishment of such a national network from a number of sources such as the CBI, the DTI, and the Bank of England. The contribution by these sponsors to ensuring the necessary resources and high profile of any such initiative is welcomed, but to date too many of these calls have been based on some of the fallacies about Angels identified, and hopefully corrected, by this survey. More attention needs to be paid to Angels' preferences highlighted in this large survey of Angels and to established Agencies' proven experience of industry best practices.

If the six different types of Angels, including the large numbers of Virgin and Latent Angels, identified by the survey are to be encouraged to invest, more action is needed to establish a national network that will provide suitable businesses with access to more Angels and thereby attract more Angels, particularly the more active and entrepreneurial type of Angels identified in this survey.

REFERENCES

BBC Money Programme (1993) Pennies from Heaven, Sunday 31 November.

BVCA (1993) A Directory of Business Introduction Services, British Venture Capital Association.

Cary, L (ed) (1995) The Venture Capital Report Guide to Venture Capital in the UK and Europe (7th ed.), Venture Capital Report, Henley-on-Thames.

Coveney, P (1994) Informal Investment in Britain: An Examination of the Behaviours, Characteristics, Motives and Preferences of British Business Angels, Unpublished MPhil Thesis, Oxford University.

The Director (1994) Heavens Above!, August, pp34–36.

DTI (1993) A Guide to Setting-up a Business Introduction Service, Department of Trade and Industry, London.

Gourlay R (1994) Financial Times Series on Business Angels, 3 May and 5 April.

Harvard Business Review (1993) Venture Capital: The Invisible Angels, July/Aug, pp8–9.

Management Today (1993) Hatching Uncle Sam's Entrepreneurs, Nov, pp54–56.

Mason C and Harrison R (1992) Promoting Informal Investment Activity: Some Operational Considerations for Business Referral Services, Venture Finance Research Project, Working Paper No 4.

Mason C and Harrison R (1993a) Strategies for Expanding the Informal Venture Capital Market, International Small Business Journal, 11, 4, pp23–38.

Mason C and Harrison R (1993b) Interim Review of Five Informal Investment Demonstration Projects, Report to Department of Trade and Industry, London.

Stevenson H (1994) 'Business Angel Investment – Matching Angels and businesses is more than a blind date', Family Business, Aug, Stoy Hayward Accountants, London.

Technology Captital Network Inc. (1994), 'A Gathering of Angels', Feb, p28.

Wetzel W (1983) 'Angels and Informal Risk Capital', Sloan Management Review, Summer, pp23–34.

Wetzel W, (1993) 'Promoting Informal Venture Capital in the United States: Reflections on the history of the Venture Capital Network', in Harrison R and Mason C (eds.), Informal Venture Capital: Information, Networks and Public Policy, Woodhead-Faulkner, Hemel Hempstead.

5.

THE STRATEGIC MANAGEMENT STYLES OF SMALL BUSINESSES

Paul Joyce, Christine Seaman and Adrian Woods

INTRODUCTION

Modernist thought in management inclines to the view that businesses can and should adapt to future circumstances, and that this requires innovation in business processes and in the products and services marketed. The consumer needs to be found in the evolving market place are, it is believed, discoverable (through market research) and the business can, and should, plan to be successful by setting targets, projecting cash flow, determining its organisation, etc. This management theory of action can be condensed into the assumptions that strategic planning will enable business to innovate and that this will lead, in turn, to a healthy and growing business.

There are, however, loud doubts being raised about this optimistic theory (Whittington, 1993). Some have warned that innovation is ungovernable; they say innovation occurs but not because management has determined it will (ibid., p87). Some challenge the ability of market research to identify the new products and services that will have value within the market place (ibid., p86). Others have suggested that businesses are very conservative and find it difficult to make the changes in their human and technological resources that are needed to exploit market opportunities (ibid., pp88–90).

Against this theoretical background this paper asks: Can different strategic management styles of small businesses be identified? This will be tackled empirically, using recent survey research evidence from Central London. At the very least, an affirmative answer to this question requires that small businesses can be classified according to their behaviour in relation to strategic planning and that there is evidence that this classification is useful in relation to innovative behaviour and business performance.

In the next section we will explore in a little more detail the theoretical considerations which have led to the unease about the orthodox or modernist conceptual model of strategic development. This is followed by a section describing the sample of businesses surveyed. In the findings part of this paper we first develop a classification of small businesses and then we explore the different records of the small businesses in business performance, process innovation and product/service innovation. Finally, the implications of the findings are examined.

It will be seen that the survey evidence suggests that the critics of modernist theories of strategic management are wrong in rejecting the possibility and importance of managing innovation. Whilst we agree that simplistic conceptual models of planning are mistaken, there are, based on the evidence we have, at least three benefits of strategic planning:
(a) it fosters the will to be dynamic and expansive;
(b) it leads to a boosting of investments which raise productivity; and
(c) it speeds up service/product innovations which are important for higher rates of return.

In consequence, we do not see effective strategic styles of management as, in a simple way, the use of techniques telling the business what to do at critical moments of strategic choice (which belongs to a heroic conception of elite decision making); rather, effective styles enhance the capacity of a business to continue to maintain itself, reproduce itself, in a way which leads to growth and development.

THEORETICAL CONTEXT

It has been argued that there 'is considerable suspicion of external experts and consultants' who are seen as 'offering short-term, simplistic and standard solutions' (Coulson-Thomas, 1992, p246). Influential writing in the 1980s was certainly critical of the technocratic and analytical approaches to strategic management which had come to dominate business schools (cf Peters and Waterman, 1982). Pascale and Athos (1981) considered that American management, for example, overfocused on the 'hard' elements of management – strategy, structure, and systems – and did so, in part because of the attention paid by academics to them. These were things which could be investigated analytically, quantitatively, logically and systematically. The Peters and Waterman characterisation of excellent firms attacked quite sharply the elitist models of corporate planning. Thus analysis was rejected: there had to be instead a bias for action. The 'high command' model was rejected; innovation had to be championed by those who were close to their customers. Top managers were not to be intellectuals; they had to be inspiring (hands-on and value driven). The model of strategic management as managing a portfolio of businesses through acquisitions and divestments was attacked; businesses had to stick to what they knew. These excellent companies were held together by values and not intellectual justifications: so they empowered those down on the shop floor but demanded commitment to the company's core values. All of this spelt a rejection of analysis and intellectual thought within business. It added up to an attack on the modernist instincts of strategic management in the 1960s and 1970s. The modernist approach is still the primary framework used in business schools, where the emphasis is on the application of analytical techniques to case studies.

What was this modernist strategic management? Ansoff's work (1965) typified this approach. He concentrated on strategy formulation and highlighted decision making about product and market choices. A major limitation with this approach is that it is usually based on experiences in large-scale businesses: few qualitative studies or case studies feature strategic management in small businesses. Key figures in this approach are the chairman, the board, the managing director, specialist corporate planners, all those who manage and control the organisation using the strategic plan. Implementation is seen as a stage which follows strategic analysis and choice; the strategists have to work out how they are going to encourage organisational members to contribute to the successful implementation of the strategy. Planning is almost seen as synonymous with strategic management. The process of decision making is planning change: business success is programmable.

This is an oversimplification of the conceptual approach to strategic management in the 1960s and 1970s, but it truly represents the spirit of the grand strategy which was commonplace. The grandness of this approach was exemplified by the neat division of labour in terms of managerial decision making. Operational decisions, by lower tiers of management, were subordinate to strategic decision making.

There has been a reaction against some of the overwhelming modernist confidence in the intellectual abilities of top managers to make and implement successful strategic decisions. Sometimes this takes the form of backing an experimental approach to innovation, allowing trial and error and organisational learning to provide a more modest approach to top down omniscience (Stacey, 1991). It can, however, go much further in rejecting rational and planned direction of strategic developments. This is to be found in the metaphor of organisational environments being chaotic and thus unknowable. Lower level employees and managers may be assigned responsibility for bringing about innovation by intuitive rather than rational thinking. Then managers at the top are left with the task of discovering what is succeeding lower down the organisation and backing it (Peters and Waterman, 1982).

This approach, which at times sounds, in a very 'simple' reading of it, like encouragement for submersion in spontaneous and intuitive action, may reassure managers feeling confused and uncertain about how to handle competitive forces, but in the end is unconvincing. The chaos paradigm may have suited the mood of the 1980s, but in the 1990s managers will no doubt look again to approaches which re-institute intellectual processes as a key aspect of strategic management. This may be inferred from the recent popularity of business process re-engineering with its updating of the scientific management framework to address concerns that organisations have become too functionally organised and need to be prepared for globalisation.

However, the development of a new modernism in strategic management will have to face a certain scepticism. Despite the existence of some evidence that strategic planning may pay off in terms of financial performance (Pearce et al., 1987; Capon et al., 1994), not all studies have corroborated such a link (Greenley, 1989; Boyd, 1991).

THE SAMPLE

In the summer of 1993, over 1,000 establishments located in Central London were surveyed as part of the CENTEC 1993 Employer Survey (Joyce, Seaman and Woods, no date). These included private and public sector organisations, large and small businesses, branch plants, head offices, and totally independent companies.

For this study of strategic management styles, a sub-sample was selected. This consisted of 301 totally independent companies. Only private sector businesses employing fewer than 25 people were included in the sub-sample. A few of the small businesses in the main sample were rejected because respondents could not give clear information about business plans, planning horizons and profit performance. Company data were collected using telephone interviews. The company respondents included: owners, partners, managing directors, directors, company secretaries, general managers, and other managers.

Nearly two-thirds of the sub-sample had very small work forces with fewer than 10 people; in only just over half of the businesses were all these employees working on a full-time basis – whilst a third of the businesses had a fifth or more of their employees working on a part-time basis. Mostly the businesses were in the private services sectors, especially business services (30%), distribution (16%) and hotels and catering (9%). Over half the businesses were selling their services (or products) to the general public; however, many were supplying other businesses. Whether selling to the public or to other businesses, the markets of these businesses typically extended beyond Central London.

A fifth (21%) of the sub-sample were said to be healthy and growing at the time of the survey. This usually meant that profits and productivity had both increased over the past three years. Indeed, the sub-sample had a group of 43 (14%) star performers, which were businesses that had increased profits and productivity over the past three years and evaluated themselves as healthy and growing. The background to this, of course, was a period of recession in business activity generally.

STYLES OF STRATEGIC MANAGEMENT

The starting point for this exploration of strategic management styles is the clarification of two contrasting approaches to strategic management. The first is a style consistent with the classic teaching of business policy and which may be labelled the 'Strategic Planner'. This style may be expressed in the production of written or formal business plans and attempts to plan at least three years ahead. Why be interested in businesses that planned three years ahead? Many organisations have financial planning on a yearly cycle and are by no means taking a forward looking view; also, Ansoff once estimated that planning horizons could range from three to 10 years ahead (Ansoff, 1965). In contrast, there are those businesses which adopt the posture that they have no real room to manoeuvre and that planning, especially that which ends in formal written business plans, is a waste of time in the real world. Since these businesses often believe that they have no choices in how they react to the exigencies of market forces, and believe that they are the result of the evolutionary effects of such forces, this style can be labelled as 'Evolutionist' (see Whittington, 1993). The Evolutionist business is operationalised as lacking a formal or written business plan, and having a planning horizon of two years or less (including businesses which claim no planning ahead at all).

However, not all small businesses are Strategic Planners or Evolutionists. There are businesses which claim they do carry out long-term planning, which we have defined as planning ahead three or more years, but which do this informally (ie they do not produce a formal business plan as such). Whilst there may be doubts about the rigour and depth of such planning, this could give rise to a strategic approach to business decisions. These are termed 'Informal Strategists'. Then there are businesses with a written business plan which deal only with the present or the next year or two. These are the 'Short-Term Planners'. It has to be remembered that written business plans may be produced for different purposes; they may, for example, be used primarily to secure capital from a bank or some other source of funds, and not be seen as having any major significance for steering the business. Thus, four distinct strategic management styles can be identified in respect of small businesses:

(a) Strategic Planners;
(b) Short-Term Planners;
(c) Informal Strategists; and
(d) Evolutionists.

In the case of this sample of very small businesses in Central London, formal or written business plans were by no means universal and long-term planning was not typical. The Evolutionist style of management was the most common of the four types identified here and fewer than one in four were Strategic Planners.

BUSINESS PERFORMANCE

The usefulness of the typology presented here depends on its ability to illuminate as many aspects of strategic behaviour and overall business performance as possible. In this and the next sections we will show that the typology is, in fact, useful in this respect.

It can be seen in Table 1 that Strategic Planners were some three times more likely than the Evolutionists to be healthy and growing. This superiority of the Strategic Planners was also corroborated by their three-year record on profitability and productivity. Over half (53%) of the Strategic Planners had increased their profits, as against less than a third (30%) of the Evolutionists. And whereas over two-thirds (69%) of the Strategic Planners had increased their productivity, only 44% of the Evolutionists had. So, the Strategic Planners were prone to be healthier in business terms than small businesses that did not plan formally and did not plan far ahead.

Table 1: Does Strategic Management Style Affect Current Trading Status of Small Businesses?

| Current trading status | Per cent Strategic Management Style | | | |
	Strategic Planners	Short Term Planners	Informal Strategists	Evolutionists
Healthy and growing	39.7	21.6	25.0	11.5
Various*	60.3	78.4	75.0	88.5
Total	100.0	100.0	100.0	100.0
(Number of businesses)	(68)	(74)	(20)	(139)

Note: * Businesses in this grouping identified themselves in various ways; for example, healthy but threatened, poor but has potential, healthy and stable, and stable but wish to grow. Healthy and growing was the most positive way of describing a company's current trading position.

There was also evidence from the past three years that Strategic Planners were more likely to be growing. Table 2 shows that they were almost three times as likely as the Evolutionists to have increased their numbers of full-time employees.

Table 2: Does Strategic Management Style Affect the Number of Full-time Employees?

| Trend in full-time employees over past 3 years | Per cent Strategic Management Style | | | |
	Strategic Planners	Short Term Planners	Informal Strategists	Evolutionists
Increased	45.6	35.1	20.0	16.5
Decreased/no change	54.4	64.9	80.0	83.5
Total	100.0	100.0	100.0	100.0
(Number of businesses)	(68)	(74)	(20)	(139)

The Short-Term Planners and the Informal Strategists showed intermediate levels of overall performance in terms of current trading position and employment over the past three years, but the Informal Strategists had a poor profile in terms of profits and productivity over the past three years. There could be an argument that the Strategic Planners had the capacity to engage in planning because of their relatively successful performance and that the poorer trends in profitability and productivity achieved by the Evolutionists denied them the time to perform planning activities. An analogous doubt was raised by Storey (1994) who pointed out that formal planning procedures might cause growth or might be a result of growth (since large businesses tend to be more formal in their management arrangements). There may be some truth in this, but, as will be seen next, the better performance of the Strategic Planners seemed explicable in terms of strategically sponsored innovation. In the light of this evidence, the plausible view that different strategic management styles are responsible for variations in performance is to some degree corroborated. So, it can be concluded that at least some of the superiority of the Strategic Planners can be associated with their style of management.

An important point needs to be made here to place these findings in context. These findings relate to our sub-sample of small businesses with fewer than 25 employees. It is not being suggested that a correlation between strategic planning and performance is found in all sizes of business; indeed, it may be that with increasing size of business the propensity to engage in strategic planning procedures increases and so do the difficulties of implementing strategies. However, it is also possible that strategic thinking is especially useful to small businesses with simple management structures, even though strategic management may be much less developed or systematic in such settings.

PROCESS INNOVATION

It has long been assumed that some successful firms are good at keeping unit costs low. This can be the result of efficient management of processes in a fairly static environment (Miles and Snow, 1978). Or it can be the result of investments which raise productivity levels. It is the second route which seems to have been the one taken by the Strategic Planners over the preceding three years.

Most (72%) of the Strategic Planners had increased their investment in new technology over the three years. Only one in three (32%) of the Evolutionists, in comparison, had increased their investment in new technology. Bearing in mind this major difference, it is therefore highly significant that productivity growth over the three years was strongly correlated with increased investment in new technology. For these small businesses in Central London, therefore, the right kind of strategic management style produced productivity growth by making technological improvements in processes.

Investment in 'soft assets' also produced productivity benefits for the Strategic Planners. One half (47%) of them had increased their investment in training, as against a sixth (17%) of the Evolutionists. Such investments in the skill levels are nowadays seen as essential for superior financial performances. Outside of the vocational education and training of craft and professional employees, traditionally there has been little development of occupational skills. In Central London, however, many businesses in recent years have been training employees in quality and customer care and in company procedures; and many have been planning to increase training in these areas (Joyce et al., no date). These kinds of training directly enhance processes within the business and are important for process innovations. There has also been a lot of Central London businesses providing training for new products and services. The small businesses which had increased investment in training over the preceding three years were markedly more likely to have training in process-related matters: two-thirds had training to achieve productivity improvements; two-thirds had training to make employees more flexible; and two-thirds of them had training to improve quality and customer care. Those that had not increased their investment in training tended not to have such training: only a third trained to improve productivity; only a third trained to raise employee flexibility; and only two-fifths trained to improve quality and customer care.

The conclusion which emerges, then, is that more strategically managed businesses, the Strategic Planners, achieved some of their productivity growth by increasing their investment in their employees' skills and knowledge, and that these businesses were especially prone to provide training which enhanced business processes within the organisation. Perhaps a very detailed point, it is nevertheless significant that businesses which had increased investments in training were very likely to have increased investment in new technology. If the changes in new technology had led to increases in training, this reinforces the point that productive investments in training were strongly related to innovations in internal business processes; however it was evident that Strategic Planners were more interested in investing in training irrespective of technological innovations.

Not all investments immediately raise productivity, and thereby expand turnover and profitability. Some investments are long term in nature and produce a stream of benefits over many years. Nevertheless, businesses which said that they invested for long term competitiveness did show a discernible propensity to have increased their productivity over the preceding three years. In this case, there was not so much an advantage for the Strategic Planners as a problem for the Evolutionists. About a third of the Evolutionists reported investing for long term competitiveness, as against a half of all the other businesses. (The Informal Strategists, who were almost as likely as the Strategic Planners to have increased investments in training and to have reported investing for long term competitiveness, had a much inferior record of productivity increases. Perhaps this points to a difference in their ability to direct their investments towards innovations in internal business processes?)

For these small businesses in Central London, the more strategically managed businesses appeared to be superior at process innovations which raised productivity performance. This was especially true in relation to technological innovations. The strategically managed businesses were better at general long term investment and had increased their investments in training, both of which were linked to productivity growth.

PRODUCT INNOVATION

Miles and Snow (1978) also identified a successful strategic formula which involved product innovation and 'being first to the market' with the new product. Those businesses which were able to do this enjoyed a period in which returns were good – until other businesses also marketed these new products and the premium was eroded by competition. There are many warnings these days that product life-cycles are falling:

> It can probably be said that competition has always been strong. But the current widespread comments about the special intensity of competition are clearly warranted. . .it is more and more frequent that even successful companies cannot sit back for a while and catch their breath. They must be innovating all the time, facing constant pressure from competitors to do so faster. (Jarillo, 1993, p7)

The obvious response to falling product life-cycles is improved management and planning of product innovation. But some have dismissed the orthodox approach to strategic planning as stultifying; they have backed an environment tolerant of craziness and chaos as likely to produce champions of new products (see, for example, Peters and Waterman, 1982). In arriving at these conclusions there is no doubt that the gurus of business have concentrated on the mega-corporations where problems of bureaucracy beset the adaptation to change. Small businesses, employing from a couple of people to a couple of dozen people, may not have the same dilemmas to balance or juggle. The question of their best approach to product (or service) innovation must be examined specifically.

Amongst the small businesses of Central London the issue of product or service innovation does appear to be amenable to a planning and proactive investment framework. Those businesses with formal or written business plans – the Strategic Planners and the Short-Term Planners – were more likely than the other businesses to have the capacity to bring a new product or service to market very quickly. Thus, a half (53%) of the Strategic Planners strongly, or quite strongly, agreed that their company could do this very quickly, as against a little more than a third (37%) of the Evolutionists. Formal planning, whether managers are working to short or long planning horizons, seems to enhance the focus and concentration that small businesses need to manage product or service innovation. Informality lessens the speedy innovation of products or services.

An orientation to long-term investment for competitiveness and an ability to bring new products or services to market very quickly are both important in the 'freshness' of products or services marketed by a business. Those small businesses which invest for the long term, for example, were more likely than the rest to derive a substantial proportion of their turnover from products or services developed in the last five years. This may well be the point that a firm's ability to be flexible in the future depends on long-term investment, and surely being flexible involves the ability to move markets and change products or services (Ansoff, 1965). As we have already noted, the companies which invested for long term competitiveness tended to be all those which were more formally or strategically managed; it was the Evolutionists which were least likely to invest for the long-term. So, two influential factors in the freshness of products or services are both dependent, in the end, on the strategic management style of the small business.

The argument that new products or services may realise higher levels of profit also seemed to fit the small businesses. Nearly a half (48%) of the businesses which had increased their profitability over the preceding three years reported a substantial proportion of turnover from products or services developed in the last five years; the comparable proportion for businesses which reported declining or static profits was less than a third (30%).

So, a strategic management style can contribute to product or service innovation in small businesses and product or service innovation also contributes to the increased realisation of profits. On the basis of the evidence, however, we would not stress the importance of product or service innovation over the importance of business process innovation which raises productivity. The health and growth of small businesses, based in part on increasing profits, is assisted by productivity growth which increases both turnover and profits. Both types of innovation can benefit the strategically managed small business.

POLICY IMPLICATIONS

The Government's 1994 White Paper on competitiveness identifies the primary importance of innovative capacity and the role of successful management in developing that capacity (DTI, 1994). It further notes the key role of very small businesses in innovation and job creation. In other words, the White Paper acknowledges the importance of both management and small businesses as vital levers for business competitiveness. Logically, these assumptions imply that the calibre and style of management in small businesses are of critical importance to the future of the economy.

This work here has shown that successful management in very small businesses is about strategic planning skills and long term thinking – not just business planning with its emphasis on short to medium term financial management (getting and using resources). It has been seen that a strategic planning style is linked to process and product innovation. Furthermore, such a style is linked to employment growth and profitability.

The implication is, therefore, that public policy for enterprise support needs to strongly recognise the importance of the development of strategic planning skills and thinking in very small businesses. The support for small businesses should not be just about helping with information and short-term problem solving (consultancy and advice), but should endeavour to develop the capacity for strategic thinking within small businesses.

CONCLUSIONS

Small businesses should plan formally and should plan long-term. However, as others have said, it is likely that strategic planning in small businesses may be very different from that found in large businesses. Strategic thinking and thinking longer term is probably what matters in the small firm. Such strategically managed businesses have proved themselves by performing better during difficult economic times and have done so by successful management of innovation. Both product or service innovation, which increases profits, and innovation in business processes, which raises productivity, have been important. If anything, innovation in business processes, especially by means of new technology, may have contributed more. However, it would be wrong to see the issue of innovation as either concerned with process or product. In practice, long-term investment has influenced both process and product innovation and, logically speaking, a productivity increase occurs in relation to specific products or services. Likewise, it would be wrong to emphasise only investments in new technology and ignore the importance of investments in training; both these kinds of investment have been strongly linked in practice and it may well be that they are interdependent in the case of successful innovation. That said, the strong linking of the two kinds of investment may show that it may be difficult to raise productivity through training investments alone, and the introduction of new technology is essential.

Whatever is the truth about the importance of strategic management in large organisations, the conclusions outlined in the previous paragraph suggest that owners or managers of small businesses need to think carefully about how they carry out strategic management. In this general sense, we have corroborated other studies showing a link between planning and success in small firms (cf Baker et al., 1993; Wheelen and Hunger, 1995). In particular, like some other studies we have shown a link with financial performance, but we have also found that growth in terms of employment has also been found to correlate with strategic style. Perhaps equally significantly the evidence for the importance of strategic planning rests on more than just a correlation between style and trends in profitability, productivity and employment: it is also based on the identification of intervening innovation processes between strategic style and productivity and profitability.

For a long time strategic management, or business policy as it was often called, emphasised the decision making process as the essence of strategic management. The two key decisions were regarded as being the choice of product (or service) to market and the choice of the market to supply. Issues of strategic investment in new technology or in the soft assets (especially the skills of the employees) were not given the same centrality in decision making. The management of the processes which determined productivity were, if anything, seen as operational or administrative decision making rather than strategic decision making.

Nowadays there is a shift of focus away from decisions regarding products and markets. The organisation itself has been getting a lot of attention. The chief required qualities of these organisations – that they be adaptable and responsive to customers – is seen as intrinsic to structures and relationships. The usual description of the desirable business structure is that it should be flat, lean and decentralised. In consequence of this shift of attention to the organisation structure, the issue of decision making and planning by top managers is downplayed. Indeed, planning itself is even distrusted (see Peters and Waterman, 1982). Innovation then becomes something that happens naturally and spontaneously by managers and employees who are close to the customer and understand the market's metrics.

What is produced and where it is marketed will never be unimportant. The old strategic planning, which was preoccupied with these matters, unfortunately simply neglected other important strategic issues. For example, it gave only cursory attention to the organisation and its people. But the strategy of creating flatter, leaner decentralised organisations is not strategic planning. Planning is important. Looking ahead, even if forecasting is not an exact science, is important. And it is important because it can help to create the capacities which are important for organisations to be profitable and capable of renewing themselves on an expanding basis. These capacities are built up through innovation processes, not through stylised organisational structures, which are in any case only really relevant to the larger organisations struggling with bureaucratic defects. (The importance of designing efficient processes is well recognised in ideas of business process re-engineering.)

Small businesses, therefore, need strategic planning as an aid to innovation in business processes, making use of new technology and training to raise productivity levels. They need strategic planning to encourage the long-term investments and the speedy marketing of new products and services which keep their products and services 'fresh'. But perhaps above all, they need strategic planning so that they have a framework for their assessments of overall performance, bearing in mind that assessment triggers the will to improve. In the absence of strategic planning businesses may be profitable, but planning enables them to compare outcomes with intentions. The comparison leads to the passing of judgement on a business: its progress is described as healthy and growing because the planning contains an ideal against which it is measured. Perhaps strategic planning reinforces the processes by which aspirations go beyond the limits of present performance, inspiring the recruitment of extra employees whose energies and talents can be harnessed to the drive for increased turnover and profits? Thus if an entrepreneurial business may be defined as more oriented to growth and innovation than other small businesses, then this may explain why some people have argued that an entrepreneurial type of small business owner is more likely to use strategic planning than other small business owners (Wheelen and Hunger, 1995, p362). This can be all summed up by saying that a modern small business needs to plan, not as a parody of corporate planning in big organisations, but as a way of spurring their own entrepreneurial motivation and their continuous interventions in, and improvements of, business processes and products.

REFERENCES

Ansoff H I (1965) Corporate Strategy, Penguin, Harmondsworth.

Baker W H, Addams H L, and Davis B (1993) 'Business Planning in Successful Firms', Long Range Planning, 26, 6, pp82–88.

Boyd K B (1991) 'Strategic planning and financial performance: a meta-analytic review', Journal of Management Studies, 28, pp353–74.

Capon N, Farley J U, and Hulbert J M (1994) 'Strategic Planning and Financial Performance: More Evidence', Journal of Management Studies 1, 1, January, pp105–110.

Coulson-Thomas C (1992) Transforming the Company, Kogan Page, London.

Department of Trade and Industry (1994) Competitiveness: Helping Business to Win, HMSO London.

Greenley G E (1989) 'Does Strategic Planning Improve Company Performance?', in Asch D and Bowman C (eds) Readings in Strategic Management, Macmillan, London.

Jarillo J C (1993) Strategic Networks, Butterworth-Heinemann, Oxford.

Joyce P, Seaman C and Woods A (no date) The CENTEC 1993 Employer Survey: Opportunities for Growth, Central London Training and Enterprise Council, London.

Miles R E and Snow C C (1978) Organization Strategy, Structure and Process, McGraw-Hill, New York.

Pascale R T and Athos A G (1981) The Art of Japanese Management, Penguin, Harmondsworth.

Pearce J A Robbins D K and Robinson R B (1987) 'The Impact of Grand Strategy and Planning Formality on Financial Performance', Strategic Management Journal, 8, pp125–134.

Peters T J and Waterman R H (1982) In Search of Excellence, Harper and Row, New York.

Stacey R (1991) The Chaos Frontier, Butterworth-Heinemann, Oxford.

Storey D J (1994) Understanding the Small Business Sector, Routledge, London.

Wheelen T L and Hunger J D (1995) Strategic Management and Business Policy, Addison Wesley, Wokingham.

Whittington R (1993) What is Strategy – and does it matter?, Routledge, London.

6.

STRATEGIC ISSUES IMPACTING ON SMALL FIRMS

Martyn Robertson

INTRODUCTION

There is a certain fascination with small businesses that has captured the imagination of both the public and politicians over the last two decades. The charisma of a self-made business person is undeniable; the press and public like nothing better than a 'local' success story. Moreover, given the apparent emphasis by the government in the 1980s on supporting new businesses, it might seem that the time has never been better for 'would-be' entrepreneurs to follow in the footsteps of the small business success stories. The tendency, naturally, of such articles to focus on successful growth . . . how the company won a major contract from a large competitor . . . the 'empowered' staff . . . the niche technical expertise . . . the personal leadership qualities . . . the caring attitude toward the community . . . are as an effective a means of spreading 'best practice' as any other.

Yet for most small business owners the reality of establishing and managing a smaller business in the competitive and turbulent world is somewhat stark in comparison. It is fraught with financial and human resource constraints, unprecedented pressures from the business environment and the growing demands of complex legislation. This is not to suggest that the media portrayal of success stories is misleading: they play a vital role in stimulating an entrepreneurial spirit of which the UK is justly proud. It does beg the question, however, that if small businesses are so desirable in both the public and politicians' eyes, why is life for the small business person so hard, and is it improving as we move into the twentieth century? Will this sector with so much potential for wealth creation fulfil the promise of meaningful and flexible work for future generations? Before attempting an answer, let us establish some facts about the size and importance of today's 'Small and Medium Sized Enterprise' (SME) and the special problems these organisations face.

The second aim of the chapter will be to explore the small firm's vulnerability to both the internal and external issues. Finally a view of the future will be put forward by examining the impact of lowering trade barriers; the importance of networks; the use of new organisational forms and homeworking; and the opportunities and threats for the SME resulting from global economic restructuring and the resurgence of the regions. This will allow for a improved understanding of the keys to successful growth.

THE ROLE OF SMES IN CONTEXT

UK: an historical perspective
As expansion and growth of industrial economies slowed down in the late 1960s, it was observed that in those countries with successful and growing economies, such as Japan and

West Germany, there was a thriving small business community which received recognition and encouragement by their national government.

The importance of small firms for the major world economies was first identified in the UK when the Bolton Committee of Inquiry on Small Firms reported in 1971 (HMSO, 1971). This was the first major step towards government awareness and acknowledgement of this sector. It remarked on the poor quality of the data on small firms and recommended that a Small Firms Division should be created within the Department of Trade and Industry (DTI), that a Minister should be responsible for small firms, and that a network of Small Firms Advisory Bureaux should be set up to provide 'signposting' and referral services.

It concluded that both the numbers of small firms and their share of output and employment were in long term decline. The entrepreneur and small business owner had been replaced in the 1960s by a new economic hero – 'corporation man', the decision-maker in the large business organisation. This person was seen as the key to industrial and economic survival and small businesses and their owners were seen as inefficient remnants of previous stages of economic development. The idea that small business owners might have some part to play in the making of Britain's economic future would have been ridiculed in the 1960s (Curran, 1987). The small business-owning stratum in industrial societies, including Britain and the United States, had lost a great deal of the prestige.

However, the decline of the small firm was seen as the consequence of strong and, on the whole, beneficial market forces and because there were also signs in the United States and West Germany that the decline might by levelling off, the Committee reached the conclusion that no drastic action was either necessary or desirable. The Government implemented some of the Bolton recommendations but failed to understand the sector's real problems.

During the 1970s the problems of small firms became even more acute: continued poor economic growth and increasing financial support for industry resulted in the appointment of the Committee to review the Financing of Small Firms (Wilson, 1979). This Committee stated that the public sector financial institutions were discriminating against small firms. Raising initial funds and development capital were fundamental problems identified by the Committee, and raising the profile of these issues contributed to the change in mood toward an 'enterprise culture' of the 1980s. Between 1979 and 1991 UK small firms were and continue to be the main source of employment growth; the numbers of self-employed rose by 52.3% during this period (Department of Employment, 1992b).

SMEs today: an international perspective

Small and medium sized businesses (ie from 1 to 499 employed) are now the backbone of British economic life. The number of SMEs with 500 or fewer employees are estimated to be a staggering 99.9 per cent of all commercial operations in the European Union (EU) resulting in 71% of all employment (Table 1).

There are 87 million jobs in the European Union (EU). 11.6 million small and medium sized organisations provide 70% of all jobs and employ more than 62 million people. As SMEs account for 99.9% of all EU organisations, the enterprises have been classified as micro enterprises (0–9 employees) and small and medium sized enterprises (10–499 employees).

The UK and French economies are characterised by a proliferation of micro organisations

Table 1: Enterprises and Employment in the European Union 1988

Size class	% no of enterprises	% employment share
Micro (1–9 employees)	92.1	29.8
Small and medium (10–499)	7.8	41.3
Large (over 499 employees)	0.1	28.9

Source: Eurostat, 1988

Table 2: Employment and Output of SMEs

	Employment	GDP
Germany	64%	50%
UK	65%	32%
Japan	80%	60%
America	50%	40%

Source: Stanworth and Gray, 1991; OECD Labour Forces Statistics, 1990; Department of Employment, 1992a.
Note: Germany does not include the former GDR.

(93%). Over 52% of these businesses have no employees whatsoever. In Italy small and medium sized companies proliferate; the big, privately owned companies quoted on the bourse are a small minority. Of the six million people working in the Italian manufacturing industry, only one million are employed by big companies (Glover, 1993). SMEs account for the great bulk of Italian industrial production: only seven Italian companies are included in Fortune 500 world list compared with 43 in the UK (Gallo, 1993).

European SMEs are dominant in the distributive trades, hotel and catering, repair and construction, where they account for more than 90% of employment. The banking, finance, insurance, rental and the other service industries are also dominated by SMEs: the SME employment share is about 65%. In the manufacturing industry, SMEs count for 62% of employment and are the main employers in the consumer goods sector.

Germany has the greatest proportion of small and medium sized organisations in the EU and employs a greater proportion of the workforce than other European states (46.7%). They have 12.6% of their enterprises in the middle sized company (10–499 employees). This is 5% above the EU average for that category.

More interesting, however, is the ability of this type of German and Japanese SMEs to produce in excess of 50% of their countries GDP (Table 2).

Simon (1992) believes that the German rates have been achieved because their small and medium sized companies, known as the Mittelstand, have a talent for export and a command of their markets that belie their small size and low profile. They account for the bulk of Germany's considerable trade surplus. The Mittelstand companies are champions of global competition and have remained hidden for two reasons. Most of their products are used in the manufacturing process or subsumed by the end product and, more importantly, they appear to relish their obscurity. Many of these companies have world market shares in the range of 70–90% (Simon, 1992).

Similarly Japanese small businesses account for 99% of all business establishments, 80% of all jobs and 60% of GDP. Between 1960 and 1986 the number of Japanese SMEs increased in every sector of the economy except utilities.

The strength of the small business in the Japanese economy can be explained in part by the influence of government policy and the concern, from the late 1950s, to reduce the dual structure of the economy (ie the difference between large and small business) (Sato, 1990). Thus from the 1950s there was a noticeable development of subcontracting to small firms, the formulation of large firm-small firm strategic partnerships, and through this, significant improvements in management quality and technological adaption within small firms. Thus by 1983 about half of all Japanese contracting firms claimed that their technological level was on a par with, or exceeded that of, their parent companies. At this stage most parent companies had changed the status of their small firm subcontractors from one of supplementary supplier to strategic partner (Sato, 1990). By the late 1980s many Japanese enterprises were establishing new plants in foreign countries rather than in the domestic market. Throughout this process the Japanese government has created the environment and conditions whereby the transformation of the Japanese small business could occur. (Sato, 1990; Kirby, 1991). The role of SMEs in the United State's economy cannot be underestimated. In 1992, 20.5 million small businesses accounted for nearly 99.8% of all

American businesses and, according to the Small Business Administration (SBA), small firms employ more than 50% of the private work-force (US SBA, 1993).

Entrepreneurship, self-employment and small firm owner management have infiltrated every segment of our society – women, ethnic minorities, senior citizens and young people. They are operating franchises, sole proprietorships, partnerships, co-operatives and companies on an unprecedented scale.

The rise of small businesses has been accompanied by efforts from governments and advisers to keep pace by providing support in the form of laws, loans and grants. The challenge has reached governments of developing countries too, where the growth of new and small businesses are a vital part of the 'second' industrial revolution. Over the last decade the growth of the small firms sector has been substantially more rapid in the UK than in other countries. As a result, the relative size of the small firms sector in the UK is now much closer to that in other countries than it was at the beginning of the 1980s.

The very rapid overall increase in self employment is not on the whole something which has been shared by our EU neighbours and other trading partners. Although there have been increases in many countries, the increase in the UK between 1979 and 1989 was more than 3 times the EU average. It could be said that the UK was starting from a low base, but so were the USA, Canada and Germany, and they have not experienced such dramatic increases (Department of Employment, 1992a).

THE PROBLEMS FACING SMALL FIRMS

Vulnerability to external influences

The stereotype small firm is generally perceived as innovative, responsive, providers of new jobs and a vital link in the supply chain to large businesses. Its strength may typically lie in low overheads, a lean organisation structure and lack of bureaucracy. The downside of being relatively small and lean can be lack of depth in certain specialisms (such as marketing), lack of managerial experience, under-capitalisation, inefficient scale of operations and inadequate resource to keep abreast of changes in market conditions and technology (Stoy Hayward/Nat West Bank, 1987; Lander, Presley and Boocock, 1993).

Larger organisations do not help the smaller firm by being late with payments (CBI 1991), expecting smaller firms to supply products and services via a formal system, only using them for small and often intermittent purchases. Ultimately, large firms will tend to consider price, quality and delivery more important than loyalty to local small firms (Blackburn, 1993). The CBI (1991) believe that the late payment of bills is endangering the survival of nearly one in five businesses.

The increasing burden of red tape on British business is partly caused by the ambivalence of the DTI and the Treasury towards deregulation (Social Market Foundation, 1992). The burden of legislation, which is an irritating and expensive inconvenience to established concerns, can be life threatening to small enterprises. Despite SMEs becoming politically fashionable, very little appears to have been done to remove the particular burdens with which they are faced.

The right business climate is vital if initiative and the application of new products or services to new or existing markets are to be encouraged. The current economic climate is characterised by economic volatility, demographic change, restructuring and downsizing within large businesses, high unemployment, short-term thinking, and disjointed government policy. Business success in the future, whatever the size of organisation, will require sensitivity, responsiveness, flexibility, and clarity (PA Consulting Group, 1992). These are not characteristics which come readily to mind when thinking of large corporations, and firms are rethinking their structures to respond to market conditions, delayering, and contracting out to other businesses.

The small firms sector represents practically all businesses so that events such as the decline in the local economy, substantial exchange rate fluctuations, increasing international competition, the collapse of communism and national budget deficits have impacted on them just as much as on the multinationals, and probably more seriously. Policy makers are unaware of small firms' needs and, unlike Germany, there are not enough good large British companies to pull small firms along with them. Even if they want to it's hard for those enterprises to latch on to foreign firms.

On a more positive note, the UK economy, along with its industrialised neighbours, is witnessing a shift toward service industries, which by their nature allow smaller businesses to play a more central role. SMEs can use their geographical dispersion, their closeness to the customer and to local culture to gain a competitive edge that larger organisations will find difficult to match.

Vulnerability to internal issues

Management competency and motivation
Small firms may lack managerial capability and have little experience of identifying and evaluating external advice and assistance (Boswell, 1973). These weaknesses contribute to the poor ability of owners to deal with bureaucratic burdens placed upon them by government, and to bargain effectively with suppliers of capital and other resources (Bonoma and Johnston, 1978; Borrie, 1986).

The 1971 Bolton report explicitly highlighted the 'fervently guarded sense of independence' which is seen to be a prime motivator for many small business owner-managers. Contrary to popular belief, and a great deal of economic theory, money and the pursuit of a personal financial fortune are not as significant as the desire for personal involvement, responsibility and the independent quality and style of life which many small business owner-managers strive to achieve. However, the pursuit and eventual attainment of independence brings with it the power to influence events and influence people peripheral to the small business and the owner-manager. Whilst there can be little doubt that the power, capability and influence of the entrepreneur is of vital importance in determining the creation and development of an organisation, the relentless drive for personal achievement may inhibit the growth potential and, ultimately, the survival potential of the small firm (Jennings and Beaver, 1993). At the same time, the stated importance of profit orientation for the business is sometimes in conflict with owners' personal objectives, which might be expressed in terms of security or lifestyle. In a number of cases a high growth strategy is perceived by the owners as threatening to the firm's existence (Stanworth and Curran, 1976).

An essential ingredient of an entrepreneur appears to be the ability to perceive opportunity through imagination and foresight. This individual is deemed to be a dynamic force with extraordinary energy – an agent of change – capable of exploiting opportunities. However in order to do this they must be capable of managing the resources at their disposal effectively.

Small business and the family
The family is of crucial importance to small firms, but these central relationships are much more complex and contested than commonly portrayed. The family acts as both a resource and a constraint: the company benefits from the flexibility afforded by familial ties, but the family also imposes obligations which occasionally contradict economic rationality. The diffuse nature of such arrangements means that 'negotiated paternalism', rather than an 'autocracy of harmony' more accurately depicts the family at work.

Finance
Small firms often have difficulty raising adequate finance to develop their business, and sometimes experience a difficult relationship with banks. In the attempt to mitigate their losses, the banks have taken an approach towards SMEs which attempts to achieve one or more of the following: minimise risk through maximising security; maximising margins through large risk premiums, or through maximum administration costs passed on to the

customer whenever possible; or lowering risk through more informed selection criteria. These practices are designed to assist the financial stability of banks, not of their small business customers.

The 1980s were an extraordinary time for growth, often with 'clever' debt structures. The practice of extending trade credit to support customers' stock holding is generally beneficial to the economy. However, these objectives have been lost from view, as trade credit is now more associated with funding trade debtors which results in a multiplier effect leading to rising financing costs and less predictable income for the majority of firms. The 1990s have seen a return to more normal business cycles and the venture capital industry, banks and other parts of the financial community are expecting lower returns (Cressy, 1992).

THE FUTURE FOR SMALL AND MEDIUM SIZED FIRMS

The impact of lowering trade barriers

The key trends for the 1990s which will shape the subsequent decade have already emerged: new technologies and fragmentation of market demand have given rise to new forms of organisation and articulation between the elements of the economy. McGowan and Hill (1993) are predicting that by 2010 there will be an 'internationalisation' of small firms. Whether these new forms will really exist may be subject to the same speculation that so-called 'global' companies are attracting.

However, some trends are clear now: as barriers to trade, particularly in Europe (for UK firms), are removed, many companies can expect to see significant changes to the size and nature of their markets, and to the standards affecting their products and services. Distribution and communication will become simpler whilst competition will be tougher, and small UK firms may find trading conditions very difficult (McGowan and Hill, 1993). The businesses formed in the 1980s will be tested through their ability to exploit these new international opportunities. They will need to access specialist skills, market information, finance and technologies to be successful in the export arena:

> The global marketplace is already a reality. Products from many countries compete for space on the shelves of major national retailers, and industrial buyers seek out the best suppliers and services: national origins have become increasingly irrelevant to producers striving to prosper in local, regional and international markets. In the UK, where exports represent 30% of GNP (against 10% in Japan), this poses special challenges.
>
> Despite the entrepreneurial revolution in Britain over the last decade, and a tradition of exporting smaller companies which account for about 25% of GNP, they are responsible for less than 15% of total exports. This disparity has commonly been explained by a lack of funds for business development, the lack of expertise (notably in marketing), a reluctance to move into foreign markets, and barriers to entry. (Cannon, 1992)

Even localised services such as refuse collection and funeral services are facing competition, as the recent incursion of French firms into these areas has shown. Smaller companies, particularly those located in the service sector of the economy, have a much more parochial attitude than large firms, and are therefore much less aware of what Europe offers, and the threats it holds (Cook, 1993). In the 'shake-out' from a highly competitive European marketplace, UK may face a high proportion of job losses. In any case, the upward trend of business insolvencies (114,000 in Europe in 1989, over 170,000 in 1990) seems set to continue (Trade Indemnity, 1992).

The importance of networks

A second 'shift' which has emerged in the 1990s is towards the importance of 'networks'. SMEs by being interwoven with large businesses as suppliers are inextricably linked to their fortunes. As Peters (1990) comments: 'Networks are changing the definition of big'.

Germany and Denmark provide powerful examples of the effectiveness of smaller firm networks. UK business people might envy the extent to which the equivalent of 'Chambers of Commerce' or enterprise agencies positively support these networks, but it is a manifestation not just of government policy, but of a deeper cultural attitude toward small businesses.

Looking ahead, new types of networks or groupings of firms will become more common, such as partnership sourcing or private public partnerships. As a result of these formations, the larger firms are now constantly reviewing the quality and performance of their suppliers' products or services. A number have changed all of their suppliers over the last five years to smaller companies. These smaller firms are generally managed and owned by younger people who have access to technology which makes them more responsive and flexible to their customers' needs.

Each time an employee within a firm moves from one project to the next, a new 'informal' network of sorts is formed. Chelsom (1992) noted that multinational companies are using fewer suppliers in their quest for international efficiency and cost benefits – but an important role exists for smaller companies. To support global operations, end producers need supplier partners with global capabilities which may include participation in design, manufacturing and servicing, around the world.

The price of admission to the supply base of a large blue chip company therefore implies a major investment in training, quality management, international communications, and probably international distribution capability. Surprisingly, this does not preclude the owner managed company. The eighth largest supplier to Ford in Europe is such a company. Taking the supply base of Ford Britain as an example, there are a few very large suppliers and many, many small ones. Ten thousand companies sold £3 billion of goods and services to Ford Britain in 1989. The top 50 suppliers between them accounted for £1.2bn of this total; the top 100, £1.6bn. The dividing line in terms of turnover between the top 1,000 and the other 9,000 suppliers comes at about £400,000 per annum (Harris, 1993).

The larger companies use alliances to spread risk. Supply partners need to adopt quality management, shared product development, advances in communications and distribution capability. Training is vital. 'A strong alliance is one where each partner gains.' A high proportion of joint ventures have fallen by the wayside because the two sides have not identified overlapping aims, but the trend toward partnership sourcing – a closer and more fruitful relationship between, typically, a large manufacturer and small business suppliers – is however to go on (Harris, 1993).

The economic climate
Recent events such as large budget deficits, restructuring in nationalised and multinational enterprises causing long term unemployment, suggest that the economic climate of the 1990s will be much more difficult for small business than it has been in the 1980s (Johnson, 1992). But the impact of world recession has been uneven: one study (ACOST, 1990) revealed that over the last 20 years, UK businesses with up to 99 employees have seen their share of net output double to 19.3%, while businesses in the 100–499 employee category have managed only to maintain their share of net output at 14.5%. The numbers reflect an overall decline in the number of medium sized businesses, while the number of small businesses has rapidly increased. Those countries characterised by strong networks of medium sized businesses have fared better.

By 2020 there will be 8 billion people in the world (United Nations, 1994), half as many again as there are now and the use of biosciences and technology will create neural networks and huge increases in the efficiency with which we manage our resources and conduct economic activity. British companies have to compete for business and capital in this global market place. To take an extreme view, if they are not encouraged and supported through positive interventionalist initiatives we could be looking at an Eastern European style economy within 10–15 years as a result of British uncompetitivenesss.

The increase in homeworking (teleworking)
With the advent of affordable telecommunications, the tremendous potential for homeworking or telecommuting can be a reality: the 'electronic cottage' is nigh. The Henley

Centre for Forecasting has studied the rise of teleworking and predicts that by the end of the century, 18% of the UK labour force will be teleworking in one form or another. This represents a three-fold increase in this mode of work. Its attractions include the ability to release individuals from the daily grind of commuting on crowded public transport or traffic ridden roads and allows additional leisure time. These benefits may however come at a price; the loss of social contact in the workplace and the re-imprisonment of women at home; the abuse of the home by demanding employers; and the psychological bullying by employers imposing unrealistic deadlines on homeworkers causing a redesignation of the home as a commercial location rather than one for social interaction.

New organisational forms

New networking arrangements
In order to speculate about the organisation of the future we require different conceptual horizons – such as culture, time, sense, space, technology, employment, organisation and location. This means new groupings of organisations and informal networks, the growth of business alliances involving joint ventures and partnership sourcing, the rise of the 'not-for-profit' sector, global economic restructuring and international markets served by local communities supported by technology, and micro multinationals using individuals with a portfolio of jobs.

   The essential feature of these types of organisations are that they will be flexible, functional and yet strategically focused. As a result there will be a need to create flexible legal structures which allow the entity to exist only for the duration of a specific short term need. New legal forms such as retail franchising will become increasingly popular, and the one-director EU firm will become a reality in the UK. Both the Germans and the French have examples of these forms of enterprises. Control for these entities could be assigned to the Euro Chambers or a development of the UK Business Link programme, designed to provide the small and medium sized business person with a single contact point for information and support. The scheme is in its infancy; its success depends on existing help agencies (TECs, Chamber of Commerce, DTI etc) cooperating and forming an alliance – a significant break from tradition. The situation in Germany, however, where all SMEs are legally compelled to register at the local Chamber of Commerce, renders legal form almost irrelevant (Bennett et al., 1994).

   Whatever type of entity is developed cultural change is needed, and the scope for governments to assist is limited. Smaller firms will have to 'think networks' before they become a real vehicle for success. 'Dating agencies' – central or networked databases of partners sought or available throughout the European Union – will be a feature of the next decade.

The micro-multi
The 'micro-multi' is a formal amalgam of highly flexible individuals utilising regional, national or global networks through sub-contract arrangements and partnership agreements to legally cooperate on a continuous basis (Ackroyd, 1993).

   These units are unlikely to follow the classical route of multi-national companies by nominating a market on a national and sectorial basis before establishing a presence overseas. They are likely to have a conceptual or visionary view of the market, develop, make or assemble their own product to meet their internationally selected clients. An example of where this form of organisation has been successful are information system providers who tailor systems to their customers' needs without being tied to proprietary products (Ackroyd, 1993).

   The features of micro multis are that they have very small staff numbers, about 30 employees; a high turnover and value added (high earnings per employee); a variety of legal forms, although the holding company is common; very few are owned by or affiliated to larger companies, ie very few spinouts or spinoffs; an unorthodox structure (matrix);

indeterminate organisation boundary (easy staff movement); informal alliances and affiliations (crucial networks); polyvalent knowledge worker staff (formal qualifications); an organisational strategy and design which follow staff competencies and interests, ie no formal managerial function; a high orientation towards customers (selective); growth by replication (not by increases in scale); and high mobility (product range, scale of activities and geography). They are likely to have developed international operations through branches, or subsidiaries overseas. The individual parties to the micro-multi may be self-employed consultants, separate companies, or operating divisions of a company (Ackroyd, 1993).

Dependent upon the type of contract undertaken, then the team for that work would be determined and the organisation shaped accordingly.

> At the level of practical organisation, these structures are matrices that link the activity of small and changing networks of highly skilled individuals. (Ackroyd, 1993, p87)

Ackroyd concludes that:

> There are a number of indications from comparative and historical research, that it is not the form of firms themselves – the way they are organised and managed for example – that makes for economic success but the way that they inter-relate with other elements of the economy. In particular a number of successful formulas in the relations of small and large firms are probably possible . . . . . . Certainly new conjunctures of regional, national and global capital flows are re-writing the basis on which economic units inter-relate. (Ackroyd, 1993, p89)

The Japanese independent
The Japanese have been very successful in developing their small firm sector and have achieved this through large company/small company involvement. Once the small entity has become strong enough it becomes independent from its parent firm.

These Japanese independents develop into small but strong global enterprises based on the most developed technologies, develop their overseas subsidiaries through foreign direct investment and become more independent from their parent firms.

The question for the UK, however, is can the process of enterprise transformation and improvement in SME business performance be enhanced by importing/imitating models of best practice so enthusiastically offered by the USA and Europe, and their derivatives of Japanese systems? (Currie et al., 1993). This surely depends on the capacity of managers to adapt to these methods and the need to recognise the broader cultural influences.

Resurgence of the regions
The resurgence of certain regions is connected with particular new patterns of economic activity. Great tracts of cities, where some of the UK's great manufacturing industries once stood, are either derelict, cleared or being reused for very different purposes, usually far removed from manufacturing industry (May, 1989). These patterns are characterised by inter-dependent activities of small, flexible units densely distributed in particular regions that inter-relate in a constructive and effective manner. This trend is likely to continue as individuals recognise the need for cooperation if the local community is to survive. Paradoxically, there is a recognition that the local economy has a reduced importance for firms challenged to survive in a competitive global marketplace (Blackburn, 1993).

Retail organisations in their fight back against the juggernaut of the international supermarkets provide a useful illustration. The spearhead against the fight against the international hypermarkets was to develop a national buying consortium embracing most of the country's medium sized independent food retailers, marshalling a buying power of £9 billion a year (Woodcock, 1993):

> Such cooperation is essential for survival in a market which is dominated by multiples – 65% of the food trade is concentrated in the hands of five chain store operators. Nisa

Today's, the buying organisation, has not only products for the 750 member companies but also helped to maintain choice and responsiveness to local needs. The organisation has developed links through a supranational purchasing organisation, European Marketing Distribution, which brings together similar operations in other countries. Among the benefits is the ability to develop products on an international scale.

The first results include a pan European brand of washing powder and washing up liquid launched in nine European Community countries but sold only through independent stores. Such international buying power enables them to offer the consumer competitive prices. It makes full use, too, of the economies of scale provided by the Single European Market. (Woodcock, 1993)

Effectively it means that the benefits of a market of 300 million people are accruing to the medium sized independent retailers in a way which is not open to the major multiples.

The opportunities of global economic restructuring

Global economic restructuring is in part made possible by transport and communications developments that enable decision makers to travel from one side of the world to another in 24 hours and to transfer information anywhere within seconds (May, 1989). Much industrial production of existing and new products moved from established locations in the First World to the Third, where cheaper and more pliant labour was available. The products were then shipped back to the First World. With advanced satellite communications, plus the fact that much of the hardware is already made there, much the same process could occur in the information industry where routine tasks can be undertaken anywhere. Indeed, it is already the case that the entire world ticketing operation of American Airlines is now located in Barbados and that Saztec, an American computer software company, has its data entry facility in China, where the wage rate is $2 a week (Kinsman, 1989; May, 1989). Large London based auditing firms are transmitting data for review so that the operation is conducted globally 24 hours a day. Much of this work is being undertaken by smaller firms. Language differences may delay the process but that is not an insuperable problem if the potential profit is big enough.

The international market is now served in part by local communities supported by technology. The new economic model of international specialisation emphasises introduction of new flexible manufacturing technology, fragmentation of markets, increasing small firm autonomy over decision making, and a renewed craft tradition manifesting itself most visibly in smaller enterprises. (Piore and Sabel, 1984; Goodman et al., 1989; Blackburn, 1993).

Improved understanding of the keys to successful growth

The true entrepreneur recognises the factors which are critical to her/his success. Most entrepreneurs have strong views and values. They set the style and culture of the business and in the early days make most of the decisions. Gray (1993) found that entrepreneurial firms achieved higher growth than firms with a proprietorial culture, but cautioned that actually wanting to grow is one necessary condition for growth but may not be a sufficient condition. A critical element is decentralisation of the decision-making process without loss of control.

The CBI (1992) recommend that firms that wish to survive or grow should aim for quality before growth, choose the right people, keep them, learn to delegate, and watch the cash flow. They add that there is a need to understand the implications of increasing globalisation and stay close to their customers, ie think globally whilst acting locally. The German Mittlestand have successfully followed this strategy. Germany's industrial prowess is irrefutable and its outstanding export performance is widely recognised (Parnell, 1993). This group has ensured the continuation of the German success story. Their philosophy, and those of their bankers, investors and managers, is orientated towards exports and the long term; subsidiaries have now been established in the East to ensure their future prosperity.

The traditional concept of a limited company or sole trader operating locally may be lost to the past. Personal objectives, so central to the development of any small business, may increasingly include travelling, studying and working abroad. In this case skilled and highly motivated individuals may be looking to internationalise their firms. Location is not important to these people. Grayson (1991) classifies them as the Nintendo Generation, technologically literate, with global culture, environmentally aware and ready to travel.

CONCLUSION

To return to the questions posed in the introduction: does the evidence indicate that life for the SME sector will improve as we move into the twentieth century, and that it will fulfil its potential to provide future generations with meaningful and flexible work? The answer has to be 'it depends'. That the potential is there is beyond doubt. The UK's declining manufacturing industries will not return – the growth of the SME sector has to be the focus for wealth creation and improved standards of living. And it is relatively straightforward to see on what it depends: effective direction of government aid to business start-ups and medium sized businesses who need help to grow, a strong competitive home economy, development of strong and supportive networks, competent managers who are able to identify and exploit opportunities across the world . . . actually achieving these things is of course much harder.

UK owners and their stakeholders will need to undergo significant mind shifts. They will need to internationalise their thinking and overcome their reluctance to move into foreign markets: overcome their fear of working with others so that high quality informal and formal networks are created to achieve added value; from this develop a strong regional entrepreneurial culture and skills base with export vision; rise to the technological challenge; be flexible, highly skilled, strategically focussed and act with vision and foresight. The next twenty years are set to be an exciting and challenging period in the development of the SME sector.

REFERENCES

Ackroyd S (1993) 'In search of the Micro Multinational', Paper presented to the European Business and Economic Development Conference, Leicester.

ACOST (1990) The Enterprise Challenge: Overcoming the barriers to growth in small firms, HMSO, London.

Bennett R, Wicks P, and McCoshan A (1994) Local Empowerment and Business Services, UCL, London.

Blackburn R (1993) 'Small Businesses and Local Networks: A Realistic Assessment', Paper presented at Leeds Metropolitan University – Enterprise in the Local Economy: Initiatives for the 1990s, 3 March.

Bonoma T V and Johnston W J (1978) 'The Social Psychology of Industrial Buying and Selling', Industrial Marketing Management, 7 October, p216.

Borrie G (1986) Restrictions on the Kind of Organisation Which Members of the Professions May Offer Their Services, Office of Fair Trading, London.

Boswell J (1973) The Rise and Decline of Small Firms, Allen and Unwin, London.

Cannon T (1992) Exporting, Keys to Growth: For Owner Managers Seeking to Expand, Price Waterhouse and Employment Department.

CBI (1991) Late Payment of Debts, a Survey of Small and Medium Sized Businesses, CBI, London.

CBI (1992) Making it in Britain, CBI, London.

Chelsom J (1992) Strategic Alliances: Keys to Growth: For owner managers seeking to expand, Price Waterhouse and Employment Department.

Cook M (1993) 'SMEs in Northamptonshire: Europe calling', European and Economic Development Conference, Leicester

Cressy R (1992) 'Loan commitments and business starts: An empirical investigation of UK data', SME Centre Working Paper No 12, Warwick Business School.

Curran J (1987) 'Small Enterprises and their Environments: A Report', Small Business Research Unit, Kingston Polytechnic, Kingston-upon-Thames.

Currie W, Helinska-Hughes E and Hughes M (1993) 'Business Performance in the US, UK and Japan: An Example to Central and Eastern Europe', Paper presented to the European Business and Economic Development Conference, Leicester.

Department of Employment (1992a) 'Planning Today for Tomorrow's Skills, A Summary of Labour Market and Skill Trends 1993/4'.

Department of Employment (1992b) Small Firms in Britain Report, Employment Department.

Eurostat (1992) Enterprise in Europe; Eurostat DGXXIII.

Gallo E (1993) 'Italy Fudges Privatisation', Financial Times, 12 January.

Glover R (1993) 'Italy's Families Lose Their Invincibility', The Guardian, 19 June.

Goodman E, Bamford J and Saynor P (1989) (eds) Industrial Districts in Italy, Routledge, London.

Gray C (1993) 'Stages of Growth and Entrepreneurial Career Motivation', in Chittenden et al. (1993) Small Firms: Recession and Recovery, Paul Chapman, London.

Grayson D (1991) Business in the Community, Small Business 2001 Megatrend.

Harris (1993) The Times, 27 April 1993.

HMSO (1971) (Bolton Report) Report on the Committee of Inquiry on Small Firms, Cmnd. 4811, HMSO, London.

Jennings P and Beaver G (1993) 'The Abuse of Entrepreneurial Power: An Explanation of Management Failure?' Paper presented to the Small Businesses and Small Business Development Conference, Leicester.

Johnson S (1992) in Robertson M (1992) Towards the 21st Century – The Challenge for Small Business, Nadamal Books, Macclesfield.

Kinsman P (1989) 'New patterns of Work, Tomorrow's Workplace – A New Lease of Life for the Regions', Paper presented to the AD 2000 Conference, INDEVO Ltd, London.

Kirby D (1991) Marketing and the Smaller Firm, Durham University Business School.

Lander D, Presley J and Boocock G (1993) 'The System of Support For SMEs in the UK and Germany', Paper presented to the European Business and Economic Development Conference, Leicester 1993.

McGowan P and Hill J (1993) 'Small Firms' Internationalisation', Paper presented to the Small Businesses and Small Business Development Conference, Leicester.

May G (1989) 'The Future of the City: Some Issues for the 21st Century', CUDEM Working Paper Series, 2 October 1989.

PA Consulting Group (1992) Mercury and CBI, Succeeding Through Information Technology in the Single European Market.

Parnell L (1993) 'Exporting by German SMEs: Small Company Perspectives', European Business and Economic Development, 1, 4, pp27–30.

Peters T (1990) 'West Germany: A Business Story for the 90s in US German Economic Yearbook', German American Chamber of Commerce Inc, pp83–92.

Piore M and Sabel C (1984) The Second Industrial Divide: Possibilities for Prosperity, Basic Books, New York.

Sato H (1990) 'Small Business in Japan: a Historical Perspective' Small Business Economics, 1, pp121–129.

Simon H (1992) 'Lessons from Germany's Midsize Giants', Harvard Business Review, March – April 1992, pp115–123.

Social Market Foundation (1992) Deregulation.

Stanworth J and Curran J (1976) 'Growth and the Small Firm – An Alternative View', Journal of Management Studies, 13, 2 pp95–110.

Stanworth J and Gray C (1991) (eds) Bolton Twenty Years On, Paul Chapman, London.

Stoy Hayward/London Business School, National Westminster Bank (1987) 'A study to determine the reasons for the failure of small businesses in the UK'.

Trade Indemnity (1992) Quarterly Business Review, London.

United Nations (1994) World population prospects; the 1994 revision, New York.

US Small Business Administration (1993) The State of Small Business, US Government Printing Office, Washington.

Wilson H (1979) The Financing of Small Firms, Report of the Committee to Review the Functioning of Financial Institutions, Cmnd 7503, HMSO, London.

Woodcock C (1993) 'Who Cares Wins: The Key for Thriving Companies in the 90s', The Guardian, 14 April.

Woodcock C (1993) 'Small is Bountiful When it Comes to Ethical Behaviour: Unsung Heroes of the Moral Majority', The Guardian 15 February.

7.

SMALL AND MEDIUM BUSINESS SECTORS IN A RECESSIONARY ECONOMY

Ted Fuller

INTRODUCTION

This chapter presents an analysis of the changes in the number of VAT registered legal units in the size range £51,000 to £5 million turnover per year. The statistics are assumed, with explicit reservations, to be a proxy for the number of small firms in the UK in this size range. Throughout the chapter the firms in this size band will be referred to as SMEs (small and medium sized enterprises), though it is recognised that the UK business population includes small firms below this size band and medium sized firms above this size band. The data source, PA1003 from the Central Statistical Office (CSO, 1993b), is described along with the limitations presented by the data source for this exercise. The population of small firms from the VAT database, within the turnover size range, is described, illustrating the differences in 'share' of the overall sector of this size band in different sectors.

The context of this analysis is a very deep economic recession. The effect of the recession on small firms is discussed. A comparison between UK Gross Domestic Product (GDP) and the reported change in sales turnover of small firms is drawn. Further analysis of the statistics in the VAT subsectors and a range of size bands is then carried out. This shows the changes in numbers of firms in each sector, the range of changes within sectors and between different sizes of firms. From this analysis conclusions about impact of the recession on the numbers of small firms are drawn.

DATA SOURCE

The source of data for the analyses in this chapter is the CSO document PA1003 which provides a detailed analysis of the number of firms (actually legal units see below) registered for VAT in the UK at a point in time. Data on firms with turnovers between £51,000 per annum and £5m have been extracted. The data from PA1003 is not a true measure of the small firms population, but data on this particular size segment closely resembles the overall population.

The VAT database is currently the most in depth published government source of statistical information on UK firms. Its main advantage is that it comprises data from all firms registered for VAT and is not based on a sample. It has been described by the Department of Employment as the most accurate illustration of the 'business population' in the UK. This assertion, however, needs to be qualified, given the high number of firms (companies and self employed people with and without employees) below the VAT threshold. For example, only 44% of self-employed people are estimated as being VAT registered (Fuller, 1992, p88).

Bannock et al. (SBRT, 1993) suggest that 64% of businesses were registered for VAT in 1991. They also estimate that although the total number of VAT registrations grew between 1989 and 1991, the total number of firms, and the number of self employed people, declined.

The reasons for the differences are mainly explained by the behaviour of firms with turnovers below the registration threshold. In sectors where VAT cannot be reclaimed by the customer of the small firm, it is usually in the firm's interest not to be registered. For instance, the catering and retail sectors are required to show the private consumer prices 'inclusive' of VAT. Assuming that firms in these sectors charge customers the same price whether registered or not, the extra margin they gain by not being registered is the going rate of VAT, ie 7/47 or approximately 15% on sales when VAT is 17.5%, eg £4,468 on a £30,000 turnover. In some sectors, such as business services, owners of small firms with turnovers under the VAT threshold are more likely to remain voluntarily registered, they can reclaim VAT charged to them and it adds to their 'credibility' with business customers (who can reclaim the VAT charged). Prices in these sectors are negotiated exclusive of VAT.

Data are available on voluntary registrations in each main VAT sector, but not in subsectors. However, VAT data on firms below registration threshold are not an adequate illustration of that part of the business population. Furthermore, the use of statistics relating to firms in the size band 'VAT threshold to £50,000 turnover' as a time series has recently been flawed by increases in the threshold level well above the rate of inflation. Inflation also has an effect on the number of firms in the other size bands. As McCann points out (1993), the turnover size bands are in current prices so firms will tend to move into higher bands over time as a result of price inflation.

The registration of a VAT Legal Unit does not always indicate one business. Two or more registered units under common ownership may elect to be jointly assessed (and therefore treated as one group registration). One company may elect to have VAT assessed separately for two or more divisions. Approximately 20,000 groups and 500 divisional companies are excluded from CSO data in PA1003 to more truly reflect the trends for small firms.

The VAT database is shown on a particular reference date which excludes some businesses which have begun trading and not yet registered and some which have ceased but not yet deregistered. Given an annual turnover in registered units of approximately 12% of the population (CSO, 1993a), slight variations in timing of registrations or deregistrations will marginally change the overall picture.

The use of sales turnover as a measure of size is, of course, only one dimension. Firms with the same turnover vary in other dimensions within sectors and between sectors. Fundamentally, sales turnover is not the same measure as added value, ie it takes no account of input costs and therefore the contribution of the firm to the economy in monetary terms.

It is with the above limitations that the following analysis should be read.

THE £51,000 TO £5 MILLION SEGMENT OF THE SMALL FIRMS POPULATION

Firms with turnovers of between £51,000 and £5 million are chosen to represent the solid core of 'established' SMEs. Most of the firms in this turnover size range will be VAT registered. In a few instances such firms may employ no other person than the proprietor, but it is likely that most will employ some people, and again very few in this turnover range will employ more than 200 people (indicating a turnover per employee of £25,000 at the maximum). Approximately 62% of all VAT registered legal units were included in this size range in 1993. The proportion varies with sector. 83% of catering legal units are in this size band, while only 46% of the agriculture sector are. The different proportions are shown in Table 1. A more complete picture is provided in Appendix 1.

Table 1: Proportion of Legal Units in the £51,000 to £5 Million Turnover Size Band in 1993 Among UK VAT Registered Population

Sector	Number of legal units	Percentage of sector population
Production	109,825	68
Construction	125,085	56
Transport	41,705	58
Wholesale etc.	96,450	67
Retailing	192,094	80
Finance etc.	91,359	51
Motor trades	56,346	73
Business services	67,440	48§
All other services	72,194	52
Agriculture etc.	78,642	46
Postal services etc.	917	54
Catering	99,621	83

§ A further 39,855 (28%) business services are voluntarily registered with turnovers below the VAT threshold (£34,000 in 1993).
Source: CSO PA1003 1993.

THE RECESSION AND ITS EFFECT ON SMALL BUSINESS

The recession in the UK, defined as a period of zero or negative growth in GDP, was between Q1 1991 and Q1 1993. The downwards trend of growth in GDP started in Q1 1989 from an overheated peak of 5% growth per annum. By Q2 1991 most respondents to the Small Business Research Trust's quarterly survey (SBRT, 1994)) put 'lack of business or low turnover' at the head of their list of problems (25.3%) compared with 21.3% for 'high interest rates'. Lack of business then became, and has remained, **the** dominant problem with SBRT respondents ever since, ie at least until Q1 1994. The perceived importance of this problem varies according to the size of firm and the sector they are in. Between 25% and 60% of firms in any given size band or sector stated this as their dominant problem compared with typically 15% in the period 1985–7 (Stanworth and Gray, 1993). The construction sector was particularly badly hit. Two surveys in 1992 suggested that almost half of building firms were working at less than half capacity (Johnson and Manser, 1992).

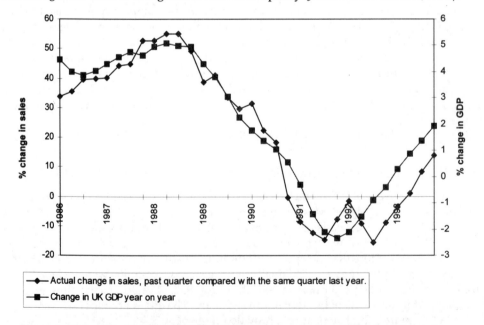

Figure 1. Change in UK GDP and the sales of a sample of small firms compared.

Data source: CSO, SBRT.

When the SBRT data on the changes in actual sales of their respondents are compared with the change in UK GDP, the level of correlation appears to be high. Evidently the recession affected many businesses by reducing the amount of business each received. This is shown in Figure 1. It is in this context of overall decline in available business that changes in the population of small firms are assessed in the next section.

Changes in the number of firms in the turnover size range £51,000 to £5 million

The rise in the number of small firms in the 1980s is well documented (Daly, 1991; McCann, 1993). Bannock et al. (SBRT, 1993) provide a number of indicators of the effects of recession on the small firms population. In particular they point out that the number of firms reduced from a high of 2.88 million in 1989 to 2.83 million in 1990 and again to 2.69 million in 1991. Overall this is a fall of 3.92% on the estimated total of 2.8 million in 1988. This fall contrasts with a rise of 22% in the numbers of VAT registered legal units with turnovers between £51,000 and £5 million between 1988 and 1991. In the period 1991 to 1993 the total number of legal units remained static, but this overall picture varies within sectors as can be seen in Table 2.

Table 2: Change in the Number of Legal Units with Turnovers Between £51,000 and £5 Million in the UK 1988 to 1993

Number of units in sector	1988	1991	1993
Production	99,326	112,770	109,825
Construction	103,375	141,824	125,085
Transport	33,454	42,246	41,705
Wholesale and dealing	86,498	96,774	96,450
Retailing	174,406	194,148	192,094
Finance, professional and property services	52,867	80,997	91,359
Motor trades	48,076	56,756	56,346
Business services	39,221	59,630	67,440
All other services	45,625	66,068	72,194
Agriculture, fishing and forestry	71,463	78,527	78,642
Postal services and telecommunications	423	802	917
Catering	84,082	97,986	99,621
Total	838,816	1,028,528	1,031,678
Percentage change on previous column		22.62%	0.31%

Source: CSO PA 1003

As the data in Table 2 indicate, there were slightly more units in 1993 than 1991, though this overall picture is quite different in different sectors. Half of the sectors peaked in number in 1991. The rise in business services, financial and all other services of 24,298 between 1991 and 1993 is similar in quantity to the fall in the number of units in production, construction, wholesale and retail sectors (22,062 units). In all sectors, overall, the number of units is greater in 1993 than in 1988.

Changes within sectors

Within each sector are different patterns of changes in numbers of firms. The classification scheme used for VAT is approximately equivalent to the 1968 SIC classification, which itself has been updated twice (1980 and 1992) to reflect more accurately the contemporary types and importance of firms in existence. These classifications reflect supply side measures, rather than demand side measures. For example leather manufacturers producing hand-crafted book bindings and leather manufacturers producing sheepskin rugs are likely to appear in the same category. There is a limit to what can be inferred from changes in any one sub-sector, though these data are likely to be more indicative of sectoral business behaviour than aggregated data.

Table 3: Range of Growth Within VTC Subsectors 1988–9

Range of growth within subsectors

Overall growth in numbers of legal units £51k to £5m turnover, 1988 to 1993		Subsectors showing greatest changes between 1988 and 1993 in each VAT Classification			
Main sector ↓	**VTC**	**Sub-sector**	**%·change**	**Abs. change**	**Comment**
Production 11%	47	Manufacture of paper and paper products; printing and publishing	17%	2,717	Largest absolute change in any subsector within main sector
	33	Manufacture of office machinery and data processing equipment	36%	291	Largest upwards percentage change in any subsector within main sector
	45	Footwear and clothing industries	-6%	-460	Smallest or most negative absolute change in any subsector within main sector
	44	Manufacture of leather and leather goods	-11%	-94	Smallest or most negative percentage change in any subsector within main sector
Construction 21%	5001	General builders	13%	5,162	Largest absolute change in any subsector within main sector
	5015	Electrical contractors	46%	3,640	Largest upwards percentage change in any subsector within main sector
	5021	Insulating specialists	-7%	-79	Smallest or most negative absolute change in any subsector within main sector
Transport 25%	7030	Road haulage contracting for general hire or reward	28%	4,440	Largest absolute change in any subsector within main sector
	7040	Other road haulage	52%	790	Largest upwards percentage change in any subsector within main sector
	7050	Sea transport	-21%	-109	Smallest or most negative absolute and % change in any subsector within main sector
Wholesale etc. 12%	8149	Other goods	25%	5,978	Largest absolute and % change in any subsector within main sector
	8311	Coal and oil merchants (not including bulk oil distributors or petrol filling stations	-14%	-455	Smallest or most negative absolute change in any subsector within main sector
	8124	Furs	-15%	-14	Smallest or most negative percentage change in any subsector within main sector
Retailing 10%	8202	Dairymen	45%	3,480	Largest absolute change in any subsector within main sector
	8228	Opticians	3450%	2,346	Largest upwards percentage change in any subsector within main sector
	8201	Grocers	-11%	-2,676	Smallest or most negative absolute change in any subsector within main sector
	8218	Retail Furriers	-70%	-76	Smallest or most negative percentage change in any subsector within main sector

Range of growth within subsectors

Overall growth in numbers of legal units £51k to £5m turnover, 1988 to 1993		Subsectors showing greatest changes between 1988 and 1993 in each VAT Classification				
Main sector	⬇	VTC	Sub-sector	% change	Abs. change	Comment
Finance, etc.	**73%**	8629/30	Other financial institutions/ property owning and managing	117%	9,782	Largest absolute change in any subsector within main sector
		8741-4	Hospital and consultant services, Local authority health services, general medical services, dentists.	181%	1,042	Largest upwards percentage change in any subsector within main sector
		8621	Stockbrokers	-31%	-77	Smallest or most negative absolute and % change in any subsector within main sector
Motor Trades	**17%**	8941	Distribution, repair and servicing of motor vehicles (including retail and wholesale)	21%	8,355	Largest absolute and % change in any subsector within main sector
		8942	Petrol filling stations	-1%	-85	Smallest or most negative absolute and % change in any subsector within main sector
Business Services	**72%**	8653	Computer services	147%	10,430	Largest absolute change in any subsector within main sector
		8655	Management consultants	152%	5,537	Largest upwards percentage change in any subsector within main sector
		8651	Industrial and commercial valuers, auctioneers and transfer agents	-24%	-587	Smallest or most negative absolute and % change in any subsector within main sector
All Other Services	**58%**	8995/6/9	Political parties and associations, services of foreign governments, OTHER SERVICES	67%	14,984	Largest absolute change in any subsector within main sector
		8814	Radio and television relay services	109%	204	Largest upwards percentage change in any subsector within main sector
		8922	Laundries	-6%	-17	Smallest or most negative absolute and % change in any subsector within main sector
Agriculture etc.	**10%**	0013	Dairying	10%	1,804	Largest absolute change in any subsector within main sector
		0020	Forestry	70%	442	Largest upwards percentage change in any subsector within main sector
		0015	Breeding of non-food producing animals (including horses)	-1%	-3	Smallest or most negative absolute and % change in any subsector within main sector
Catering	**18%**	8852	Fish and chip shops, sandwich and snack bars etc. selling food partly for consumption off the premises	64%	8,476	Largest absolute change in any subsector within main sector
		8880	Catering contractors	74%	677	Largest upwards percentage change in any subsector within main sector
		8860	Public houses	-2%	-631	Smallest or most negative absolute and % change in any subsector within main sector
Postal Services etc.	***117%***	*7080*	*Postal services and telecommunications*	*117%*	*494*	*Largest absolute and % change in any subsector within main sector*

Data source CSO PA1003

The range of change in the number of firms (legal units are taken as a proxy for the number of firms) in subsectors is shown in Table 3. This table shows the percentage changes in numbers of firms in the size band £51,000 to £5 million among the subsectors in each main VAT Trade Classification (VTC). For each VTC the subsectors showing the maximum rise in numerical and percentage terms and the subsectors with the greatest decrease are shown.

As Table 3 shows, the variation in growth in VAT subsectors ranges from a rise of 3,450% (opticians) to a fall of 70% (retail furriers). The increase in opticians is mainly due to deregulation of optician services, the inclusion of spectacles under the scope of VAT, plus increased demand from an ageing population and increased expenditure on personal goods. Such a percentage rise is untypical. The largest absolute rise in the size band is 14,984 units in VTC 8995/6/9 (other services, political parties and associations), reflecting the trend in other service sectors and an increased formalising of not-for-profit enterprises. There are also increases of 10,430 in the number of computer services (8635), unsurprising given the increased use of computers, and 9,782 in 'other' financial institutions, property owning and managing (8629/30). The recently (semi) deregulated postal and telecommunications sector showed an increase of 117%. Identifying growth in 'other' sectors is frustrating as it is likely to indicate the emergence of new classes of enterprise which in themselves are of considerable interest.

The largest fall in numbers was 'grocers' which reduced by 2,676 (11%); this is symptomatic of changes in the retail sector, the impact of the supermarkets and a shift towards 'convenience' retailing in general stores and franchised petrol stations. In the production sectors, which might have been expected to decrease in numbers, the types of business which are important today (computers and packaging) both grew substantially in numbers. The established sectors affected by lower cost imports, such as footwear, leather and clothing, declined in numbers.

GROWTH OF NUMBERS WITHIN SIZE BANDS

There has been considerable emphasis in UK small firms policy of late on the 'growth business'. The apparent reduction in the overall numbers of small firms with the apparent increase in firms with turnovers between £51,000 and £5 million would add weight to the argument that 'established' businesses are robust in the face of recession. The final question addressed in this analysis is therefore whether there is any evidence of a higher concentration of (larger) small firms in the sectors. One indicator of this would be a reduction in the overall number of firms with a proportional increase in the number of larger sized firms. In a growing sector, only the latter indicator will register as the overall numbers of firms would be expected to grow. In a declining market, a shift in market share rather than turnover would indicate a higher concentration. For this purpose the data have been analysed to determine the proportion of each main VTC of the size bands £51,000 to £100,000, £101,000 to £500,000 and £501,000 to £5m.

There is little change in the proportion of firms in each of these size bands in any sector. If anything the evidence suggests that in most sectors it is the smaller sized firms which have held up in numbers through the recession, compared with larger ones (Table 4). This could merely reflect a movement downwards in turnover among the larger firms and would be consistent with a downturn in business in the recession. There are three sectors which show an opposite trend to this. In retailing, agriculture and catering the proportion of firms in the £51,000 to £100,000 turnover segment declined (shown by the boxed areas in Table 4). Only in these sectors is a clear increase in concentration of ownership implied by the data.

The data also reveal interesting trends when the period 1985 to 1993 is considered. Since 1985 there has been an increase in the proportion of firms (legal units) in the £51,000 to £100,000 turnover size band in only the transport and business services sectors. There have been increases in the proportion of larger small firms (£0.5m to £5m) in all sectors except business services. This indicates that the high rate of start up in the 1980s is feeding through into an increased number of 'established' businesses in the 1990s.

Table 4: Number of Firms in Different Size Bands.

UNITED KINGDOM: NUMBER OF LEGAL UNITS t/o £51k to £5m
Share of segments of different size bands within overall sizeband

Sector		1985	1988	1991	1993
Production	51k-100k	28.7%	26.3%	22.3%	23.5%
	101k to 500k	47.2%	47.4%	48.6%	48.5%
	501k to 5m	24.1%	26.4%	29.1%	28.1%
Construction	51k-100k	40.9%	38.5%	36.1%	37.6%
	101k to 500k	46.2%	46.7%	46.7%	47.2%
	501k to 5m	12.9%	14.8%	17.2%	15.2%
Transport	51k-100k	32.3%	32.6%	35.4%	35.8%
	101k to 500k	46.9%	45.3%	43.1%	42.2%
	501k to 5m	20.8%	22.1%	21.6%	21.9%
Wholesale etc.	51k-100k	22.8%	20.8%	17.6%	19.3%
	101k to 500k	46.2%	45.2%	43.9%	43.7%
	501k to 5m	31.0%	34.0%	38.5%	37.0%
Retailing	51k-100k	47.2%	42.2%	34.6%	32.3%
	101k to 500k	47.4%	51.2%	56.9%	58.6%
	501k to 5m	5.4%	6.5%	8.5%	9.1%
Finance, etc.	51k-100k	38.1%	35.0%	35.0%	38.1%
	101k to 500k	45.9%	47.8%	45.9%	44.5%
	501k to 5m	15.9%	17.2%	19.1%	17.3%
Motor Trades	51k-100k	26.7%	27.2%	25.5%	25.9%
	101k to 500k	46.7%	45.5%	45.9%	46.2%
	501k to 5m	26.6%	27.3%	28.6%	28.0%
Business Services	51k-100k	35.3%	35.5%	36.2%	40.2%
	101k to 500k	45.7%	44.6%	43.4%	41.5%
	501k to 5m	19.1%	19.9%	20.4%	18.3%
All Other Services	51k-100k	46.2%	44.6%	43.7%	44.2%
	101k to 500k	43.7%	44.1%	45.5%	45.4%
	501k to 5m	10.2%	11.4%	10.8%	10.4%
Agriculture etc.	51k-100k	48.1%	45.8%	42.5%	41.3%
	101k to 500k	46.8%	48.5%	51.0%	51.8%
	501k to 5m	5.0%	5.7%	6.5%	6.9%
Postal Services etc.	51k-100k	35.9%	31.4%	30.5%	29.1%
	101k to 500k	45.7%	44.7%	42.8%	44.3%
	501k to 5m	18.5%	23.9%	26.7%	26.6%
Catering	51k-100k	57.4%	50.1%	40.2%	37.4%
	101k to 500k	40.0%	46.3%	55.1%	57.0%
	501k to 5m	2.6%	3.6%	4.7%	5.5%

Analysis of size bands and sectors reveals a wide range of growth rates. While all of these cannot be described within the scope of this chapter, two examples are given. Figure 2 illustrates the variation in the growth rates of size bands within the main VTC headings. For example, the range of change in catering is from –11% in the £51,000 to £100,000 size band to 89% in the £501,000 to £1 million size band. The growth in the number of units in construction in any size band is between 18% and 30%. Variations within subsectors are greater than illustrated by this aggregated data. The scope of this chapter allows for only two examples to be given. These examples are drawn from the more comprehensive analysis in Small Business Trends 1994–8 (Fuller, 1994).

The changes in number of units within business services is shown in Figure 3. The range is from –40% in industrial and commercial valuers, auctioneers and transfer agents (VTC 8651) with turnovers of £250k to £500k, to 227% in computer services (VTC 8653) with turnovers of £51k to £100k. (NB some data are missing from PA1003 in very small

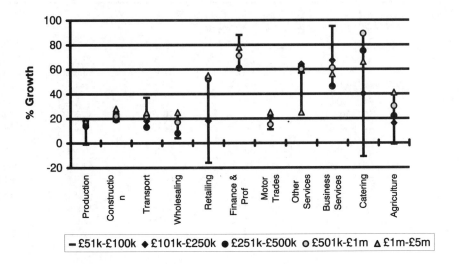

Figure 2 Growth in number of firms in each size band by VTC 1985-1993

Data source: CSO PA1003 / Small Business Trends 1994-8

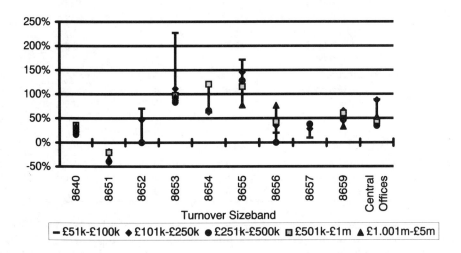

Figure 3. Business services: % growth in number of legal units 1985 to 1993

Data source: CSO PA1003 / Small Business Trends 1994-8

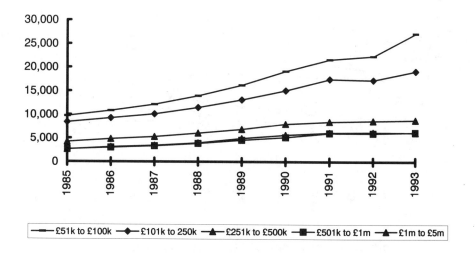

**Figure 4 Business services: growth in number of businesses
in different turnover sizebands – 1985–1993**

Data source: CSO PA1003 / Small Business Trends 1994-8

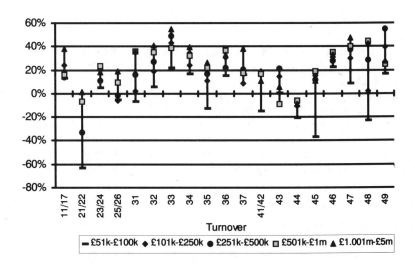

Figure 5. Production industries: % growth in number of legal units 1985 to 1993

Data source: CSO, Small Business Trends 1994-8

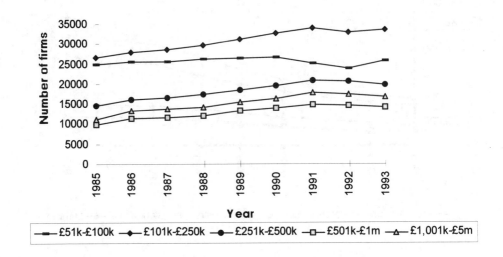

**Figure 6 Production industry: growth in number of businesses
in different turnover sizebands – 1985–1993**

Data source: CSO, Small Business Trends 1994-8

segments). The trend in aggregate by size band is shown in Figure 4. This shows the impact of the considerable rise in smaller computer services and management consultants on the total number of units.

The change in numbers of units in the production industries is shown in Figure 5. The range is from –63% in firms in the extraction industries (VTC 22) with turnovers of £51k to £100k to +55% in manufacturers of office machinery and data processing equipment firms (VTC 33) with a turnover of £1m to £5m and in 'other' manufacturing industries (VTC 49) in the £250k to £500k size range. The trends in aggregate numbers are shown in Figure 6, illustrating the slow rise in overall numbers and the fall away in the smallest size band.

CONCLUSIONS

The data shown in this chapter are taken from VAT registrations. It is cautiously proposed that VAT data of the number of legal units in the size range £51,000 to £5m can be taken as a proxy for the number of firms of this size in most sectors. Explanations for changes in the number of registrations may be different from explanations for changes in numbers of firms, ie regulatory rather than market oriented. The evidence from this source shows an increase in the number of firms in this size range over the period of the recession. The rate of increase is not as great as in the period before recession. There is some evidence of a possible downwards shift through the turnover size bands caused by a general loss of business, but the 'losers' seem, in aggregate, to be the smaller firms, ie those with turnovers below £100,000 and especially below £50,000 (though the latter is difficult to measure because of the change in VAT registration threshold). Throughout the recession there appears to have been a continuation in the trend in the growth of professional and technical services, probably linked to the restructuring of the major markets for such services, larger public and private organisations (Jones-Evans and Kirby, 1993).

REFERENCES

CSO (1993a) VAT Registration and Deregistrations in the UK (1980 – 1991) 5/93

CSO (1993b) Business Monitor PA 1003.

Daly M (1991) 'The 1980s – A decade of growth in enterprise; Self employment data from the Labour Force Survey', Employment Gazette, March.

Fuller E (1992) Small Business Trends 1992–1996, Durham University Business School.

Fuller E (1994) Small Business Trends 1994–1998, Durham University Business School.

Johnson A and Manser J (1992) 'Effects of the recession of small building firms' (sic), Paper presented at the Small Firms Policy and Research Conference, Southampton, November.

Jones-Evans D and Kirby D (1993) 'Technical Entrepreneurs in the service sector', in Chittenden F, Robertson M and Watkins D (eds) Small Firms Recession and Recovery, Paul Chapman, London.

McCann A (1993) 'The UK enterprise population 1979–91', NatWest Review of Small Business Trends 3, 1, Small Business Research Trust, Milton Keynes.

SBRT (1993) 'Estimates of the Business Population', NatWest Review of Small Business Trends, 3, 2, Small Business Research Trust, Milton Keynes.

SBRT (1994) NatWest SBRT Quarterly Survey of Small Business in Britain 10, 1, Small Businesses Research Trust, Milton Keynes.

Stanworth J and Gray C (1993) 'Problems and Preoccupations', in Stanworth J and Gray C (eds) Bolton 20 Years On, The Small Firm in the 1990s, Paul Chapman, London.

Appendix 1.

Table 5: Proportion of VAT Registered Legal Units in Different Size Bands in the UK

UNITED KINGDOM

	1985 Number	%	1988 Number	%	1991 Number	%	1993 Number	%
Production								
Those in range £51k to £5m	87,166	55%	99,326	61%	112,770	65%	109,825	68%
Those in range Threshold to £50k	42,540	27%	38,264	23%	32,499	19%	12,974	8%
Those above £5m t/o or voluntarily registered	27,724	18%	25,693	16%	27,097	16%	38,992	24%
All legal units	157,430	100%	163,283	100%	172,366	100%	161,791	100%
Construction								
Those in range £51k to £5m	87,471	39%	103,375	43%	141,824	51%	125,085	56%
Those in range Threshold to £50k	93,374	42%	93,531	39%	92,010	33%	31,105	14%
Those above £5m t/o or voluntarily registered	42,535	19%	41,146	17%	44,184	16%	66,017	30%
All legal units	223,380	100%	238,052	100%	278,018	100%	222,207	100%
Transport								
Those in range £51k to £5m	27,598	42%	33,454	47%	42,246	54%	41,705	58%
Those in range Threshold to £50k	26,994	41%	27,286	38%	25,096	32%	11,022	15%
Those above £5m t/o or voluntarily registered	11,046	17%	10,597	15%	11,126	14%	18,852	26%
All legal units	65,638	100%	71,337	100%	78,468	100%	71,579	100%
Wholesale etc.								
Those in range £51k to £5m	78,581	63%	86,498	67%	96,774	68%	96,450	67%
Those in range Threshold to £50k	26,928	22%	23,121	18%	22,580	16%	10,602	7%
Those above £5m t/o or voluntarily registered	18,735	15%	19,716	15%	23,353	16%	36,768	26%
All legal units	124,244	100%	129,335	100%	142,707	100%	143,820	100%
Retailing								
Those in range £51k to £5m	157,163	59%	174,406	66%	194,148	74%	192,094	80%
Those in range Threshold to £50k	91,647	34%	74,661	28%	51,917	20%	22,273	9%
Those above £5m t/o or voluntarily registered	19,757	7%	16,166	6%	17,784	7%	26,775	11%
All legal units	268,567	100%	265,233	100%	263,849	100%	241,142	100%
Finance, etc.								
Those in range £51k to £5m	40,322	36%	52,867	40%	80,997	44%	91,359	51%
Those in range Threshold to £50k	43,167	39%	50,633	38%	65,209	36%	26,355	15%
Those above £5m t/o or voluntarily registered	27,196	25%	29,783	22%	36,737	20%	63,190	35%
All legal units	110,685	100%	133,283	100%	182,943	100%	180,904	100%
Motor Trades								
Those in range £51k to £5m	43,646	57%	48,076	61%	56,756	68%	56,346	73%
Those in range Threshold to £50k	24,495	32%	22,163	28%	18,677	22%	7,902	10%
Those above £5m t/o or voluntarily registered	8,630	11%	8,051	10%	8,592	10%	12,633	16%
All legal units	76,771	100%	78,290	100%	84,025	100%	76,881	100%
Business Services								
Those in range £51k to £5m	27,550	36%	39,221	38%	59,630	43%	67,440	48%
Those in range Threshold to £50k	33,185	43%	43,594	42%	50,055	36%	22,296	16%
Those above £5m t/o or voluntarily registered	16,411	21%	20,249	20%	28,325	21%	51,994	37%
All legal units	77,146	100%	103,064	100%	138,010	100%	141,730	100%
All Other Services								
Those in range £51k to £5m	33,092	32%	45,625	38%	66,068	45%	72,194	52%
Those in range Threshold to £50k	47,797	47%	52,635	44%	55,654	38%	22,770	16%
Those above £5m t/o or voluntarily registered	21,275	21%	21,323	18%	25,267	17%	43,882	32%
All legal units	102,164	100%	119,583	100%	146,989	100%	138,846	100%

Agriculture etc.								
Those in range £51k to £5m	68,406	37%	71,463	40%	78,527	45%	78,642	46%
Those in range Threshold to £50k	53,035	29%	45,699	26%	35,554	20%	16,868	10%
Those above £5m t/o or voluntarily registered	61,338	34%	61,458	34%	61,225	35%	75,225	44%
All legal units	182,779	100%	178,620	100%	175,306	100%	170,735	100%
Postal Services etc.								
Those in range £51k to £5m	184	40%	423	47%	802	49%	917	54%
Those in range Threshold to £50k	191	41%	328	37%	519	32%	210	12%
Those above £5m t/o or voluntarily registered	88	19%	143	16%	310	19%	559	33%
All legal units	463	100%	894	100%	1,631	100%	1,686	100%
Catering								
Those in range £51k to £5m	71,224	57%	84,082	66%	97,986	75%	99,621	83%
Those in range Threshold to £50k	47,601	38%	39,346	31%	27,666	21%	12,677	11%
Those above £5m t/o or voluntarily registered	5,830	5%	4,774	4%	5,396	4%	7,992	7%
All legal units	124,655	100%	128,202	100%	131,048	100%	120,290	100%

Source: PA1003

Appendix 2. VTC headings used in figures

Production
11/17	Energy and water supply industries
21/22	Extraction and preparation of metalliferous ores and metal manufacturing
23/24	Extraction of minerals not elsewhere specified and manufacture of non-metallic mineral products
25/26	Chemical industry and production of man-made fibres
31	Manufacture of metal goods not elsewhere specified
32	Mechanical engineering
33	Manufacture of office machinery and data processing equipment
34	Electrical and electronic engineering
35	Manufacture of motor vehicles and parts thereof
36	Manufacture of other transport equipment
37	Instrument engineering
41/42	Food, drink and tobacco manufacturing industries
43	Textile industry
44	Manufacture of leather and leather goods
45	Footwear and clothing industries
46	Timber and wooden furniture industries
47	Manufacture of paper and paper products, printing and publishing
48	Processing of rubber and plastics
49	Other manufacturing industries

Business Services
8640	Advertising and Market Research
8651	Industrial and Commercial Valuers, Auctioneers and Transfer Agents
8652	Chartered or Company Secretaries (firms acting as)
8653	Computer Services
8654	Contract Cleaning
8655	Management Consultants
8656	Staff Bureaux and Employment Agencies
8657	Duplicating, Calculating and Typewriting Agencies
8659	Other Business Services
	Central Offices

8.

THE ROLE OF ESTABLISHED SMEs IN REGIONAL AND LOCAL ECONOMIC DEVELOPMENT: A CASE OF NEGLECT?

David North and David Smallbone

INTRODUCTION

This chapter aims to assess the potential contribution of established small and medium enterprises (SMEs) to economic development at the subnational scale. Using evidence from a recent study of the survival and growth of mature manufacturing SMEs during the 1979–90 period, it is argued that established SMEs do merit greater attention from an economic regeneration standpoint than they have received hitherto. The aim of this chapter is to give a balanced assessment of their potential, identifying the ways in which they are capable of contributing to the growth and competitiveness of regional and local economies, as well as identifying various limitations that they have.

In recent years, the concern for the economic regeneration of regional and local economies within the UK has become both more widespread and more urgent. The 1990s recession combined with other changes, such as reductions in defence expenditure, have had severe consequences for local economies in what were previously considered to be fairly buoyant regions, including the South East and the South West. This has been recognised in recent changes to the coverage of Assisted Areas and the Rural Development Areas. The increasing interest in economic regeneration has become associated with a growing recognition across the political spectrum that any credible economic regeneration strategy needs to include measures which stimulate and support business activity. This might be directly in the form of assistance aimed at individual businesses, or indirectly in the form of premises provision, infrastructure investment and training initiatives. Implicit in most economic regeneration policies in the 1990s is the view that businesses are the main agents of economic change and therefore the most important source of future growth, competitiveness, and job creation within regional and local economies.

Given the need to stimulate business activity, policy-makers are faced with a number of alternative courses of action. Sometimes this is presented as a choice between strategies concerned with attracting inward investment and those concerned with releasing indigenous potential in the form of encouraging entrepreneurship and helping existing businesses to realise their expansion potential. The advantages of the inward investment approach are said to include those of technology transfer and local multiplier effects such as creating markets opportunities for local SMEs as well as the chance that a single project may provide several hundred additional jobs. The disadvantages revolve around the arguments to do with external control, the repatriation of profits, and the lack of a long-term commitment to the local economy.

In broad terms, the indigenous potential approach can be equated with support for both new and existing SMEs within a regional or local economy. The arguments in favour of such an approach are similar to those which have been used in favour of support for small firms at the national level and include the role that small firms play in stimulating competition and innovation as well as generating employment (Employment Department, 1992).

Until fairly recently, the main thrust of those strategies concerned with releasing indigenous potential has been to encourage new firm formation. For example, the activities of enterprise agencies and innovation centres in the 1980s were predominantly concerned with assisting aspiring entrepreneurs in setting up their businesses. This focus on new firm creation was of course consistent with the Thatcher Government's active promotion of the principles of self-help and enterprise during the 1980s. From an economic development perspective, new firms were seen as bringing a much needed dynamism to local and regional economies, being a source of new ideas, new products and services, and, in the process, creating new jobs.

In comparison with new firms, established SMEs appeared less attractive politically as well as often lacking in growth aspirations. This lack of interest in established SMEs may have been influenced by the accepted wisdom 'that most small businesses grow only in the first few years after start-up and then stabilise' (Burns, 1989). Although the limitations of life cycle models have been frequently emphasised (eg O'Farrell and Hitchens, 1988; Storey, 1994), their influence remains, not least because of the absence of alternative theories of small business development. An additional reason for established SMEs being given a low policy priority was the commonly held view that they were less in need of external support than new businesses. For these reasons therefore, the potential role that they can play in indigenous economic regeneration has tended to be disregarded. In the last few years however, there have been signs of both an increasing interest in the potential contribution of established SMEs to economic development, and also a growing recognition that mature firms do have external support needs if they are to maintain and improve competitiveness (ACOST, 1990). Moreover, it has been argued that putting more money into start-ups is less cost effective than helping established SMEs grow faster, especially if resources are targeted towards encouraging the growth of a small proportion of existing firms (Storey, 1993).

KEY COMPONENTS OF REGIONAL AND LOCAL ECONOMIC DEVELOPMENT

In assessing the contribution of SMEs to economic regeneration, it is also necessary to consider the aims of regional/local economic development itself and here the framework provided by Turok and Richardson (1991) is potentially helpful. Whilst stressing the problems in defining the concept of local or regional economic development that arise from the variety of theoretical positions which can be used as a starting point, Turok and Richardson state that most definitions include three components: a growth component, an equity component and a capacity building component. Since the nature of our data does not permit an evaluation of an equity component in this chapter, we shall focus on growth and capacity building.

It has to be recognised that economic development policy-makers and business managers may have different priorities in relation to the achievement of growth. Ever since the publication of the Birch study (Birch, 1979), it is the contribution of SMEs to employment growth which has been the focus of particular interest from policy-makers and practitioners from the local/regional scale through to the national and the European levels. For individual businesses which are seeking growth, on the other hand, it is growth in sales turnover and/or growth in profitability that is more likely to be the objective rather than employment growth per se. Whilst job creation may seem a more appropriate focus for public policy than contributing directly to increasing profits or sales in individual privately owned businesses, there is a danger that if policy becomes too narrowly focused on job generation, this may be at the expense of the competitiveness of both firms and their local/regional economies in the longer term.

With regards to regional/local capacity building, there are a number of ways in which established SMEs may be expected to contribute. First, there is their ability to sell outside the region and thereby contribute to the economic base of a region. Whilst recognising that some SMEs may contribute indirectly to a region's exports by supplying components or services to other exporting companies, in this chapter the focus is on assessing the extent to which established SMEs have been able to develop an 'export capability' themselves. Second, SMEs are frequently considered to be a source of innovation, being more flexible, dynamic and responsive to shifts in demand and changes in economic conditions than larger firms. Innovation is important to local and regional economies since it represents an opportunity to gain competitive advantage which is potentially more sustainable than that based mainly on price (Porter, 1990). Third, Porter also stresses the importance of increasing productivity as a means of achieving sustainable growth in national and subnational economies. In the rest of this chapter, an assessment is made of the contribution that established SMEs can make to regional and local economic development using recent research evidence and making the above distinction between growth and capacity building.

DATABASE AND METHODOLOGY

The evidence used in this chapter comes from a broader longitudinal study of adjustment processes in mature manufacturing SMEs which formed part of the ESRC's Small Business Research Initiative.[1] This chapter brings together findings from the project relevant to assessing the contribution of established SMEs from an economic development perspective.

Full details of the methodology employed in the study can be found elsewhere (North et al., 1992a). Suffice to say here that the panel comprises 306 SMEs which were in existence in 1979 and at that time were independently owned, employed fewer than 100 employees, and were in 1 of 8 manufacturing sectors. The SMEs were drawn from 3 contrasting geographical locations: London (126 firms), the outer metropolitan area (OMA) (100 firms), and remote rural locations in northern England (80 firms). In depth interviews were conducted with the owners and managers in all 306 firms in 1990/91 supplemented where possible with data drawn from annual reports and accounts. In addition, a preliminary round of recontact telephone calls was made in 1994 to try to establish survival rates.

There remains the definitional question of what constitutes an established SME. Storey (1993) uses a 3 year cut-off to distinguish between short-life businesses and those which become established and this can be supported by the trend in new business failure rates: 36% cease to trade within 3 years whereas only 37% cease in the following 7 years (Employment Department, 1992). On this basis, firms in this particular study could be considered to be 'well established' in that they were all at least 10 years old at the time they were interviewed in 1990/91. However, if considered at the base year, ie 1979, the panel does include young firms which had only been in existence for a few years, as well as more established businesses. This means it is possible to make some comparison in this chapter between relatively young firms (founded in the 1970s) and more established firms (founded before 1970).

THE CONTRIBUTION OF ESTABLISHED SMES TO THE GROWTH OF REGIONAL/ LOCAL ECONOMIES

Survivability

Once SMEs become established, their resilience and ability to adapt to economic change is an important asset from an economic development perspective. In comparison, low survival rates reduce the contribution that young firms can make. For firms that are at least ten years old, age appears to be no longer a factor influencing survival.

It is well known that there is a high risk of failure in the first few years of establishing a business and that new businesses are most vulnerable between 12 and 30 months after registration (Employment Department, 1992). Whilst this particular study has not been concerned with the prospects of new firms, the longitudinal nature of the database for London SMEs has made it possible to measure accurately the survivability of firms over 10 years and in addition, to compare the survival rates of firms of different ages (for a full discussion see North et al. 1991; 1992b).

Although there was considerable variation in the rates of firm survival between the sectors, the overall survival rate between 1979 and 1990 was an impressive 58%. However, the ability of firms established in the 1970s to survive the 1980s was significantly lower than that of older firms: just under half of the 1970s firms were still in existence in 1990 compared with nearly two thirds of those set up before 1970. Whilst it might be tempting to argue that this emphasises the importance of measures designed to increase the survival rates of young firms, this is not justified by the employment implications of non-survival since the older firms that did go out of business were typically larger than the younger firms that ceased trading.

The resilience of established SMEs can also be demonstrated with evidence drawn from a follow-up contact made with firms in the summer of 1994. Table 1 shows that at least[2] 82% of firms that were trading in 1990 had survived until 1994 despite the recession of the early 1990s; indeed for firms located in remote rural areas, the survival rate was a remarkable 96%. These findings must remove any doubts about the underlying resilience of established SMEs in view of the hostility of the external economic conditions during this period.

By 1990 all surviving firms can be considered established businesses in that they had all been trading for at least 11 years. By this stage, age is no longer a factor influencing a firm's ability to survive. Unlike the 1979–90 period, there was little difference between the age groups in the survival rates of firms between 1990 and 1994. As we have demonstrated elsewhere, by 1990 firms founded in the 1970s were largely indistinguishable from older firms in a number of respects such as the extent to which they had broadened the geographical base of their markets and their involvement in export activity, and this contributed to a convergence of survival rates between firms of different ages (Smallbone and North, 1995).

There are two other aspects of the survivability of SMEs which deserve a brief mention since they can affect their contribution to local and regional economic development. First, established SMEs show a high propensity to stay within their original regional/local economy in that when they relocate, they show a preference for short distance rather than long distance movement. From an economic regeneration standpoint therefore, there is a high probability, certainly at the regional scale, that support for locally-based SMEs will be rewarded in terms of benefits (eg jobs) which accrue locally in the longer term. The one exception appears to be in inner city economies as there was a tendency for the more dynamic, expansionist SMEs that were located in inner London in 1979 to move elsewhere during the 1980s. 'Company retention' is becoming an increasingly important objective of those inner city economies which are unlikely to be attractive to inward investment and particular efforts are likely to be needed to retain the more growth orientated SMEs, once again illustrating the need to tailor economic regeneration policies to local circumstances.

Table 1: Firm Survival Rates 1990–94

	London	OMA	Rural	All Firms
Trading 1994	92 73%	83 83%	77 96%	252 82%
Not trading*	34 27%	17 17%	3 4%	54 18%
All firms	126 100%	100 100%	80 100%	306 100%

Note: * these figures include firms that we were not able to trace

Second, our evidence suggests that the commitment of SMEs to a regional/local economy is unlikely to be threatened by ownership changes such as acquisitions which may result in the absorption of their activities into the parent company and the eventual loss of the SME to the local economy. Only 10% of the 306 surviving firms were taken over between 1979 and 1990; even if management buy-outs are included, a change in the majority shareholding only affected 14% of companies over the period. Moreover, the best performing firms were no more likely to experience takeover than were the stable and declining ones between 1979–90. The risk of takeover should not be a major consideration therefore when policy makers are assessing the potential of established SMEs for regional/local economic development.

The output growth of surviving SMEs

There is a high propensity for surviving SMEs to achieve growth over a ten eyear period and thereby contribute to the growth of regional/local economies. Although younger firms are more likely to grow than older firms, some established SMEs are capable of achieving significant growth.

In order to analyse the growth performance during the 1979–90 period, each firm was assigned to one of 5 performance groups[3] based on the change that had occurred in the value of real sales turnover over the period. Additional criteria (minimum size and consistent profitability) were used to distinguish the best performing firms in order to identify those whose growth performance was soundly based and suggesting continued viability.

On this basis, more than half (54%) of all firms increased real turnover between 1979–90, 37% doubled it and 23% were also able to achieve the consistent profitability and minimum size (£0.5m) by 1990 to suggest they had become substantial high growth businesses. As we have shown elsewhere there was little difference between locations in the extent to which firms had been able to achieve growth although there were differences in the means by which growth had been achieved (Smallbone et al., 1993; North and Smallbone, 1995).

However, as Table 2 shows, younger firms in the study did show a higher propensity to grow than older firms: 70% of firms founded in the 1970s were able to achieve real turnover growth in the 1980s and 56% more than doubled it, compared with 44% and 25% respectively of firms founded before 1970. Although the lower absolute turnover of these younger firms in 1979 increased their ability to grow in proportional terms they were typically more growth orientated than the older firms.

Whilst younger firms may have a higher propensity to be both aiming for growth and actually achieving it, it is clearly a mistake to write off all mature firms as stagnant, low growth businesses. In fact, 57% of the SMEs which achieved high growth during the 1980s were established before the 1970s so that in terms of any targeting strategy related to economic regeneration, it would be wrong to treat age as a determinant of a firm's growth potential.

The longitudinal nature of the database for the SMEs located in London enables a

Table 2: Age of Firm and Growth Performance 1979–90

Age of Firm	Grp. 1 Firms No. %	Grp. 2 Firms No %	Grp. 3 Firms No %	Grp. 4 Firms No %	Grp. 5 Firms No %	All Firms No
Pre-1950	13 (19)	3 (4)	13 (19)	22 (31)	19 (27)	70
1950–69	26 (23)	4 (3)	23 (20)	21 (18)	41 (36)	115
1970–79	30 (25)	36 (31)	17 (14)	22 (18)	14 (12)	119
Total	69 (23)	43 (14)	53 (17)	55 (18)	74 (24)	304*

*Note: * there are 2 firms for which we do not have accurate age data*

comparison of firms' growth performance in the 1980s with that for the late 1970s. This analysis shows that a significant minority of the firms which performed well in the 1980s were going through a difficult period at the end of the previous decade involving sluggish performance or even apparent decline. More detailed examination of these cases emphasises the extent of the adjustments made by some firms subsequently in order to achieve growth. This supports the idea that growth is not a smooth and continuous process and that firms which may be successful in the longer term may go through phases of indifferent performance over shorter periods of time. Factors such as a change in management or the loss of a major customer can result in a period of crisis which may stimulate some re-appraisal of the business followed by a period of strong growth. One implication for policy is that the status of individual firms from a targeting perspective may change over time and that recent performance is not necessarily a reliable indicator of future growth prospects in SMEs.

Employment generation

> Over a ten year period, surviving SMEs are likely to prove to be a source of new jobs within a regional/local economy. Their ability to generate employment is closely tied to their ability to grow in output terms, although a substantial proportion of new jobs will be created by relatively few firms. Whilst surviving younger firms are responsible for most of the net increase in employment, the contribution of older, mature firms should not be overlooked.

Although few would argue with the conclusion that small firms in the UK are creating jobs at a faster rate and more consistently than larger firms (Storey, 1994, p201), the nature of their contribution has been the subject of more debate. One aspect concerns the number of SMEs which are employment generators. Some research evidence suggests that overall job growth in the small business sector is due to increased employment in a large number of firms (Daly et al., 1991). On the other hand, other research suggests that relatively few SMEs actually create employment on a significant scale (Storey, 1982; Storey et al., 1987). The issue is an important one since it raises the question of whether or not there is a case for targeting firms which have job generating potential and if so, how this can be achieved (Storey and Johnson, 1987).

Our evidence suggests that if SMEs can survive the critical early years after formation, they are capable of generating additional jobs over an extended period of time. In aggregate the 306 surviving SMEs provided more jobs in 1990 than in 1979, there being a net increase of 18% (1106 more jobs). Just over half of the surviving firms (52%) increased their employment over the period compared with just over a third (36%) which decreased it. Employment in surviving firms grew in all sectors except clothing, with the best employment performance being in the instruments sector (Table 3).

Table 3: Employment Change 1979–90 In Surviving Firms by Sector

Sector	No. of firms	% change 1979–90	Mean change per firm	Median change per firm
Clothing	31	−17.7%	−4.9	+0.5
Electronics	44	+30.2%	+6.4	+2.0
Furniture	64	+10.0%	+1.3	+1.0
Ind. Plant	51	+21.0%	+2.9	0
Instruments	28	+50.8%	+13.0	+5.0
Pharmaceuticals	10	+15.2%	+8.0	+0.5
Printing	63	+21.1%	+5.0	+2.0
Toys & Games	15	+45.5%	+3.1	0
All Firms	306	+18.4%	+3.8	+1

One of the key findings of the study as a whole is that job creation during the period 1979–90 was closely related to the growth of the firm in output terms (measured in terms of deflated sales turnover 1979–90) (see North et al., 1994). However, because of productivity improvements, a firm had to typically increase its real sales turnover by two and a half times in order to double its employment. As a result, the best performing firms in terms of output growth accounted for nearly three-quarters of all new jobs which were created: in fact, the 70 firms which achieved high growth status (23% of all firms) contributed 71% of all new jobs between 1979–90, an average increase of 25 jobs per firm. From an economic regeneration perspective therefore, it would appear that the best way of generating employment in the longer term is to focus support on firms with the greatest output growth potential.

Whilst the younger firms (ie, those established during the 1970s) undoubtedly contributed most to net job creation within the panel, it would be a mistake to assign all older firms to Storey's (1993) 'trundler' category (ie businesses likely to survive for a considerable period of time but which are unlikely to create significant numbers of jobs). As Table 4 shows, older firms have a much higher propensity to reduce employment (and survive) than younger firms, but it also shows that firms founded before 1970 were responsible for almost half of the total jobs gained. It would therefore be unwise to make younger firms the sole focus of policy attention simply because of their superior contribution to net job creation.

Before leaving this discussion of the employment generation potential of established SMEs, it should be mentioned that it is not just the numbers of jobs created which are important from an economic development perspective, but also the quality of the employment provided by SMEs. In fact, in the past some development agencies have been reluctant to support small businesses because it is considered that the jobs provided are of a poorer quality to those provided by larger firms. In a recent review of the research evidence it is concluded that

the evidence from both the UK and the USA suggests that, according to most measures, the job quality provided by small firms is lower than that in larger firms . . . wages are lower, training is less frequent and the evidence for a compensating higher level of job satisfaction is weak. (Atkinson and Storey, 1994 p11)

However, the evidence from this study (which is admittedly based solely on manufacturing sectors) tends to portray SMEs in a more favourable light. For example, the majority of firms made only marginal use of peripheral sources of labour (such as part-time workers, home-workers, and casual workers) in 1979 and this was still the case a decade later (North et al., 1994). Moreover, the data on wages for different occupations indicate that there is a wide range of levels of pay amongst SMEs within any one sector, with many of them paying rates which are above the national average. Many SMEs do already provide good quality jobs, and with the right kind of support others are capable of improving their working conditions and pay levels, especially when this goes hand in hand with the growth of the business.

Table 4: Jobs Gained and Lost 1979–90 By Age of Firm

	Pre 1950	*1950–69*	*1970–79*	*All firms*
Jobs gained	437 (17.5%)	778 (31%)	1289 (51.5%)	2504 (100%)
Jobs lost	625 (46.5%)	557 (41.4%)	163 (12.1%)	1345 (100%)
Net change	-188	+221	+1126	+1159
No. of firms	70 (23%)	114 (38%)	116 (39%)	300* (100%)

Note: it was not possible to classify 6 firms because of inadequate data

THE CONTRIBUTION OF ESTABLISHED SMES TO 'REGIONAL CAPACITY BUILDING'

From a regional/local economic development standpoint, an underlying objective of small business policy must be to facilitate the contribution of SMEs to the development of competitive economies. Such a strategy emphasises the ability of firms to sell outside their local areas/region, to innovate, to increase productivity, to upgrade their human resource base and to contribute to the external competitiveness of other firms with whom they may have supply relationships. In this section of the chapter, survey evidence is considered in relation to some of these criteria in order to make some assessment of the contribution of established SMEs to the building of 'regional capacity'.

Ability to generate external income for the region

> Established SMEs make an important contribution to the economic base of regional/local economies through exporting and selling in other areas. However, their ability to do this varies between sectors and according to the opportunities and constraints within the type of geographical environment in which the firm is based.

One of the factors which influences the contribution of SMEs to regional economic development is their ability to generate sales outside their region since this is a mechanism for generating additional regional income and also minimising any displacement effect within the region. Whilst recognising that some SMEs may contribute indirectly to a region's exports by supplying components or services to other exporting companies, the focus here is on assessing the extent to which firms in our panel have been able to develop this 'export capability' themselves.

Overall, the evidence from the study is that the propensity of established SMEs to sell outside their regional markets varied between sectors and to some extent between locations. As Table 5 shows, there is considerable variation between the sectors in the geographical market orientation of firms and also in their propensity to be involved in exporting. For example, in pharmaceuticals, instruments, electronics and toys a majority of firms were selling at least 50% of sales outside their region by 1990 and a majority were also involved in exporting. In printing, furniture and industrial plant on the other hand, most firms were dependent on local or regional markets for at least half their sales and only a minority were exporting at all.

One of the themes in the study overall is a comparison of the opportunities and constraints on SMEs in contrasting types of location. Our evidence is that young growing firms

Table 5: Sectoral Variations In Geographic Market Orientation

Sector	% of firms natn/ internat markt orient.		% of firms exporting		Number of firms
	1979	1990	1979	1990	
Printing	15	17	8	13	63
Instruments	75	79	68	86	28
Pharmaceuticals	100	100	90	100	10
Clothing	52	52	23	48	31
Indust. Plant	34	35	26	28	51
Toys & Games	87	93	67	80	15
Electronics	53	68	46	68	44
Furniture	27	31	25	23	64
All firms	37	46	32	42	306

Note: A firm is considered to be national/international market orientated if more than 50% of sales is outside its region.

in remote rural areas face the need to extend their geographical markets at an earlier stage in their development than urban-based firms (Smallbone et al., 1993). In London by contrast, the size and diversity of the regional market meant there was good scope for growth without a need for firms to change their regional market orientation (particularly in printing and furniture). London-based firms which did extend their geographic markets over the decade tended to be in either instruments or electronics, which are both sectors where many firms need to sell outside the region because of the highly specialised market segment they were aiming to serve.

Two main implications for policy can be drawn from these findings. First, that business support policies need to be sensitive to geographical variations in the opportunities and constraints facing SMEs as well as to differences in sectoral conditions. In this case it needs to be recognised that remote rural firms will have to grow by market extension at an earlier stage and often from a smaller initial size base than similar urban firms. Second, that the extent to which established SMEs are generating additional regional income through external sales shows considerable sectoral variation. This has important implications for a sectoral targeting strategy if economic growth is a prime policy objective.

Ability to innovate

> Established SMEs can be an important source of new product innovation within a regional/local economy and there is a clear link between innovativeness and the growth of the business. SMEs appear less active when it comes to making production process innovations although again the more active firms tend to be the most rapidly growing ones.

SMEs are often said to be a source of innovation, being more flexible, dynamic and responsive to shifts in demand and changes in economic conditions more generally than larger firms. Our evidence suggests that a firm's propensity to have developed products or services which could be considered innovative in some way varies considerably between industrial sectors. On the one hand, in the medium-high technology sectors a majority of firms did so (pharmaceuticals 70%; instruments 68%; electronics 52%) but in the more craft-based sectors the development of innovative products was the exception rather than the rule (clothing 19%; furniture 14%; printing 13%). The explanation is that instruments and electronics were technology driven sectors in which innovative products and ongoing product development were an important part of the way in which firms attempted to gain a competitive advantage. In pharmaceuticals also the importance of product characteristics in affecting a firm's competitive position meant that innovation was invariably a requirement if it was to survive in the marketplace.

The evidence suggests that SMEs tend to be less innovative in terms of making changes to production processes. Only a fifth of the firms in the panel moved to a new technological base involving a shift to new production processes or new ways of organising production over 10 years, the majority of firms ending the decade with essentially the same production methods as they had in 1979. Not surprisingly, it tended to be the better performing firms which were most active in making changes to their production processes, with the high growth firms typically investing four to five times as much per employee as declining firms.

Although the panel of firms used in this study is comprised more of low- and medium-technology rather than high-technology sectors, the realisation of the technological potential within firms is important for regional growth regardless of the industrial sector (Alderman et al., 1988). In those regional/local economies with little chance of attracting firms in high-tech sectors, their technological capacity depends upon being able to upgrade and modernise SMEs in the more traditional sectors. This would appear to be a particularly important issue for remote rural economies since our results confirm those of other researchers

(Keeble et al., 1992) in showing that remote rural firms were lagging behind their urban counterparts in terms of both product and process innovation (Smallbone et al., 1993).

Ability to increase productivity

> SMEs are shown to contribute to the increasing competitiveness of regional/local economies by means of raising productivity levels, although there are indications that SMEs in remote rural locations may be lagging behind their urban counterparts in this respect. In the best performing firms, major improvements in productivity are consistent with employment generation.

As well as innovation, Porter (1990) stresses the importance of increasing productivity as a means of achieving sustainable growth in national and sub-national economies. In view of the concern expressed by some authors that encouraging and supporting the growth of SMEs may be associated with lower levels of productivity than is typically found in larger companies (Hughes, 1991), the productivity trends demonstrated by surviving firms in our panel are examined during the 1979–90 period.

On average, SMEs in the panel increased their productivity[4] during the 1980s, with the highest increases being in the printing sector and the lowest in the craft-based sectors. Moreover, the majority of firms (75%) which achieved an increase in real turnover over the decade also increased productivity, and in a third of cases the increase was at least 100%. Thus from an economic development perspective, an important feature of high growth firms as a group was their ability to increase productivity at the same time as they were generating employment. The development path followed by these mature 'high growth' firms suggests that employment generation in SMEs can be compatible with the development of increasingly competitive businesses which in turn can contribute to the development of competitive local and regional economies.

However, an examination of the productivity trends in the panel of firms as a whole reveals some variations between locations which may have implications for the kinds of policy pursued in different types of regional/local economy. Labour productivity in remote rural SMEs was generally lower than that of firms in similar sectors in other locations and, with the exception of printing, average productivity levels actually declined in rural firms between 1979–90. The fact that high rates of job generation were associated with declining productivity for firms in the rural panel as a whole emphasises the dangers of measuring the contribution of SMEs to economic development solely in terms of employment change. Unless these productivity trends are reversed, some of the rural SMEs may find it increasingly difficult to compete in the longer term. It is clearly important that firms are encouraged to develop in ways which lay the basis of their long term competitiveness if their capacity to generate employment and to contribute to economic regeneration is to be maintained.

CONCLUSION

On the basis of the above evidence from our study of the growth and survival of manufacturing SMEs over the 1979–90 period, it can be argued that established SMEs made an important contribution to regional and local economic development. It would be wrong to portray them all as stable, 'trundler' businesses with only a limited role to play in economic regeneration. A substantial number of surviving SMEs have been shown to grow and create employment over a 10 year period, thereby contributing to the growth of their regional and local economies. Unlike the branch plants of some larger companies, they also show a commitment to particular locations, thereby increasing the chances of long term benefits from any support which is provided. They have also been shown to be capable of contributing to regional/local capacity building and competitiveness through developing non-local markets, engaging in innovation, and raising productivity levels.

Finally, it should be stressed that the key proposition of this chapter is not that established SMEs should suddenly become the sole, or even the dominant, focus of regeneration policies compared with other options such as inward investment or new business formation, but rather that their role should not be neglected. Established SMEs have been the Cinderellas of regional and local economic development policy for too long, a position which has been shown on the evidence of this chapter to be undeserved and in need of some reappraisal. Clearly their economic growth and capacity building potential will depend very much upon the nature of the regional/local economy and the existing strength of the SME sector. In many circumstances we can expect their role to both complement and interrelate with that of new businesses on the one hand and larger firms on the other, in effect occupying the interstices of the regional/local economy.

NOTES

1. The research on which this paper is based was part of the Economic and Social Research Council's Small Business Research Initiative which included financial contributions from Barclay's Bank, The Commission of the European Communities (DG XXIII), the Employment Department and the Rural Development Commission. The views expressed do not necessarily reflect those of the sponsoring organisations.
2. The contact made in July 1994 was a very brief telephone interview to establish if the firm was still trading. Firms which were no longer trading with the same telephone number were checked with directory enquiries. Firms we were not able to trace are considered to be no longer trading.
3. Definition of the 5 performance groups:
   Group 1 'High Growth Firms': firms that more than doubled their real turnover 1979–90, reached £0.5m turnover by 1990 and were consistently profitable in the late 1980s.
   Group 2 'Strong Growth Firms': firms that at least doubled their real turnover in real terms 1979–90 but failed to reach either the minimum size and/or the consistent profitability needed to be in the high growth group.
   Group 3 'Moderate Growth Firms': firms which increased their real turnover by between 1.5 and 2 times 1979–90.
   Group 4 'Stable Firms' : firms that stayed at about the same size, ie not more than a real growth of 1.5 times 1979–90.
   Group 5 'Declining Firms': firms which declined in real turnover 1979–90.
4. Productivity is defined in terms of the sales/employment ratio. To measure productivity change over the period we deflated the 1990 sales turnover (to allow for inflation since 1979) to give a measure of real productivity change 1979–90.

REFERENCES

Advisory Council on Science and Technology (ACOST) (1990) The Enterprise Challenge: Overcoming the Barriers to Growth in Small Firms, HMSO, London.
Alderman N, Wynarczyk P and Thwaites A (1988) 'High Technology, Small Firms and Regional Economic Development: a Question of Balance?' in Giaoutzi M, Nijkamp P and Storey D Small and Medium Size Enterprises and Regional Development, Routledge, London.
Atkinson J and Storey D (eds) (1994) Employment, the Small Firm and the Labour Market, Routledge, London.
Birch D (1979) The Job Generation Process, MIT, Cambridge, Massachusetts.
Burns P (1989) 'Strategies for Success and Routes to Failure', in Burns P and Dewhurst J (eds) Small Business and Entrepreneurship, Macmillan, London.
Daly M, Campbell M, Robson G and Gallagher C (1991) 'Job Creation 1987–89: The Contribution of Small Firms and Large Firms', Employment Gazette, November pp589–596.
Employment Department (1992) Small Firms in Britain Report 1992, HMSO, London.
Hughes A (1991) 'UK Small Businesses in the 1980s: Continuity and Change', Regional Studies, 25, 5, pp471–479.

Keeble D, Tyler P, Broom G, and Lewis J (1992) Business Success in the Countryside: the Performance of Rural Enterprise, PA Cambridge Economic Consultants, HMSO, London.

North D, Leigh R, and Smallbone D (1991) 'A Comparison of Surviving and Non-Surviving Small and Medium Sized Manufacturing Firms in London During the 1980s', ESRC Small Business Research Initiative, Middlesex University Project Working Paper No. 1.

North D, Smallbone D, and Leigh R (1992a) 'A Longitudinal Study of Adjustment Processes in Mature Small and Medium Sized Manufacturing Enterprises', End of Award Report to the Economic and Social Research Council, Centre for Enterprise and Economic Development Research, Middlesex University.

North D, Leigh R, and Smallbone D (1992b) 'A Comparison of Surviving and Non-Surviving Small and Medium Sized Manufacturing Firms in London during the 1980s, in Caley K, Chell E, Chittenden F, and Mason C (eds) Small Enterprise Development: Policy and Practice in Action, Paul Chapman, London.

North D, Smallbone D, and Leigh R (1994) 'Employment and Labour Process Changes in Small and Medium Sized Manufacturing Enterprises during the 1980s', in Atkinson J and Storey D (eds) Employment, the Small Firm and the Labour Market, Routledge, London.

North D and Smallbone D (1995) 'Employment Generation and Small Business Growth in Different Geographical Environments', in Chittenden F, Robertson M, and Marshall I (eds) Small Firms: Partnerships for Growth, Paul Chapman, London.

O'Farrell P and Hitchens D (1988) 'Alternative Theories of Small Firm Growth: A Critical Review', Environment and Planning A, 20, pp1365–82

Porter M (1990) The Competitive Advantage of Nations, Macmillan, London.

Smallbone D, North D and Leigh R (1993) 'The Growth and Survival of Mature Manufacturing SMEs in the 1980s: an Urban-Rural Comparison', in Storey D and Curran J (eds) Small Firms in Urban and Rural Locations, Routledge, London.

Smallbone D and North D (1995) 'Targeting Established SMEs: Does their Age Matter?' International Small Business Journal, 13, 3, pp47–64.

Storey D (1982) Entrepreneurship and the New Firm, Croom Helm, London.

Storey D (1993) 'Should We Abandon Support for Start-Up Businesses?', in Chittenden F, Robertson M and Watkins D (eds) Small Firms: Recession and Recovery, Paul Chapman, London.

Storey D (1994) Understanding the Small Business Sector, Routledge, London.

Storey D, Keasey K, Watson R and Wynarczyk P (1987) The Performance of Small Firms, Croom Helm, London.

Storey D and Johnson S (1987) Job Generation and Labour Market Change, Macmillan, London.

Turok I and Richardson P (1991) 'New Firms and Local Economic Development: Evidence from West Lothian', Regional Studies, 25, 1, pp71–83.

9.

THE PRIVATISATION OF LOCAL AUTHORITY SERVICES AND MARKET OPPORTUNITIES FOR SMALL FIRMS

Brian Abbott, Robert A Blackburn and James Curran

INTRODUCTION

One of the contributing factors to the revival of small-scale enterprise has been the restructuring and rationalising activities in the private sector. It is widely argued that this has created new opportunities for small business, for example through an increase in outsourcing especially in sectors such as consultancy (Keeble et al., 1993) as well as providing a supply of redundant employees with the need to seek alternative employment. One major deficiency in research to date, however, is the absence of attention given to restructuring activities in the public sector and their effect on small-scale enterprise. A central element of Conservative government policy since 1980 has been the privatisation of local authority services, through the 1980 Local Government Planning and Land Act and the 1988 Act. This has run in concert with the Government's policies of privatisation and asset sales (Marsh, 1991). The aims of compulsory competitive tendering (CCT) as expressed in the legislation and Government manifestos, are to reduce the size of the public sector, increase efficiency, encourage competition and provide opportunities for private enterprise (IPM/IDS, 1986; Beaumont, 1992; Employment Department, 1992; Abbott, 1993).

Of course, the connections between the activities of the private and public sectors and smaller businesses are complex. Even in the relatively well researched area covering contracting-out in the private sector, debate exists on the extent and type of business-to-business relationships (Curran and Blackburn, 1994). However, the absence of research on the impact of CCT on small business is curious given that the policy has been established for over a decade and that small business owners are often held up as the personification of many of the values and beliefs of the Conservative Party and the objectives underlying CCT.

This chapter assesses the extent to which CCT has created opportunities for small scale enterprise. It focuses on the responses of local authorities to CCT and its implications for small businesses. This involves an analysis of the role of small independent businesses in undertaking local authority contracts directly and identifying their sub-contracting relationships with other private sector contractors serving the public sector. A central theme of the chapter is that small firms have not made significant in-roads into this work. Changes in the tendering process and legislative developments including BS5750, the transfer of undertakings protection of employment (TUPE) and local management of schools (LMS), mean that this situation could change. The extension of CCT into professional services in the 1992 Local Government Act for example could provide new opportunities for small businesses in accountancy, housing management and architecture (Labour Research, 1994).

CCT AND THE ROLE OF THE PRIVATE SECTOR: AGGREGATE DATA

It is estimated that the total value of local authority work under contract is £2,147.6 million per annum, of which Direct Service Organizations (DSOs) have won about 82% (Local Government Management Board (LGMB), 1994). Evidence on the ability of the private sector to win contracts reveals mixed success (see Table 1). Building cleaning has the highest level of private sector involvement, with 56.9% of all contracts being won by private contractors although in-house DSOs have won 74.2% of work by value where known (LGMB, 1994, p15). This is followed by ground maintenance where over a third is provided by the private sector. For this reason, these two sectors were selected for investigation together with professional services which have received recent attention under CCT in the 1992 legislation. This is an area where there has traditionally been a high level of small firm involvement.

Two main points emerge from the aggregate data when considering the role of smaller businesses. First, the average value of contracts is high for any small business wishing to compete (although this average figure does include DSOs). Second, a more detailed break-down by minimum size of contract (see the last column in Table 1) does reveal that the values of some contracts are very much lower than the average. However, even where contracts are relatively small, although this increases opportunities for small firms, it is not guaranteed to benefit them because many smaller contracts are won by subsidiaries of large businesses. First evidence suggests therefore that small firms have been unsuccessful in the CCT market overall:

> UK experience indicates that it is clearly unrealistic to expect public monopolies to be replaced by a diverse market of small, locally owned competing entrepreneurs. (Thomas, 1988, p64)

However, there are no aggregate data sources analysing the size of business involved in contracting and this makes any statements about the role of small firms difficult to make with any precision.

SURVEY METHODOLOGY

This chapter is based on 40 interviews with private contractors, councillors and senior local authority personnel involved in the management of contracts between April and

Table 1: Summary of Compulsory Competitive Tendering Data

Sector	Number of contracts	Average value (£000)	Won by Private Sector By no. of Contracts (%)	By value (%)	Min value (£000)
Building Cleaning	914	284.7	56.9	25.5	28.7
Ground Maintenance	1320	263.4	35.2	21.4	49.4
Refuse Collection	376	1,314.9	29.5	25.4	402.5
Refuse and Other (Street) Cleaning	107	2,218.3	25.2	22.6	835.5
Other Cleaning	344	483.2	28.8	20.1	42.7
Vehicle Maintenance	233	532.2	21.0	13.9	73.7
Catering (Other)*	192	174.3	29.2	17.7	16.9
Sports & Leisure Management	400	529.7	14.2	7.7	51.7

Note: All data derived from LGMB (1994). Data cover England and Wales.
* Excludes Education and Welfare, for which statistics are incomplete.

September 1993. All four local authorities were located within Greater London. Local authority representatives (both officers and councillors) and representatives of businesses in grounds maintenance, building cleaning and professional services took part in the research programme.

Since the respondents were selected from four contrasting London boroughs, caution must be applied when interpreting the results as there are considerable regional variations in relation to levels of competition and the impact of CCT. Due to the sensitive nature of the information and guarantees of confidentiality, the identities of all participants have been concealed. The four local authorities were selected to represent different political mixes to show any variations in strategies in implementing CCT. They consisted of two inner London authorities – one Labour, one Conservative – and two outer London authorities, one controlled by the Liberal Democrats and the other with no overall control, decisions being passed on the casting vote of the Conservative mayor (Table 2).[1] The survey included face-to-face, tape recorded interviews with nine councillors: four Conservatives, three Liberal Democrats and two Labour. Six local authority contract managers representing client and contractor roles were also interviewed. A further seven telephone interviews were also undertaken with a mix of contract managers and councillors to up-date information, for example, on the number of contracts awarded.

To ascertain the contractors' perspectives, 18 contract managers employed by large and small private sector businesses were interviewed (see Table 3). Seven worked in ground maintenance, nine in building cleaning and two in professional services (housing management and information technology). These businesses were identified through a 'snowball' strategy initiated through contacts with council representatives and other sources. However, the research revealed a dearth of businesses in the lower employment size bands and in order to recruit sufficient businesses the initial upper size criteria of 50 employees or fewer was increased to 100 employees or full-time equivalents. This reinforced the initial impressionistic evidence that small firms were not securing local authority CCT work to any large degree.

CONTRACTING-OUT IN THE FOUR BOROUGHS AND THEIR RESPONSES TO CCT

The responses of local authorities to CCT has been described as ranging from hostility to

Table 2: Summary of Face-to-Face Council Interviews

Location	Overall Control of Council	Number of Councillors	Number of Officials
Westborough	Lib/Dem	2	2
Southborough	Marginal/Conservative	3	1
Eastborough	Conservative	2	1
Northborough	Labour	2	1
Total		9	5

Table 3: Summary of Face-to-Face Interviews With Contractors

Sector activity	Number interviewed
Grounds Maintenance	7
Building Cleaning	9
Professional Service	2
Total	18

fear and pragmatism, to neutrality and even enthusiasm (Shaw et al., 1994). In discussions with councillors and officers in all four Boroughs, most reported that prior to the introduction of CCT there was already a culture of using private contractors, albeit to varying degrees. For example, one Liberal Democrat in Westborough commented that '. . . tenders were used but not in all cases before CCT'. Echoing this point a Labour councillor in Eastborough commented:

> In one sense the whole argument is bogus, there is no council in the country that has ever done all its work in-house. When we [Labour] were in control lots of building construction work, repair work was done by private contractors . . .

Before CCT, therefore, private contractors were used to provide a range of services including highway and building maintenance, refuse collection and street cleaning and professional services, such as solicitors and surveyors. They were often used when there was no in-house provision or expertise. The use of external contractors in the surveyed boroughs prior to CCT largely echoes the findings of similar studies (Ascher, 1987; Walsh, 1991; Common et al., 1993) but some have suggested that tendering has generally been unpopular and restricted to Conservative controlled authorities (Beaumont, 1992; Colling, 1993). Prior to CCT, the approach adopted by the four local authorities surveyed towards contractors varied. For example, in Westborough a system of competitive quotes was used with tenders awarded to the lowest bidder. In another local authority, Northborough, an approved list was in operation.

The imposition of CCT did, however, represent a sea-change in the activities of local authorities. Whereas local authorities had previously used their discretion and adopted very different approaches to the use of private contractors, CCT legislation compelled them to tender work. For example, as part of their criteria for selecting suppliers before CCT, some local authorities had insisted that contractors had to meet health and safety criteria and nationally negotiated rates of pay. However, Section 17 (5) of the 1988 Act defines these as 'non-commercial' (Thomas, 1988) and consequently local authorities can no longer insist on contractors' compliance (Painter, 1991).

Table 4: Extent of Contracting-Out Under CCT to Private Businesses in the Four Boroughs

	Building cleaning	*Ground maintenance*	*Professional services**
Northborough	Minority	Minority	None
Southborough	Mixed	Minority	None
Eastborough	All	Majority	Minority
Westborough	Majority	Mixed	None

Note: *This was under review at the time of the research and only recently subject to CCT.

In line with the range of responses to CCT discussed by Shaw et al. (1994), the four local authorities involved displayed a variety of reactions (see Table 4). Political allegiance was one of the main factors influencing different practices. In Conservative Eastborough, CCT was greeted with zealous enthusiasm and many services such as refuse collection and housing management were tendered even before required by legislation. In Labour controlled Northborough, reaction to CCT was hostile and every effort was made to support the DSOs. Clearly, opportunities for the private provision of local authority services are likely to have varied according to the political composition of the local authority before the introduction of CCT.

SMALL FIRMS AND LOCAL AUTHORITY WORK

The smaller businesses surveyed in ground maintenance had relatively long histories of doing work with the four local authorities prior to CCT as well as for other government bodies. Most of the small ground maintenance firms reported a strong preference for local work when tendering which meant that the DSO was usually their main competitor. This was dictated by the actual equipment and labour capacity of the businesses. The contracts awarded to the businesses varied tremendously in value ranging from £20,000 to £900,000 per annum. The numbers employed in these firms ranged from 45 to 95, although the seasonal nature of the work led to fluctuations and the use of self-employed labour and sub-contractors. Not all the staff were employed specifically on local authority contracts, which varied employing from 2 to 27 people.

Building cleaning has been described as the sector receiving the highest level of interest from the private sector (IPM/IDS, 1986; Ascher, 1987) although as shown earlier DSOs have retained nearly 75% of contracts by value (see Table 1). This is a very competitive market, partly explained by low start-up costs and the labour intensiveness of the work (Rees and Fielder, 1992, p351; *Financial Times* 9.8.93). Owner-managers of the three small building cleaning firms reported that they had been working for local authorities for only a short time. Their contracts involved school cleaning and window cleaning in civic buildings. The businesses employed between 40 and 178 staff, although well over three-quarters were part-time. Despite their appreciable size, as with grounds maintenance, they undertook work for only a few authorities and on a local basis only. Contracts tended to be valued at around £50,000 per annum. Owners pointed out that there has been a trend to break up previously large contracts which had favoured large firms. Although larger contracts are in the short-run more cost effective and less time consuming from the point of view of the local authorities, there have been reports of poor performance by large providers in the past (Labour Research, 1994).

The selection of professional services was, with hindsight, premature since at the time the research was initiated these services were not to be fully subject to CCT until 1995. However, the research identified a small estate agent involved in housing management performing CCT work and a large computer company providing data and invoice management services to local authorities. The data from these interviews do not form a major part of this chapter because so few professional firms involved in CCT were identified. The fact that the small estate agent was able to secure a contract from the local authority does however, illustrate further the connection between the size of the contract and the ability of small firms to pick up CCT work. It can be argued that the CCT of professional services will provide more opportunities for small businesses given their strong presence in such areas as legal services and architecture (Labour Research, 1994).

THE CCT TENDERING PROCESS

One key aspect of CCT is the tendering process. In practice, there is scope for local authorities to influence the ability of outside contractors to win contracts and this has important ramifications for small businesses. One of the first stages in the tender process is to define the tender specification. These are written by client departments. The council then seeks quotes for the cost of providing its service. This involves advertising contracts, in local, national, and relevant trade journals. Interested contractors then apply for details and submit a tender. In the authorities researched, the process prior to tenders going out involved going through a select list process.

Once a contractor is on the select list they are in a position to make a bid. If they meet the specifications it is irrelevant who is appointed, because they are all assumed to be able to do the job to the same standard. The final decision is therefore usually dictated by the lowest price. Tenders are assessed by a panel comprising representatives from legal, financial management services and client departments. They make recommendations based on their assessment of the resources and financial stability of the firm to the client committee which awards the contract. Although CCT legislation attempts to ensure that those tendering are treated equally, avoiding anti-competitive behaviour, the research identified anomalies. These sometimes prejudiced the chances of the smaller businesses winning contracts.

Cost of tendering and the complexity of CCT

The experiences and views of both officers and councillors provided insights into the difficulties of small businesses winning CCT contracts. A reason advanced by councillors is that small firms have inadequate resources to bid for contracts. This view was put succinctly by a council officer:

> The tendering process is a barrier to entry for small firms because small firms characteristically have less resources and less experience than large firms . . .

For example, one local authority in the first tranche of ground maintenance work from January 1990 to December 1992, had enquiries from 16 contractors. The firms employed from 38 to 200. In the second round of tendering, only two of the 14 firms invited on to the select list employed fewer than 50 employees. One council officer, involved in the management of contracts in Southborough, commented:

> Our experience is universally that a minority of pre-selecting enquiries are from small firms, under 10%. There is a very small proportion of small firms who actually make it through to the select list stage and that seems to be the general experience.

This view was emphasised strongly by business owners themselves. Although many had undertaken work with the Councils before CCT, the actual CCT tendering process was a painful experience in terms of time and money. This deterrent to small firms is verified independently by wider evidence (Walsh, 1991). A recent report by the Audit Commission indicated that three-quarters of businesses that expressed an initial interest in contracting, failed to bid (*Financial Times*, 31.3.93). These findings are supported by the experiences of the smaller businesses interviewed. Generally, they found CCT to be too costly and drawing up the specification too time consuming and complex:

> . . . the last tender we got from them [local authority] cost me about eleven hundred pounds to just do the tender . . . you do not want to be doing 10 tenders a month to get one, it's not economical . . . it's because their tenders are so complicated, they run into reams for the smallest little job, you really have to get a consultant to fill them in, someone who's familiar with council tendering . . . To go through a tender document is like going, well it's a minefield, the way they lay it out. You do not just price a job, they then want to know how much per 5 metres cleaned does this cost and how much per 5 metres cleaned does that cost . . . (Large cleaning firm)

This was reinforced by a further respondent:

> [It] takes quite a few days on each tender, so it is a very expensive process, in time . . . if you think of each one taking perhaps a day to do and look at then maybe 2 days to work out and then a day to fill in all the different features, it takes six to 7 man days per contract, which is expensive. Financially, this equates to about £1,000 per contract in terms of lost opportunities that could be earned elsewhere. (Ground maintenance owner-manager).

Having few resources was one fact that many small businesses cannot alter. However, some business owners also argued that the sheer complexity of the language of CCT specifications deters contractors from bidding. Government guidelines have attempted to overcome this problem, stressing that specifications:

> . . . should provide clear, adequate and precise details of the nature of the work to be done or service to be provided in order to ensure that the DSO does not obtain an unfair competitive advantage . . . (Department of the Environment, Circular, 10/93).

It was pointed out by business owners that a difference between CCT and other bidding processes was that local authorities write the specification with the potential contractor having no input. In contrast, with commercial contracts, the contractor and client often write the specification in partnership. Instead, the small businesses which were interested in tendering for work had to meet the requirements of standardised but complex forms. The complicated forms added a further barrier to the ability of the private sector to win CCT contracts.

Finally, there was some evidence of bias against small and especially new firms, when awarding contracts. Smaller firms were perceived as less stable than larger enterprises and new firms had no track record to convince the council that they could carry out the work successfully.

Size of contracts

A more fundamental problem for small businesses is the large value of the contracts under CCT. For example a councillor in Westborough commented:

> It's partly a function of how you chop up your contracts. Obviously the more parcels you can put it out in, the better it is for small companies.

Echoing this point, the Labour councillor interviewed in Eastborough reported:

> The deals are so big most small companies can't handle it. The average small company does not have the legal or administrative back-up to go through that thickness of document and work out all the pros and cons, does not have the experience of having done it elsewhere, just does not have the time and can't afford to respond to tenders of that scale and lose. There is so much time and effort in doing them.

A main reason for the large size of the contracts is the economies of scale this affords councils. Officers pointed out that breaking up contracts into smaller units involves more resources devoted to evaluating tender documents, invoice systems, quality control records and monitoring procedures.

From the small business owners' perspective, there was recognition that size of contracts strongly affected the ability of the smaller contractor. One large private contractor summarised this:

> The success of small firms depends on the size of contract that the local authority is putting out . . . but when you have got councils like Southborough letting £50,000 to £100,000 then they have every chance of picking those up. (Large grounds maintenance firm)

A further problem relates to the way contracts are packaged. For instance, a number of unrelated activities, such as grave digging and toilet cleaning, were being put into ground maintenance contracts. There is also other evidence to suggest that ground maintenance contracts were being combined with activities, such as building cleaning, vehicle maintenance and sports and leisure management (LGMB, 1993, p48). If this trend towards multifunctional contracts accelerates, then it is likely to militate against small firms securing contracts directly simply because they do not have the resources or breadth of expertise to undertake them. In contrast, large cleaning firms welcomed the trend towards multifunction contracts and were forming alliances with other large firms or their own subsidiaries in security and ground maintenance.

Recent government guidelines have suggested that the packaging of contracts into large units could be anti-competitive:

> For example, packaging large amounts of work over a wide geographical area may deter competition from small locally based companies. This is particularly important when seeking tenders for activities such as ground maintenance, building cleaning and jobbing maintenance, where many potential contractors are likely to be small companies. (Department of the Environment, Circular, 10/93, 1993, p2)

Owner-managers reinforced this suggestion and felt that they were at a disadvantage to the DSO or large organisation under these circumstances. However, this should not be overstated. Many of the small businesses owners saw their main competitors as other small and large firms rather than the DSOs and there is strict legislation to deter anti-competitive behaviour (Shaw, et al., 1994).

Lowest price tenders

A further criticism by owner-managers was that those awarding contracts were legally compelled to award the contracts to the lowest price bidder and lacked an understanding of the nature of the work and its monitoring. Under 5% of contracts nationally, approximately 170, have not gone to the lowest bidder (Local Government Chronicle, 1992). When bidding for work, many small business owners complained that they could not match the lower bids from the large organisations. They viewed the low bids by some large organisations as a way of extending their markets but with little concern for quality – as exemplified by the high incidence of contract terminations.

Overall, we argue that the CCT process militates against small firms successfully winning contracts. This is not necessarily a result of deliberate attempts at anti-competitive behaviour but is mainly a direct result of the large size of the contract packages put out and the complexities of the tendering process.

THE MONITORING PROCESS

All the local authorities had monitoring officers responsible for inspecting work. A simple pass-fail system based on the tender specification usually operated. Where work did not meet required standards, correction notices were usually issued and the length of time given to bring the work up to standard depended on the service and local authority. For example, in the cleaning of schools in Eastborough, contractors not meeting the specification were given two working hours to rectify the problem. If the work was not rectified in the time period, then defaults were applied and a percentage deducted from the contractor's monthly invoice. Nationally, between 1988 and 1992, the private sector won about 40% of building cleaning contracts of which one quarter experienced problems and almost 1 in 10 was terminated (Public Services Privatisation Research Unit, 1992).

Overall, however, monitoring did not pose major problems for the smaller businesses interviewed and in some cases was actually beneficial since it appeared to be the larger businesses which were not able to comply with contracts. Each local authority interviewed provided an example of a contract that had been terminated. In one local authority a building cleaning contract was awarded to a large firm with responsibility for all cleaning throughout the borough. However, the contract was terminated after six weeks because the firm could not meet the tender specification. This was then re-tendered and awarded to a number of smaller, locally based firms.

One perceived advantage of smaller contracts for councils was that they are easier to locate and deal with if a problem develops because the area of responsibility is likely to be limited geographically. Contractors also monitor each other closely. For example, if one contractor responsible for ground maintenance in a group of schools was aware of another contractor not performing satisfactorily in another part of the area, it is likely that the council would be informed. Breaking contracts into smaller units also potentially helps the DSO as it needs to bid more frequently, increasing familiarity with the tendering process. If the DSO loses a small contract it has also less impact on employment in the local authority. Thus, there were also advantages to the local authority if contracts were smaller scale.

SUBCONTRACTING, SMALL FIRMS AND CCT

Although small businesses have not been successful in winning appreciable amounts of local authority CCT contracts directly, they may be recipients of work through subcontracting. Contracting out is a well established feature of the private sector and is widespread for a number of functions and industries. Small firms, for example, have been identified as closely linked to primary contractors in clothing manufacture and electrical and mechanical engineering (Rainnie, 1992). Therefore, it is interesting to investigate subcontracting relationships developing as a result of CCT and the role of small scale enterprise in this activity.

Interviews with the large, corporate businesses in ground maintenance and building cleaning revealed frequent use of subcontractors. This included the use of other businesses as well as labour-only contract staff. In both sectors, subcontracting was common irrespective of CCT work. Subcontractors were recruited for conventional reasons: overflows in work but mainly for specialist tasks. For example, in grounds maintenance weed spraying, a specialist operation performed by qualified personnel, is often subcontracted. This is particularly common with the rise in multi-function CCT contracts and where a particular task forms part of the total contract but does not justify employing someone in-house. In building cleaning, responses from representatives of large employers illustrated these themes. For example one contractor commented:

> We do subcontract . . . that tends to be special services where we haven't got that in-house, pest control . . . whereby we might subcontract that to a sister company . . . Subcontracting is a means of meeting the peaks and troughs. If we have a steady business coming through from the local authority then we know what the needs are, then frankly we wouldn't subcontract. It's where we're jumping around and seasonal variation that we might think about subcontracting . . . (Representative, large contract cleaning Company)

There are two qualifications to this picture of large firms subcontracting work. First, large businesses are more likely to have a subsidiary capable of performing the work and the opportunities for smaller firms may therefore be limited. Second, large firm representatives often pointed to a loss of control over the quality of the work subcontracted and this loss was more acute because of the monitoring associated with CCT.

It was significant that subcontracting was not exclusive to large firms. Indeed, given the relatively limited capacity of smaller businesses, and the rise in multi-functional CCT work, there may be strong pressures on the small business to subcontract. Three of the four grounds maintenance firms and one of the three cleaning businesses had subcontracted work. Subcontracting was used in grounds maintenance mainly for seasonal work or specialist tasks.

One business acted as subcontractors to a large firm on CCT work, providing specialist arboricultural services, and had approached a number of large CCT contractors as part of their marketing strategy. In this case, the small firm assisted the large firm by pricing the arboricultural work to be included in the prime contractor's tender and would receive work on a subcontract basis if the bid was successful. Collaborative ventures therefore existed but were the exception rather than the rule.

Despite the pressures to subcontract, there was a strong resistance among smaller employers. For some employers, subcontracting was considered to increase costs and a shedding of owner-managers' responsibilities. One cleaning business owner-manager commented:

> If you've been awarded that contract I would think that's up to you to look after [it] . . . if you can't handle it you should not have taken it on in the first place . . . In fact they [local authority] do not like you to subcontract anyway, they do ask you that and the answer would be 'no' anyway, so I would not subcontract.

'Going it alone' and avoiding dependence on others has been identified in other research as characteristic of small business owners (Scase and Goffee, 1987; Curran and Blackburn, 1994, Ch 4) and clearly those involved in CCT work were no different.

One major regulator of the use of subcontractors in the CCT market is the local authority. Representatives of two of the local authorities expressed the view that it was unacceptable for contractors to win a contract and then subcontract. If a firm needs to subcontract, they have to seek approval from the local authority. In an attempt to monitor the use of non-direct employees, three of the four councils reported that they asked about the use of subcontractors and self-employed labour. Information requested included reasons why the main contractor wanted to subcontract, the financial stability of the firm, references from previous clients, and how the prime contractor intended to control the subcontractor in meeting tender specifications. One interviewee commented that if a firm had too heavy a reliance on subcontractors, they would not be awarded the contract. This was because councils found subcontractors difficult to control:

> . . . we found we were quite ineffective and he [the subcontractor] would not take any instructions or anything from us . . . you lose control the moment it goes subcontract, you've lost the control. (Local authority officer, Westborough)

The interviewee reported that it would be cost effective and afford more control to go direct to the subcontractor, missing out the 'middle men', offering the subcontractor more competitive rates.

A further response by local authorities to subcontracting is to leave the decision on which subcontractors are employed to the prime contractor. Insisting on particular subcontract firms weakened relations between the council and the prime contractor. If a contract develops a problem and the council has specified a particular subcontractor, then the prime contractor can use this in their defence. Responsibility had to lie with the prime contractor and any sanctions levied against this firm. Overall, therefore, there was some evidence of subcontracting in the CCT market but the close regulation by the clients, and the resistance by some smaller business owners to becoming part of a contracting chain, suggest that this is relatively underdeveloped.

DEVELOPMENTS IN CCT AND IMPLICATIONS FOR SMALL FIRMS: BS5750, TUPE AND LMS

There are currently three major developments in the CCT market which have ramifications for the involvement of smaller businesses: quality standards, TUPE and the local management of schools (LMS).

Quality standards, chiefly in the form of BS5750, are becoming increasingly recognised by large firms and public sector organisations as a way of regulating their own processes as well as a standard to be achieved by their suppliers (North et al., 1993). However, in general, small businesses have tended to resist adopting formalised quality standards primarily because of the associated bureaucracy and costs. In the survey, the adoption of BS5750 by both councils and businesses was mixed. Only one council was working towards BS5750 approval while the others were aware of the standard but were not seeking to adopt it themselves.

Legislation prevents local authorities from stipulating that suppliers have BS5750 because this is viewed as anti-competitive. However, in dealing with their contractors, local authorities encouraged suppliers to be working towards certification. National data report that 96 local authorities (21%) have included the requirement that contractors should achieve certification in one or more of their contracts during the lifetime of the contract (Local Government Management Board, Survey Report No 5, 1992, p10).

This puts further pressures on those small firms interested in tendering for CCT work. Both ground maintenance and building cleaners acknowledged the potential importance of BS5750, although moves towards certification varied. Two of the small businesses interviewed were expecting to achieve certification, both in ground maintenance. This low level of certification among small firms contrasts with the high level among the larger firms interviewed and is likely to reduce the chances of the former winning contracts. Much, therefore, depends on the rigidity of local authorities in applying BS5750 standards to CCT work and the ability and willingness of smaller firms to apply for the standard.

One reason for the contracting out of local authority services is to reduce costs. If a former in-house service is contracted-out and employees transferred to the private sector, this can lead to a deterioration in wages and conditions of employment (Labour Research

1994, p13). However, in 1992 the European Commission, prompted by the European Court of Justice, forced the Government to clarify the law relating to the rights of employees transferred from the public to the private sector.[2] Initially, TUPE included the word 'commercial' and on this basis British courts ruled against public sector staff transferred to the private sector who claimed pay and conditions had been eroded through the transfer. The effects of the Trade Union Reform and Employment Rights Act 1993 may change the situation by extending the TUPE regulations to cover public sector workers (*Financial Times*, 20.5.94; 22.6.94). The implications of this development have shed some uncertainty over the ability of private sector contractors competing for contracts, especially where the greatest savings are related to wage rates and conditions of employment, particularly in labour intensive sectors such as building cleaning.

The reaction of the local authority representatives to TUPE (the interviews for this research were conducted prior to the European Court's decision) was one of uncertainty but varied from strong resistance to applying TUPE, to waiting for a clear ruling.

The reaction of smaller firms to TUPE was one of dismay and claims that it undermined the whole CCT process were common. Greater efficiency and associated lower unit labour costs were one advantage some small business owners emphasised. This was particularly stressed by cleaning firms. One owner of a small building cleaning firm commented:

> It's made a mockery of competitive tendering. I should think a good 80% of all quotes for that type of work is manpower, so how can it be competitive . . . ?

Overall, however, the response of the smaller employers to TUPE was varied. Some stated that they would pull out of the CCT market while others were reacting by developing strategies to cope with any new requirements.

A third major development in the CCT market with possibly more favourable implications for small firms is LMS. Schools which have opted-out of local authority control and are managing their own budgets may provide a new market for smaller businesses, for example, by providing smaller packages of work for ground maintenance and building cleaning services. There were already examples in the survey of contractors working with schools. Schools which had opted-out had a much more direct relationship with the contractor, circumventing the need to liaise with a local authority contracts manager. Overall, however, the extent to which schools will opt-out of local authority control appears unlikely to be great. Retaining the existing contracts with local authority providers may also prove, in the immediate future at least, to be a safe option for schools that have opted out given that they have little experience and resources to design, implement and monitor contract specifications. Opportunities deriving from LMS are more likely to occur in primary rather than secondary schools since the latter are larger. It is possible also that larger schools may opt for a 'total service' approach rather than have separate contracts for specific functions. Consequently, while LMS has the potential to create a new CCT market for smaller firms, this will be contingent on the number of schools opting-out and the way they package work contracted-out.

CONCLUSIONS

The compulsory competitive tendering of local authority activities has been an important feature of government policy aimed at increasing efficiencies, reducing costs and cutting the size of the public sector. This market is estimated to be worth over £2 billion per annum. The private sector has had mixed success in winning CCT contracts, but has been most successful in building cleaning and ground maintenance.

Reaction by local authorities to CCT has also varied tremendously, but smaller contracts were viewed as more expensive to develop and smaller firms were often viewed as lacking continuity and the resources to be able to deal with the larger contracts on offer. At the same time, the advantages of awarding contracts to small firms were acknowledged by councillors and contract managers. Small firms were perceived as having a greater contribution to the local economy in terms of income and jobs, possessed local knowledge and were easier to monitor.

From the smaller businesses' perspective, the biggest barrier to undertaking CCT work was the tendering process. This was viewed as expensive, time consuming, bureaucratic and rigid. The large size of the contracts and their sometimes multi-functional nature also deterred some smaller businesses from tendering. The system of awarding tenders to the lowest bidder was also viewed as placing small firms at a disadvantage to large. The CCT market was considered extremely competitive and it was especially difficult for small firms to match the low tender prices of the large private sector organisations.

However, the monitoring process did provide positive outcomes for small firms. Some large firms, in their attempts to expand their portfolio of work, had bid unrealistically low prices and were not complying with contract specifications. In some cases, these contracts were divided among specialist or along geographical lines and often awarded to smaller businesses.

Subcontracting was a strategy used by both large and to a lesser extent, small employers, mainly for seasonal or specialist work purposes. However, there was no clear pattern of large firms winning prime contracts and then subcontracting to smaller firms. Subcontracting was regulated strongly by the local authorities acting as a brake on its potential development. This brake was reinforced by the views of some smaller business owners who expressed a resistance to subcontracting.

There was some uncertainty expressed by owner-managers regarding their future involvement in the CCT market. Although the market was viewed as here to stay, BS5750 and the application of TUPE cast a shadow on the development of the market for private sector firms. The resistance of small businesses to adopting BS5750 has been documented elsewhere (North et al., 1993) but the small businesses interviewed in this survey showed a higher level of acceptance. However, implementing BS5750 was yet another burden to overcome in entering the CCT market and is likely to deter some small firms from tendering for contracts. TUPE is a further factor which is likely to deter small firms from participating in the CCT market.

Evidence presented in this chapter suggests that there are opportunities deriving from CCT for smaller businesses but, to date, these have been limited. In building cleaning and ground maintenance, unless CCT contracts are packaged into smaller units and the tendering process simplified, the involvement of small firms is likely to remain limited. However, the extension of CCT may offer greater opportunities for small firms in professional services given their predominance in these sectors.

NOTES

1. However, since the completion of the research control of this authority switched to the Liberal Democrats in the May 1994 local elections.
2. This emanates from the European Court's Acquired Rights Directive, 1977 which laid down that employees whose jobs were transferred from one employer to another took with them their same rates of pay and conditions. This was incorporated into the Transfer of Undertakings Protection of Employment Regulations, 1981.

REFERENCES

Abbott B (1993) 'Patterns of Privatisation and the Provision of Local Authority Services', Kingston Business School Working Paper, Kingston University.

Ascher K (1987) The Politics of Privatisation Contracting out Public Services, Macmillan, London.

Beaumont P B (1992), Public Sector Industrial Relations, Routledge, London.

Colling T (1993) 'Contracting Public Services: The Management of Compulsory Competitive Tendering in Two County Councils', Human Resource Management Journal, 3, 4, pp1–15.

Common R, Flynn N and Mellon E (1993) Managing Public Services Competition and Decentralisation, Butterworth and Heineman, London.

Curran J and Blackburn R (1994) Small Firms and Local Economic Networks: The Death of the Local Economy?, Paul Chapman, London.

Department of the Environment (1993) Circular 10/93.

Employment Department (1992), Small Firms in Britain Report, Enterprise in Action, HMSO, London.

Financial Times (1993) 'Watchdog Criticises Council's Tendering', 31 March.

Financial Times (1993) 'Private Sector Wins Big Share of Council's Cleaning', 9 August.

Financial Times (1994) 'EU Ruling Hits Contracting Out Programme', 20 May.

Financial Times (1994) 'Contractors Urge Tendering Rules Shake-Up', 22 June.

Institute of Personnel Management, IDS Public Sector Unit (1986) Competitive Tendering in the Public Sector, Unwin Brothers, Old Woking.

Keeble D, Bryson J and Wood P (1993) 'The Rise and Fall of Small Service Firms in the United Kingdom', International Small Business Journal, 11, 1, pp11–22.

Labour Research (1994) 'Local Services – A Contract Killing', May, 83, 4, pp11–13.

Local Government Chronicle (1992) 'Contract Survey Refutes High Private Sector Share', 12 June.

Local Government Management Board (1992) CCT Information Service, Survey Report No 5, June, LGMB, London.

Local Government Management Board (1994) CCT Information Service, Survey Report No 9, June, LGMB, London.

Marsh D (1991) 'Privatisation Under Mrs Thatcher: A Review of the Literature', Public Administration, 69, Winter, pp459–480.

North J, Curran J and Blackburn R A (1993) 'Small Firms and BS5750: A Preliminary Investigation' paper presented at the National Small Firms Policy and Research Conference, Nottingham, November.

Painter J (1991) 'Compulsory Competitive Tendering In Local Government: The First Round', Public Administration, 69, pp191–210.

Public Services Privatisation Research Unit (1992) 'Privatisation Disaster for Quality', March.

Rainnie A (1992) 'Flexibility and Small Firms: Prospects for the 1990s' in Leighton, P and Felstead, A (eds) The New Entrepreneurs, Kogan Page, London.

Rees G and Fielder S (1992) 'The Services Economy, Subcontracting and the New Employment Relations: Contract Catering and Cleaning' Work, Employment and Society, 6, 3, pp347–368, September.

Scase R and Goffee R (1987) The Real World of the Small Business Owner, second edition, Croom Helm, London.

Shaw K, Fenwick J and Foreman A (1994) 'Compulsory Competitive Tendering For Local Government Services: The Experiences of Local Authorities in the North of England', Public Administration, 72, Summer, pp201–217.

Thomas C (1988) 'Contracting-out: Managerial Strategy or Political Dogma?' in Ramanadham V V (ed) Privatisation in the UK, pp153–170, Routledge, London.

Walsh K (1991) 'Competitive Tendering for Local Authority Services, Initial Experiences', May, Department of the Environment, HMSO, London.

10.

GROWTH IN SMALL MANUFACTURING FIRMS: AN EMPIRICAL ANALYSIS

Richard Barkham, Mark Hart and Eric Hanvey

INTRODUCTION

This chapter presents the results of an investigation into the causes of growth in small manufacturing firms in the UK and is organised into 6 sections. Section 2 explains the background to the study. Section 3 deals briefly with the approach to small firm growth adopted by this research. Section 4 outlines the methodology of the study and Section 5 presents and discusses the results. Section 6 contains conclusions and policy implications.

BACKGROUND

It is well established that the small firm sector can create jobs and contribute, albeit with some regional variations, to employment growth. This has been revealed, in particular, by two reports produced by the Northern Ireland Economic Research Centre (NIERC) which examine the components of employment change in Northern Ireland, the Republic of Ireland and Leicestershire (Gudgin et al., 1989; Hart et al., 1993). Gudgin et al. (1989) show that, in the period 1973 to 1986, small firms made an appreciable contribution to job generation in Leicestershire but this contribution was missing in Northern Ireland and the Republic of Ireland. In particular, during this period the growth of surviving small manufacturing firms in Leicestershire was twice as rapid as in Northern Ireland and almost six times as fast as in the Republic of Ireland. An important feature of this study is that market conditions and industrial structure do not appear to account for the observed differences between regions in the growth of the small firm sector. In the light of research by Hitchens and O'Farrell (1987; 1988a; 1988b) it is possible that the inferior manufacturing capabilities of Irish firms, in particular those located in Northern Ireland, might account for some of the differences in the aggregate performance of small firms, in the period 1973 to 1986.

Drawing on the same databases Hart et al. (1993) show a change in the situation with regard to the aggregate growth of small manufacturing firms in the period 1986 to 1990. During this period surviving small firms in Northern Ireland grew much faster than their counterparts in the Republic of Ireland and Leicestershire. So, in 1986 small manufacturing firms contributed 25.3% of total manufacturing employment in Northern Ireland but by 1990 their share had increased to 27.6%. This represents an increase in employment from 27,233 to 30,418. This finding raises the intriguing possibility that the intensive support for small firms that is a feature of the Northern Ireland economy is bearing fruit.

In attempting to explain regional variations in small firm performance it quickly becomes apparent that there is a need for research of a more fundamental nature into the process of small firm growth itself. Not only has economic theory failed to explain why some small firms grow and others do not; it has not even adequately addressed the issue (O'Farrell and Hitchens, 1988). Nor have the many detailed univariate studies arrived at a convincing explanation of the small firm growth process (Storey, 1994). There is an obvious need for a comprehensive multivariate empirical analysis of small firm growth from which theoretical development, regional analysis and policy prescription may proceed. Meeting the need for this type of analysis of small firm growth was the primary aim of this research.

CONCEPTUAL FRAMEWORK

Over the last 20 years, in a variety of disciplines, considerable work has been carried out into the causes of small business growth. However, the conclusion of three review articles is that as yet our theoretical and empirical understanding of the small firm growth process is poor (Chell, 1986; O'Farrell and Hitchens, 1988; Storey, 1994). A particular deficiency of the literature, as Storey (1994) notes, is in the area of multivariate analysis. Too many studies have concentrated on examining the impact of individual variables, such as psychology or education, on small firm growth when the factors that affect the development of a small organisation are obviously myriad.

The approach adopted in this research is similar to that outlined by Storey (1994). Growth in small firms is conceptualised as the result of the direct and indirect influence of four separate but interrelated sets of factors: the characteristics of the entrepreneur, the nature of the firm, the objectives and strategies adopted by the entrepreneur and the constraints imposed on the small firm by the economic environment.

A priori, considerable importance was attached to the objectives and strategies of the entrepreneur. Some entrepreneurs, perhaps the majority, are not interested in the long term growth of their enterprises but are content with a reasonable 'living' and the independence that comes with running a small firm (Stanworth and Curran, 1976). Even those entrepreneurs that do pursue growth may choose different strategies to achieve it. For instance some may seek to develop their firms through product innovation whilst others may concentrate on marketing. The success of different groups of strategies depends partially on their being appropriately chosen and partially on the skill with which they are executed.

The major influences on business strategy are the characteristics of the entrepreneur.[1] The literature suggests that age, ambition, family background, education, overseas experience, and career history are important characteristics. In terms of education, area of specialisation is influential as well as level of achievement and degree of vocational training (Gilmore, 1972; Schultz, 1980; Cross, 1981; Fothergill and Gudgin, 1982; Sweeney, 1987). Regarding career history, functional specialisation and level of managerial experience appear to be important variables (Smith, 1967; Barkham, 1989). The characteristics of the entrepreneur determine the goals of the firm and, to an extent, the strategic options at its disposal.

In addition to a direct influence on goals and strategy the characteristics of the entrepreneur have an independent influence on the growth of the firm. The characteristics of the entrepreneur not only determine strategy but also how well it is carried out. It is possible for an entrepreneur to select the right strategy but to carry it out badly. Related to this is the issue of energy and commitment. The correct strategy may be pursued with energy and commitment or with a relatively low level of motivation. Furthermore, the abilities and motivation of the entrepreneur may be enhanced or extended if he or she works as part of a team.

The literature on small firm strategy is less profuse than that on the characteristics of the entrepreneur (Storey, 1994). Utilising this literature and our own intuition it was possible to define a range of strategies which had the potential to influence small firm performance. A priori, considerable importance was attached to the overall strategic aims of the organisation such as sales growth or profit growth. With regard to production the hypothesised influences, defined to include the way in which these activities are financed and supported by research and development, were product and process development. In the area of marketing a range of variables appeared important including sales methods, utilisation of market research and other sources of information as well as the overall approach of the firm to bringing its products to the attention of customers.

Research has identified certain 'firm' variables, termed in this analysis company characteristics, which appear to affect firm growth. For instance, sector of operation and region of operation appear to have an influence on small firm performance (Storey, 1994). To a certain extent these variables proxy the state of the market but they may also represent systematic variations in access to key resources such as premises, labour, information and finance. Another business characteristic that has been shown to affect growth is business size. In aggregate studies small firms appear to grow more quickly than large ones. There is also evidence to suggest the age of the business is important.

The fourth group of variables that affect the performance of the small firm are the constraints placed upon it by the economic environment in which it operates (DTI, 1991). In general, a small firm may be constrained because it does not have access to the resources it requires or it cannot sell as much of its product as it would like. The resources required by a small firm include capital, premises, information, suitable labour and suitable management. To a certain extent, as has been said, business characteristics such as sector and location act as proxies for supply and demand constraints but it is important to consider these influences specifically when analysing the causes of business growth.

DATA AND METHODOLOGY

The data used in this study were derived from a questionnaire survey of 174 small firms located in four regions of the UK. The study regions, Northern Ireland, Leicestershire, Hertfordshire and Wearside, were selected because previous work indicated that they represent areas of contrasting small firm performance (Gudgin et al., 1989; Hart et al., 1993) and because in each region it was possible to draw a sample of firms from a comprehensive industrial database.[2] These databases contain information on a range of business characteristics including employment.

The initial criteria for firms to be included in the study were that they should employ fewer than 50 people at the start of the study period, 1986–1990, and have been in existence for more than five years prior to this time. To control for any sectoral effect on growth, firms were drawn from five specific industrial sectors representing a balance between low-tech and high-tech activity: electrical engineering, clothing, mechanical engineering, chemicals and other manufacturing.

Within these parameters firms were selected on the basis of stratified random sampling. The stratification was made on the basis of employment growth.[3] Within each stratum firms were selected on a random basis. The aim was to arrive at a sample of firms equally weighted in terms of fast, medium and slow growing firms. It was not the aim to produce samples that reflected the actual distribution of fast, medium and slow growing firms in the study regions, since this information was contained in the databases that underpinned the study[4] but to gain adequate coverage of each growth category. The regional balance of fast, medium and slow growing firms is shown in Table 1.

The firms that conformed to the criteria and agreed to be interviewed were visited by members of the research team during 1992. The interviewers usually worked in pairs[5] and the interviewees, by prior arrangement, were always the firm's most senior decision makers. Every interviewee was asked 60 questions[6] covering the following topics:

background company characteristics,
growth in assets, turnover, employment and profits,
owner-manager qualifications and work-experience,
owner-manager objectives,

business development activities,
constraints on growth.

Working from the questionnaire an extensive list of variables was created which were
tested for their possible influence on firm growth.[7]

Table 1: Breakdown of Survey Firms by Region and Growth

Region	Fast growth		Medium growth		Slow growth		All firms
	No.	%	No.	%	No.	%	No.
Northern Ireland	18	36.0	15	30.0	17	34.7	50
Leicestershire	10	20.4	22	44.9	17	34.7	49
Hertfordshire	9	18.7	15	31.2	24	50.0	48
Wearside	5	52.0	13	52.0	7	28.0	25
Total	42	24.4	65	37.8	65	37.8	172

Source: NIERC Small Firms Survey

The approach to analysing the data adopted in this research might be described as
'guided model-building'. Within the framework of the three influences on firm growth,
company characteristics, entrepreneur characteristics and business strategy, an iterative
procedure was adopted for the identification of an equation which had the ability to explain
the largest proportion of the variance in the dependent variable. The statistical framework
for this procedure was multivariate regression analysis.

Although data on the growth of assets, employment and profits[8] were collected, the
preferred dependent variable was growth in turnover. In accounting terms, turnover is the
variable which is least influenced by variations in accounting policies. The use of employment growth was rejected because of the potentially distorting effect of the use of subcontractors and because, in reality, few businessmen relate the success and development of
their enterprise to the number of people it employs.[9]

The use of OLS regression techniques for analysis necessitated certain transformations of
the data. For instance, the variable percentage change in turnover is highly skewed. To
overcome this problem change in turnover enters the model as the log of the ratio of 1990
turnover to 1986 turnover which is the 4 year growth rate, continuously compounded.[10]
The qualitative nature of the independent variables necessitated their transformation, in
many cases, into dummy variables indicating the presence or absence of a characteristic. In
certain cases, where a variable was composed of a number of categories, a group of dummy
variables was formed with one category acting as the base. The process of transformation
yielded 270 potential independent variables. Many of these potential independent variables
were similar in nature and could not therefore be included in the same equation. The
approach to estimation that was adopted may be termed 'guided model building'. Our
hypothesis was that firm growth depended on Business Characteristics, Entrepreneur
Characteristics, Business Strategy and Constraints. The equation was developed iteratively
by estimating and re-estimating the model, having regard to overall fit of the equation (R-
squared) and the model significance as well as the coefficients on individual variables and
their significance and, importantly, the overall plausibility of the regression. In some cases,
due to the weight of previous evidence, variables were retained in the model even though
they were not significant. However, in general, non-significant variables were dropped
from the model.[11]

RESULTS AND DISCUSSION

Table 2 contains the results of the statistical analysis in the form of a regression equation.[12]
The equation contains 26 variables[13] and, inevitably, an equation of this size is complex in
its interpretation. In discussing the results two important themes are explored: the meaning
and relative importance of the individual variables and the significance of the model as a
whole.

THE INDIVIDUAL VARIABLES

Company characteristics
The variable 'initial size', measured as the log of 1986 turnover, is clearly an important influence on the subsequent growth of the firm. The coefficient is negative and this indicates that the larger the firm at the start of the period, the slower the subsequent growth. This finding is in line with other research (see, for instance, Evans, 1987a; 1987b).

Despite the emphasis on sector and location in the literature, within a multivariate framework in which managerial and strategic variables appear, these variables, with one exception, are not significant. It appears that sector and region influence are much fewer than was previously thought. These variables are retained, in view of previous research, to demonstrate their relatively limited effect.[14]

The exception to this statement is the Northern Ireland dummy. Northern Ireland firms show significantly better growth over the period than firms in Hertfordshire (which acts as the base category) whereas firms in Leicestershire and Wearside do not. This finding mirrors that of Hart et al. (1993) that Northern Ireland firms are strong performers over the period 1986 to 1990. It requires further research to substantiate the fact that support policies are the cause of this strong performance but it is worth noting that the majority of small firms in the Northern Ireland sample have received Local Enterprise Development Unit (LEDU) or Irish Development Board (IDB) assistance in the period 1986–1990.

Table 2: Small Firm Growth Equation

Variable Group	Variable	Coefficient
Business characteristics	Initial size	(0.14)**
	Northern Ireland	0.26**
	Leicestershire	0.0
	Wearside	0.16
	Mech Eng	(0.23)
	Chem	(0.2)
	Other manu	(0.02)
	Elec Eng	(0.14)
Owner characteristics	AGE	(0.01)*
	Professional	0.35**
	Organisation Founder	0.12
	Other businesses	0.26**
	Other businesses (Adv)	0.43**
	Other owners	0.19**
Business strategy	Profit growth	0.19**
	Marketing	0.24**
	Price flexible	0.40*
	Production process	0.19*
	Market research	0.26**
	Agent	(0.36)**
	New products	0.03*
	Capital success	0.21**
	Capital failure	0.34*
	New machinery	0.15*
	Diversification index	(0.19)**
Constraints	Demand	(0.29)**
	Constant	1.83**
Regression statistics	Cases	138
	Adjusted R-square	0.51
	F-statistic	6.48
	S.E. model	0.38

Full variable descriptions can be found in Appendix 1
Source: NIERC Small Firms Survey

The base category for the group of dummy variables representing sector of operation is clothing.[15] None of the sector variables is significant indicating that such sector influences are accounted for by the other variables in the model. There appear to be no influences operating at the level of broad industrial sector which have an influence on the growth of the small firm. This is in line with our a priori conceptualisation of firm growth in which the entrepreneur and the strategy he or she pursues are thought to be the most important influences.

Entrepreneur characteristics

The second section of the model contains the characteristics of the entrepreneur found to be associated with growth. Together they present a plausible picture of the type of entrepreneur associated with rapidly growing small firms.

The variable indicating the age of the entrepreneur is significant, has a negative coefficient but is relatively small in its impact. Each additional year of age is associated with a 1% decrease in the growth of the firm. Age is positively related to experience and skill but negatively associated with motivation and flexibility. It appears that the decline in motivation and flexibility that age brings dominates any gains from experience in the running of a small firm.[16]

Twenty seven interviewees indicated that they were members of a professional organisation. A dummy variable indicating membership of a professional organisation indicates that this characteristic is strongly associated with growth. Entrepreneurs who were members of a professional organisation are associated with firms that grow 35% faster than those with no such membership.

A limitation of this study is that we were unable in all cases to gather information on the nature of the professional organisations concerned. On the basis of rather limited evidence[17] it appears that membership of a professional organisation implies high technical competence. For instance, a frequently mentioned professional organisation is the Institute of Engineers but the list also contains the Institute of Chemistry. There appear to be few accountants and solicitors running small manufacturing firms.

The membership of professional organisation variable is important because variables representing education are not found to be significant in this equation. However, there does appear to be a link between qualifications and membership of a professional organisation. Thirty seven per cent of entrepreneurs who are members of a professional organisation have a degree compared with only 15% in the rest of the sample. This finding illustrates an important point, namely certain variables have a strong but indirect effect on firm performance. One such variable is education. Although education is insignificant in the equation it is highly correlated with other variables. Membership of a professional organisation is one variable that is correlated with education. Others so linked are discussed below.[18]

The variable 'founder' indicates that the owner-manager was the founder of the firm. Although insignificant in formal statistical terms the t-value indicates a level of significance not far below the 5% level. The variable was retained in the equation because of a strong a priori expectation that having the founder in control affects the performance of the firm because of the commitment the founder has to the enterprise he or she has created. A number of studies have found a link between the presence of the founder and the performance of the firm (Storey, 1994).[19]

Twenty eight per cent of business owners in the survey indicated that they owned other enterprises. This group could be differentiated according to whether or not the other firms gave the survey firm an advantage. Entrepreneurs who own other firms achieve higher growth than entrepreneurs with no additional business interests. It is our view that the literature has completely neglected this aspect of small firm entrepreneurship. It seems likely that the most capable entrepreneurs seek to expand their activities not through developing one business but by creating a whole network of enterprises. Our work indicates that approximately 65%[20] of these 'other' business interests are related to the survey firm. It is as if one business is not enough for the highly active entrepreneur. Research into entrepreneurship urgently needs to address the issue of multi-business entrepreneurs. In particular the characteristics of this group should be studied and the linkages between businesses investigated. Very little information in the current study was collected on this issue.

The variable 'other owners' indicates that the firm had more than one owner-manager active in the business.[21] In the sample, 53% of firms had more than one owner active in the business so the image of the lone entrepreneur is somewhat misplaced at least in the area of small manufacturing firms. Multi-owner firms grow more quickly than single owner firms. Our impression from the interviews was that the disparity in growth between the single business owner and multiple business owner firms is related to the benefits of specialisation and team-working.[22] However, although beneficial to the small firm, entrepreneurial teams seem to emerge from long term working relationships and cannot be created 'overnight'. Thus it is not possible for all small firm owner-managers to adopt this method of running a firm.

The picture that emerges from the statistical results is that the entrepreneur associated with the more rapidly growing small firm is relatively young, a member of a professional organisation, the owner of a network of small firms and part of a team. Contrary to expectation, education and career history (including functional specialisation and managerial experience) do not appear to have a direct influence on small firm growth although, as has been indicated, education appears to be an important indirect influence.

Business strategy

In this research the variables representing entrepreneurial objectives are considered as part of the set of strategic variables despite their link with motivation, and, therefore, their possible classification as entrepreneur variables. The reason for this is that it is not always possible to draw a hard and fast distinction between the objectives and strategies of entrepreneurs. For instance, growth is an end in itself for some entrepreneurs whilst for others it is merely a means to achieve higher profits or market dominance. To ensure the correct identification of the entrepreneur's most important objectives we asked a number of questions on this subject so that the answers could be cross referenced. Table 3 summarises the results of these questions.

One important feature of this table is that it indicates that the ambition to grow is widespread, perhaps more widespread than has been appreciated by other researchers (Storey, 1994; Stanworth and Curran, 1976). The data in the table were used to create dummy variables that were tested in the model. Only profit growth, which indicates that a high importance is attached to growth in profits, has explanatory power and significance.

Table 3: Entrepreneurial Objectives

	Frequency	%
Section A: Aim to Grow		
Aimed to Grow	121	70
Section B: Focus of growth		
Asset growth important	32	18
Turnover growth important	81	47
Profit growth important	107	62
Employment growth important	23	13
Section C: Main aims		
Expand firm	139	50
Restrain growth	62	36
Improve products/Product range	47	27
Improve production	29	17
Other business development	14	8
Other personal	19	11

N = 174

Source: NIERC Small Firms Survey

An important issue therefore is why 38% of small businessmen do not rate the growth of profits as highly important.

The variable 'capital success' in Table 2 indicates that the owner-manager successfully sought loan capital from outside the firm whilst the variable 'capital' indicates that although an effort to raise loan capital was made, this was unsuccessful. The equation shows that growth is 21% higher in firms where the entrepreneur seeks outside capital and obtains it than in firms where the entrepreneur chooses to finance the firm from internal sources only. However, in firms where the entrepreneur seeks finance from outside and does not obtain it, growth is 34% higher. This suggests that it is the openness to outside finance that distinguishes the entrepreneur rather than the receipt of the finance alone. It is also interesting to note that certain firms are unable to obtain capital despite being capable of achieving growth.

There are two important qualifications to be made at this point about the relationship between the capital variables and ambition. First, in some cases, in particular in Northern Ireland and Wearside, external finance will have been sought from public sector agencies such as, in Northern Ireland, IDB and LEDU. In these cases it cannot necessarily be said that the owner-managers are accepting a higher level of risk since public sector assistance is often in the form of grants. However, in areas where finance is available at below market rates it might be expected that attempts to access this form of funding will still differentiate the ambitious from the non-ambitious entrepreneur although perhaps less so than in the case of private sector funding.

The second caveat is that there is a potential confusion of cause and effect in the capital failure and capital success variables. The greater the growth of the company, it might be argued, the more likely the management is to seek access to outside finance and to succeed in obtaining it. This interpretation cannot be refuted although our preference is for the explanation linking the search for outside capital to the ambition and capabilities of the entrepreneur. It is worth noting that dropping these variables from the model has a small effect on the R-square but no effect on the level of significance of the other variables.

The remaining strategy variables may be divided into those relating to production: production process, new products, new machinery; and those relating to the marketing activities of the firm: marketing, price flexibility, market research, agent, diversification. Those relating to production will be dealt with first.

The variable 'production process' indicates that the entrepreneur attaches a high degree of importance to improving the production process as a means of achieving given strategic objectives. Since only 52 owner-managers indicated that this was an important strategy, *vis-à-vis* the 122 that actually invested in new machinery, it is clear that improving the production process was associated with a broader range of activities than investing in new plant and machinery. 'New machinery' is the dummy variable that identifies those firms that invested in new plant and machinery. The coefficient on the new machinery variable is positive and significant as is that in the production process variable. This indicates that upgrading plant and machinery is associated with increased growth. On average those installing new machinery had 15% greater growth than those not doing so. However, controlling for the effects of improved machinery the strategy of improving production process still brings about an improvement growth of 19%. The 'production process' variable can best be described as a constant pressure to improve the production capabilities of the firm utilising anything from small changes in factory layout to improvements on worker training and morale.

The other aspect of production on which we have evidence is the introduction of new products. 'New products' is not a dummy variable and indicates, for each firm, the number of new products introduced by the firm over the study period. The definition of 'new product' is broad: it includes innovations, the introduction of products new to the firm and improvements made to existing products. Although this variable is significant the coefficient shows that it has relatively little impact on growth. Two other definitions of new products were tested in the equation, one indicating the number of pure innovations and the other pure innovations plus products new to the firm. Neither of these variables was significant indicating that it is in the adaptation and improvement of existing products that small firms are able to generate growth.

An important finding of this research is the importance of market related variables in explaining variations in small firm growth relative to production, entrepreneur and firm variables. As will be demonstrated, the firm will always be subject to the influence of the overall growth of the market but the way in which the firm positions itself within a market has a crucial impact on its growth performance.

The strongest marketing variable and indeed the strongest variable in the model is the presence of formal 'market research' within the firm.[23] The commitment of the firms to seek out new market information is strongly associated with growth. An equation containing the 'market research' dummy by itself explains 15% of the variance in growth. In relation to earlier comments made about education it is interesting to note that 48% of graduate entrepreneurs conduct market research as opposed to only 12% of non-graduates. The importance of education lies in the fact that it affects the type of strategies adopted by the entrepreneur.

The variable marketing indicates that within the firm a high importance was attached to marketing. Only 62 firms in the sample had this strong marketing orientation and it can be seen that these firms increased their growth by 24% over the period. This additional growth is over and above gains from conducting market research.

Interestingly only six firms indicate that they use price as a strategic variable, that is, they used price cuts to generate growth. This is illustrative of the extremely competitive markets faced by most small firms. A dummy variable differentiating these firms from the others, price flexibility, is significant and has a large coefficient. Firms indicating that they could vary price so as to achieve strategic objectives had 40% higher growth rate than non-price-flexible firms. Apart from the obvious impact of price reductions on sales this variable possibly indicates those few firms capable of making major productivity advances.

Two of the market variables had negative coefficients: 'agent' and 'diversification index'. The variable agent indicates that the firm uses agents to assist in the marketing and sale of their products. There are two possible interpretations of this variable. First, since the entrepreneur is relying on an agent they are not greatly motivated to achieve sales. Against this is the fact that establishing a distributor network takes a good deal of time and resources. It is probable that it is just too difficult for the small firm entrepreneur to oversee and get the best out of a network of agents and this accounts for the poor performance of firms using them.

The variable 'diversification index' indicates the degree to which the small firm is diversified.[24] The higher the number, the more diversified the firms in terms of a weighted average of the number of products it sells. It can be seen that diversification is associated with slow growth. The more products the firm sells, the lower the growth. Each unit increase in the diversification index is associated with a 19% reduction in growth. One explanation of this result is that a major motivation for diversification is falling demand in the core business. However, the impact of falling demand is controlled by the demand variable. A more plausible explanation is that diversification is a difficult process for the small firm because it requires entry into markets with which the management is unfamiliar.

Constraint variables

The variable 'demand' is a dummy variable based on the question how important is demand as a constraint on growth. It indicates those entrepreneurs that said demand was a very important constraint. Entrepreneurs were asked about the influence of a range of other constraints on growth but these were not generally found to have any statistically significant influence on growth. The main problem with the demand variable is that it may simply proxy the entrepreneur's own deficiencies which they are not prepared to discuss. The inclusion of the variable has a strong impact on the equation's R-square and generally improves the significance of the other variables. Demand makes a strong and independent contribution to the model and as such indicates the important impact of market changes in the growth of small firms.

Taken at face value the significance of this variable indicates that whatever the characteristics of the entrepreneur and the strategies he or she adopts a strong influence on the performance of the firm is the growth of the market. Poorly run firms will do well in periods of market growth and well run firms will suffer in times of recession.

The complete equation

The complete equation shows that the entrepreneur associated with fast growth is relatively young, sufficiently well qualified to be admitted to a professional organisation, has outside business interests and works as part of an entrepreneurial team. In terms of strategy, fast growing firms are active in both product and process improvement, invest in new machinery, seek and obtain finance outside the company, engage in market research, place a high level of importance to bringing their products to the attention of the market and have the flexibility to adjust prices to achieve sales. Growth is reduced if firms face a declining market, produce and sell a range of products and or use agents. However, this review of the independent variables should not obscure the importance of the complete equation.

The first thing to note is the R-square of the equation. The variables we have identified jointly explain 51% of the variance in small manufacturing firm growth rates. Table 4 gives summary statistics for the small firm growth variable. The highly divergent performance of any sample of small firms means that there is a high degree of variance to be explained. The explanation of 51% of this variance can be taken as confirmation of the essential correctness of this approach to small firm growth. The performance of any small firm is due to four broad factors: the characteristics of the firm, the characteristics of the entrepreneur, the business strategies adopted by the entrepreneur and the specific market conditions faced by the entrepreneur. Of these groups of factors the most important are the strategies adopted by the firm and the specific market conditions. It is worth noting in this regard that the 2 most important variables in the equation are market research and demand as a constraint and these 2 variables alone account for 24% of the variance.

The success of the equation in explaining the variance confirms the approach taken in several other important respects. First, as Storey (1994) points out, research on small firm performance must be multivariate in its approach to statistical testing. It is not realistic to look at the influence of individual variables such as location, or entrepreneurial motivation or marketing strategy. This research shows that there is a considerable difference between the univariate and multivariate regression coefficients. Certain variables appear to have no significance unless they are included within the multivariate model whilst others such as education, whilst significant in a univariate regression, are insignificant in the full equation. Research on small firm performance has to be predicated on the finding that growth is the result of a multiplicity of factors.

Although the R-square of 51% is high for complex cross-sectional analysis the implication

Table 4: Summary Statistics: Growth Variable

mean	.30
standard deviation	.54
maximum value	1.96
minimum value	−1.40
N=138	

Source: NIERC Small Firms Survey

is that 49% of the variance in the data is unexplained. One area that might have been explored in more depth is the psychological characteristics of the entrepreneur. Although the evidence is mixed (Leff, 1979; Chell, 1986) some studies show this to be an important factor in business performance (Smith, 1967; Collins and Moore, 1964). Arguably we have captured many of the ways in which the highly motivated entrepreneur is differentiated from the poorly motivated entrepreneur in the analysis of the business development variables but it is possible that some of the residual variance might be explained by motivational variables. In addition the impact of chance factors that affect all firms for better or worse may mean that it is impossible to fully explain variations in firm growth rates in terms of tangible economic variables.

CONCLUSIONS AND IMPLICATIONS

The first conclusion of this research is that it is possible to explain growth in small firms in terms of the characteristics of the company, the characteristics of the entrepreneur, the business strategies adopted and the dynamics of specific markets. Within this framework it appears that strategies and markets are the most important factors. In particular 'market research' and 'demand as a constraint' appear to be important single variables. However, the overall picture is that growth in small firms is an extremely complex process defying simple conceptualisations. A large number of variables influence growth. Changes to any one of the variables, even if appropriate, will have a relatively small impact on the annual growth rate of a firm.

From a policy perspective the results of this research are particularly interesting. The complexity of small firm growth means that there is no single means of boosting the aggregate performance of small firms except insofar as market constraints might be removed by macro-economic policy. A corollary of this finding is that small firm advisers need to adopt a sophisticated and individualistic approach to helping small firms. For example, at the level of the individual firm there is a range of strategic variables that seem to have an impact on growth rates. Advisers and entrepreneurs seeking to expand the firms they are connected with need to make certain that:

1. profits are the sole motivating factor in business decision taking[25],
2. good business opportunities are pursued even if outside finance is required,
3. every opportunity is taken to improve the productivity of the firm and continually seeking productivity improvement becomes a way of life,
4. the product range is kept as narrow as possible and as close as is feasible to the main area of expertise of the entrepreneurs,
5. within the constraints of 4. a flexible approach to product development is adopted where every attempt is made to meet changing customer requirements by the adaptation of existing products,
6. they adopt a cautious approach to the development of totally new products,
7. a percentage of the firm turnover is devoted to market research, the aim of which should be the generation of information on the requirements, budgets and location of potential customers,
8. marketing should be a formal strategy of the firm,
9. firms take responsibility for selling their products themselves and avoid the use of agents.

This research has uncovered several areas that require further investigation. One potential research project is to use the equation we have developed to predict the future performance of a sample of small firms rather than account for previous performance. The variables that have been identified could be used to identify the firm that might be expected to do well and the performance of these firms could be monitored over a period of time.

A second important project is to examine the way in which entrepreneurial teams boost the growth of small firms. It is clearly beneficial for entrepreneurs to work in pairs or threes and the reasons for this appear to be related to skill-complementarity and specialisation in decision making. Previous research has not fully investigated this issue and further research on this issue might uncover additional important ways in which entrepreneurial teams create growth.

ACKNOWLEDGEMENTS

The research was funded by the Northern Ireland Economic Research Centre which is itself partially funded by the ESRC. The research team, under the chairmanship of Dr Graham Gudgin, comprised individuals from 4 institutions: Dr R J Barkham, University of Reading; Dr John Fagg, Worcester College; Dr Mark Hart, University of Ulster; Dr Ian Stone, University of Northumbria.

NOTES

1. In this research the term owner-manager is used interchangeably with entrepreneur.
2. These databases have been specially created by NIERC for the purpose of examining the components of employment change. For further details see the full report of this study, Barkham et al., 1994.
3. Fast growing firms are defined as those with a 100% growth in employment over the period, medium growing firms as those showing between 1% and 99% growth and static or declining firms as those with zero or negative growth.
4. In fact, the composition of the regional samples, with regard to growth, is similar to that distribution found in the underlying populations.
5. This practice was departed from in the case of Leicestershire where interviewing was contracted out to a market research firm. The Leicestershire questionnaires, though usable, were less well completed than those for the other regions where the interviews were conducted by academics.
6. A copy of the questionnaire can be found in Barkham et al., 1996.
7. A list of these variables can be found in Barkham et al., 1996.
8. For accounting and survey reasons our data on profitability were not considered to be of sufficient quality for inclusion in this study.
9. A fuller discussion of the relative merits of the various measures of size and growth is contained in the full report of the project as is an indication of the levels of correlation between them.
10. The effects of inflation have been removed using the GDP deflator. Thus turnover growth is in real terms.
11. More details of the dropped variables can be found in Barkham et al. (1996).
12. The full report of this research contains several variants of this model. In some of the alternatives the impact of dropping variables is explored and in others the significance and explanatory power of individual and groups of variables is shown and, in particular, a reduced form model gives an indication of the most important number of variables in the model. This model contains the largest number of variables and has the highest explanatory power.
13. The model is based on 138 observations. The reduction in the number of observations from the full 172 is due mainly to missing data. Not all of the questionnaires were correctly completed in full. In particular a number of companies failed to provide data on turnover change despite persistent requests. In addition 6 cases have been dropped because we suspect the data on product are wrong.
14. Dropping the regional and sectoral dummies from the model has little impact on the coefficients and significance of the other variables.
15. The selection of the base category has no influence on the results.
16. It was been suggested in the literature that age take a quadratic form in multivariate analysis. This was tried but the variable was not significant. This is possibly because there are relatively few young entrepreneurs in the sample.

17. We have detail for only 16 entrepreneurs.
18. Barkham et al., 1996, contains a fuller account of the interrelationships between the variables in the equation and those which have an important though indirect effect.
19. Certain 'reduced form' equations also indicate that founder is an important explanatory variable.
20. Fifty-two entrepreneurs in the study had other business interests and of the 34 on which there are data, 22 were interrelated with the survey firm.
21. The variable specifically omits owner of the firm not active in the business. A variable including non-active entrepreneurs is significant in the equation but its inclusion reduces the R-square of the model.
22. Although data were collected on all of the management team it was generally possible to identify a lead entrepreneur. In the model building stage of the research we experimented with variables that encapsulated all the skills of the group but found that these had very little explanatory power.
23. The strength of the variable is gauged by its contribution to the proportion of variance explained by the model as indicated by the R-square.
24. As measured by Utton's diversification index.
25. This suggests the effective use of discounted cashflow techniques incorporating the appropriate discount rate.

REFERENCES

Barkham R J (1989) Entrepreneurship, New Firms and Regional Development, unpublished PhD Thesis, Department of Economics, University of Reading.

Barkham R J, Gudgin G , Hart M, Hanvey E and (1996) The Determinants of Small Firm Growth: An Inter-Regional Study in the UK, 1986–90, Jessica Kingsley/Regional Studies Association, London.

Chell E (1986) 'The entrepreneurial personality: a review and some theoretical developments', Survival of the Small Firm Vol 1: The Economics of Survival, Curran J, Stanworth J and Watkins D (eds), Gower, Aldershot.

Collins O F, Moore D G and Unwalla D B (1964) The Enterprising Man, Michigan State University Business Studies (Bureau of Business and Economic Research), Graduate School of Business Administration, MSU, East Lansing.

Cross M (1981) New Firm Formation and Regional Development, Gower, Farnborough.

DTI (1991) Constraints on the Growth of Small Firms, HMSO, London.

Evans D S (1987a) The relationship between firm growth, size and age: estimate for 100 manufacturing industries, Journal of Industrial Economics, XXXV, 4, pp567–81, June.

Evans D S (1987b) Tests of Alternative Theories of Firm Growth, Journal of Political Economy, 95, 4, pp657–674.

Fothergill S and Gudgin G (1982) Unequal Growth – Urban and Regional Employment Change in the UK, Heineman Educational, London.

Gilmore J B (1972) An investigation of selected entrepreneurial models: ability to predict successful entrepreneurial behaviour, unpublished PhD dissertation, University of Oklahoma, Graduate College, Norman Oklahoma.

Gudgin G, Hart M, Fagg J, D'Arcy A and Keegan R (1989) Job Generation and Manufacturing Industry 1973–1986, A Comparison of Northern Ireland with the Republic of Ireland and the English Midlands, NIERC, Belfast.

Hart M, Scott R, Gudgin G and Keegan R (1993) Job Creation and Small Firms, NIERC, Belfast.

Hitchens D M W N and O'Farrell P N (1987) Inter Regional Comparisons of Small Firms Performance: the case of Northern Ireland and South East England, Regional Studies, 21, pp543–55.

Hitchens D M W N and O'Farrell P N (1988a) The Comparative Performance of Small Manufacturing Companies in the Mid-West and Northern Ireland, Economic and Social Review, 19, 3, pp177–98.

Hitchens D M W N and O'Farrell P N (1988b) The Comparative Performance of Small Manufacturing Companies Located in South Wales and Northern Ireland, Omega, 16, 5, pp429–38.

Leff N H (1979) Entrepreneurship and economic development: the problem revisited, Journal of Economic Literature, 17 (1), pp46–64.

O'Farrell P N and Hitchens D M W N (1988) Alternative theories of small firm growth: a critical review, Environment and Planning A, 20, pp1365–83.

Schultz T W (1980) Investment in Entrepreneurial Ability, Scandinavian Journal of Economics, 82, pp437–48.

Smith N R (1967) One Entrepreneur and His Firm, Bureau of Business and Economic Research, University of Michigan, Illinois.

Stanworth M J K and Curran J (1976) Growth and the Small Firm – An Alternative View, Journal of Management Studies, 13, 2, pp95–110, May.

Storey D J (1994) Understanding the Small Business Sector, Routledge, London.

Sweeney G P (1987) Innovation, Entrepreneurs and Regional Development, Frances Pinter, London.

APPENDIX 1

Full variable descriptions

Variable	*Description*	*Type*
Initial size	Log of turnover in 1986	Continuous
Northern Ireland	Location in Northern Ireland	Dummy
Leicestershire	Location in Leicestershire	Dummy
Wearside	Location in Wearside*	Dummy
Mech Eng	Sector of operation: Mechanical Engineering**	Dummy
Chem Eng	Sector of operation: Chemical Engineering**	Dummy
Other Manu	Sector of operation: Other Manufacturing**	Dummy
Elec Eng	Sector of operation: Electrical Engineering**	Dummy
Age	Age of the entrepreneur	Continuous
Professional Organisation	Member of a professional organisation	Dummy
Founder	Entrepreneur is firm's founder	Dummy
Other businesses	Entrepreneur has other business interests which are not directly advantageous to the firm	Dummy
Other businesses (adv)	Entrepreneur has other business interests which are directly advantageous to the firm	Dummy
Other owners	Other owners active and influential in the firm	Dummy
Profit growth	Importance attached to growth in profits	Dummy
Marketing	Importance attached to marketing	Dummy
Price flexible	Price used as a strategic weapon	Dummy
Production process	Importance attached to improving the process of production	Dummy
Market research	Firm conducts market research	Dummy
Agent	Agents used for sales	Dummy
New products	Number of new or modified products introduced	Continuous
Capital success	Entrepreneur successfully sought outside loan capital	Dummy
Capital failure	Entrepreneur unsuccessfully sought outside loan capital	Dummy
New machinery	New machinery installed	Dummy
Diversification index	Weighted average of number of products	Continuous
Demand	Demand an important constraint on growth	Dummy

* Base category Hertfordshire

** Base category Clothing

11.

BS5750 AND QUALITY MANAGEMENT IN SMEs

Francis Chittenden, Syeda Masooda Mukhtar, and Panikkos Poutziouris

INTRODUCTION

> Quality does not have to be defined. You understand it without definition. Quality is the direct experience independent of and prior to intellectual attractions. (Robert Pirsing, in Tom Peters' Liberation Management, 1992)

Quality constitutes an important vehicle in the development of competitive advantage in the era of 'New Competition' (Best, 1990). Consequently, there has been an increase in the interest of governments and industrial institutions in upgrading the quality of industrial products and services in order to further the international competitiveness of the economy. One manifestation of this interest in the UK has been the promotion of the BS5750 Quality Standard by the British Standards Institute (BSI) and the Department of Trade and Industry (DTI, 1987).

However, BS5750 is not a quality standard per se. In fact BS5750 is a management control procedure which involves businesses in documenting their processes of design, production and distribution in order to ensure that the quality of those products and services consistently meets the intended purposes. Since publication of BS5750 by the BSI in 1979[1] it has been intended that the standard should be applied to firms of all sizes and from all business activities. BS5750 has been applauded by some business commentators, but also widely criticized especially by the small business community (Gourlay, 1994a;1994b; Sepsu, 1994).

In the words of BSI chairman at the launch of a new service to demystify BS5750 for small business:

> BS5750 is an undoubted UK success story. Over 28,000 organizations have been registered to the standard in the UK alone and a further 17,000 worldwide. With this comprehensive package we aim to make the benefits of BS5750 accessible to all companies no matter what the size, without in any way devaluing the standard or providing a second rate alternative. This service is the result of listening, learning and acting on the needs of smaller businesses. (BSI Chairman, Vivian Thomas, April 1994)

The announcement of BSIs recognition that small firms face difficulties in registering for BS5750 may be regarded as a positive development. Unfortunately, introducing cost reductions for those businesses where initial assessment for the standard can be undertaken in one day (typically small businesses employing fewer than ten employees) does not fully address the problems surrounding the application of BS5750 to small businesses.

The criticism directed to BS5750 for failing to meet the needs of smaller firms is reflected in a number of statements (SBRT,1992; SEPSU, 1994) such as: 'There are many enterprises going bust where the last flag as they go under is their (quality) certificate' (Jacques MacMillan of DGIII, quoted in Gourlay (1994a)).

BS5750 AND SMALL FIRMS: OTHER STUDIES

The early discussions of BS5750 and small firms have been conducted through the media and the management consultancy literature. These studies have identified some of the concepts and issues associated with BS5750 and quality management in SMEs (Halliday, 1992; Woodcock, 1992; 1994). For example, Bannock (1991) concluded that there was 'no rush for small firms to register' with BS5750 since early criticism of the standard drew attention to the complex quality management procedures which were thought to be inappropriate for small-scale operations. The formality of these required procedures resulted in high financial and time costs associated with developing and operating the BS5750 quality management system.

The problems with regard to BS5750 and small firms have been confirmed by other preliminary investigations such as an SBRT Survey (1992) and the recognition by the BSI that only a very small proportion of registered firms were small businesses. More recently academic research has focused on the underlying problems associated with BS5750 in the context of the small business sector. North et al. (1993, 1994) cite some evidence of the factors which have led to the unpopularity of the standard amongst the small business community. These two studies were based upon a sample of 120 service firms and 30 manufacturing businesses who were interviewed by telephone. Only five of these small firms were found to have registered under BS5750.

These studies identified the following issues relating to BS5750 and small firms:

1. Two thirds of the small business respondents were either unaware of or did not intend to register with the standard;
2. Of those firms not intending to register, almost a third considered the standard irrelevant because of the small size of their businesses;
3. One third of small business owners not pursuing BS5750 said it was too costly;
4. A fifth of the firms described BS5750 as over-bureaucratic and incompatible with their informal management style.

Those businesses which were either considering or in the process of implementing BS5750 reported the following motives for pursuing registration under the standard (in descending order of importance):

1. Reaction to external market conditions (eg pressure from larger customers);
2. Procedural benefits relating to their internal systems (eg training); and
3. The desire for an improved market image.

Based upon these preliminary studies it may be hypothesized that the majority of small firms operate informal quality management procedures which are tailored to their small scale operations and are not externally controlled by market agents or customers.

Following the results reported above a large scale study of the attitudes and experience of small businesses relating to BS5750 was undertaken in the spring of 1994. The research objectives of this large scale study were to:

1. Obtain a better understanding of the nature and extent of quality management practised in the SME sector (whether this involved adopting a formal standard or not).
2. Identify the key issues relating to BS5750, especially for those businesses employing fewer than 20 staff (as these represent in excess of 90% of all firms and account for over 30% of private sector employment (Storey, 1994).
3. To investigate the differences, if any, between the business and market characteristics of firms using or not using BS5750.
4. To establish the motivations for and the consequences of registration under BS5750.
5. To identify the barriers that inhibit small firms from adopting the BS5750 quality assurance standard.

METHODOLOGY

Data collection was conducted by a postal survey. Thirty thousand questionnaires were sent to randomly chosen members of the Forum of Private Business (FPB), the Federation of Small Businesses (FSB) and the Rural Development Commission (RDC). In addition 1,000 questionnaires were posted to a sample of registered businesses from addresses provided by the Department of Trade and Industry (DTI).

The 88-question survey was divided into four separate sections and participants were encouraged to complete those parts relevant to their stage of involvement with BS5750, and then return the questionnaire. The four sections dealt with the profile of respondent businesses, the investigation stage that business-owners must go through in order to decide if BS5750 is relevant to their firm; the process of implementing the standard and, finally, the registration and assessment procedure for adopting and operating the standard.

The following analysis is based on 4,091 completed questionnaires which were received and processed within six weeks of posting.[2] The average number of responses per section was:

Section 1 :	Business Information Stage	3,517
Section 2 :	Think Through Stage	2,517
Section 3 :	Implementation Stage	537
Section 4 :	Registration Stage	191

The sample used in this research is broadly representative of the small firms sector (the size distribution of the sample suggested that 94.6% of sample firms were employing fewer than fifty employees), but like most surveys, has some biases. Manufacturing firms and firms registered for BS5750 are over-represented and very young firms are under-represented. A comparison was made of responses from the clients of the RDC and the members of FPB and FSB to test if there was any evidence of bias in the response of 'joiners' versus 'non joiners'. No bias was evident in the sample data. Comparison was also made of the responses of firms in the DTI sample and the registered firms from the random sample. There is a high degree of uniformity in the results from both of these samples of registered firms. Where there are any differences these are identified in this chapter.

In order to minimize the risk of bias in the sample, a telephone survey of non-respondents was also carried out by selecting at random members from each organization participating. Six questions were selected from the questionnaire and the owners of the small businesses who had received (but not completed) the survey were asked to respond to these questions. Two hundred and thirty seven telephone interviews were completed. There is no evidence of significant differences between the questionnaire results and the analysis of non-respondents.

Comparison was made of the characteristics of BS5750 users and non-users in order to identify their motives for implementing or rejecting the standard and to explore the perceived barriers to the use of BS5750. The following sections summarize these results. In order to gain an insight into the detailed operations of the businesses and the impact of BS5750, the analysis in each section is further broken down by the size, legal structure and business activity of respondents. The dynamics of served markets and the impact of owners management styles on the management of quality are also considered.

BACKGROUND SURVEY RESULTS

Business characteristics
The results show that BS5750 users tend to be larger than those firms which do not register. The median number of employees for BS5750 users was 21 (full-time) compared with 6 full-time employees for unregistered firms. Figure 1, which provides a comparison of users and non-users by size in terms of sales turnover, further emphasises this point.

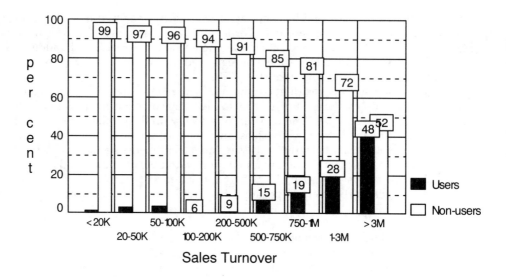

Figure 1 Firms using BS5750 by size

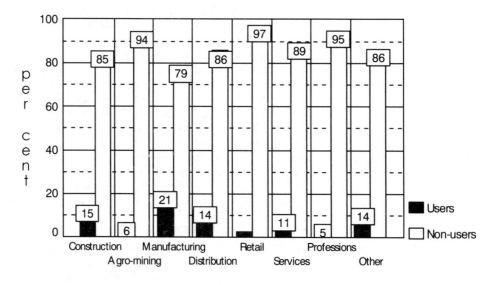

Figure 2 Business activity

This difference in the scale of operations between those firms which do or do not adopt BS5750 is manifested in a number of other ways. For example, 80% of 'BS5750 users' are incorporated compared with 46% of non-registered businesses. The median age of BS5750 users (17 years) is 33% higher than for the unregistered respondents.

Cross-tabulations employing the chi-square statistical test revealed significant differences (p=.00) in the proportion of businesses using BS5750 between industry sectors. Figure 2 shows that BS5750 is particularly appealing to manufacturing firms, and less attractive to businesses operating in Retailing, Agriculture/Mining and the Professions.

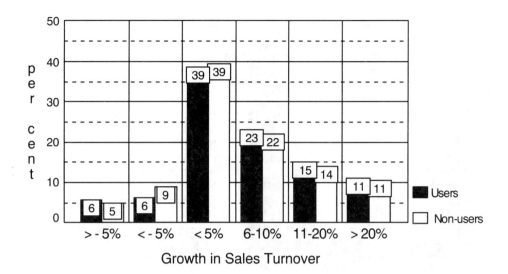

Figure 3 Business expectations

Table 1: Customer Base-Marketing Channels

		BS5750 Users %	Non-users %
Q18: How would you best	Domestic	6.1	26.2
describe the majority	Smaller than yours	11.9	10.2
of your customers ?	Your size	10.1	11.8
	Bigger businesses	59.7	42.1
	Government	6.4	2.5
	Other	5.8	7.1
Q19: How do you sell	Over the counter	6.4	19.2
to your customers?	Direct mail	6.5	15.3
	Sales staff	49.0	32.8
	Sales agents	11.0	10.8
	Other	27.0	39.9
Q20: Where are the majority	Local	30.7	55.2
of your customers?	UK/National	65.3	41.9
	Export	4.0	2.9

There appear to be few differences in the recent sales growth rates experienced by BS5750 users versus unregistered firms, as may be seen from Figure 3.

This similarity is also reflected in the degree of concentration of the customers of BS5750 users and unregistered firms. In both cases the median number of customers accounting for 80% of the sales of respondent firms was around 20. The median number of active customers on a weekly, monthly or annual basis were also similar.

However, the customer types, sales methods and geographic location of customers were significantly different (Table 1). In addition only one in five of the BS5750 users described themselves as being a single product business, compared with almost 30% of unregistered respondents.

There were statistically significant differences (p=.00) in the management styles adopted by the relatively smaller unregistered firms compared with the larger BS5750 users in the

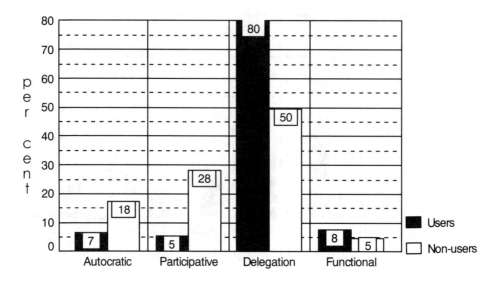

Figure 4 Management style of firms

sample. As shown in Figure 4, almost 45% of the owners of unregistered firms stated that their management style involved no delegation of authority, compared with one in eight of the BS5750 users.

Almost 90% of BS5750 users operated with a formal management structure although fewer than one in ten of these used performance targets for *all* levels of management. Even so, the apparently more hierarchical BS5750 users operated with relatively flat structures with 90% stating that there were three or fewer levels of authority (90% of unregistered firms had two or fewer levels of authority).

Financial planning and management accounting information were widely used throughout the sample. However, stock control and computer systems were less widely used by unregistered businesses. The unregistered firms were also less likely to use other formal management techniques such as production control, sales forecasting and formalized company objectives.

Inevitably every business is concerned about the quality of its products and services. Customers, especially those dealing with smaller firms in highly competitive markets, are able to express dis-satisfaction by selecting alternative suppliers. As a result over 80% of all sample firms utilized some form of specified quality standard and in one case in five quality assurance was the direct responsibility of the business owners (Figure 5).

However the way in which quality was managed in the sample differed between the BS5750 users and unregistered firms, as shown in Table 2.

The extent of formality of the quality management system did not appear to determine the effectiveness with which these systems operated. For example, at least 85% of all respondents were satisfied with their present quality procedures. Despite this, there was evidence to conclude that there is a strong association between perceived satisfaction with the operation of quality systems and the level of formality adopted. Firms with very informal quality systems were significantly more likely to express satisfaction with their present quality (p=.00). Using BS5750 may, therefore, be seen as a response to dissatisfaction with product or service quality when informal systems cease to be adequate. Thus it is not surprising that so few small firms do, in fact, register for BS5750 as the relative

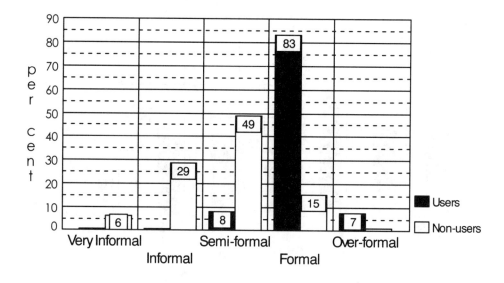

Figure 5 Quality management systems

Table 2: Level of Standardization

Quality Standard used for major products, goods or services	BS5750 Users %	Non-users %
Unwritten	18.8	2.4
Internally-specified	19.5	19.7
Customer-specified	24.3	23.9
Trade standard	18.4	9.7
British Standard	10.0	28.1
International/EU	5.3	11.6
Other	3.7	2.6

simplicity and small scale of their operations ensure that informal methods are the most effective.

The high level of satisfaction with informal quality systems is reflected in the similar rates of historic and projected sales growth achieved by both BS5750 users and unregistered firms (Figure 6).

SURVEY RESULTS ON USING BS5750: MOTIVATIONS AND CONSEQUENCES

This section presents data on the reasons why firms decided to adopt BS5750 and their assessment of the subsequent impact of that decision. Respondents were invited to identify, on a scale of 1 to 5, the extent to which they agreed or disagreed with a series of possible reasons for which firms might or might not wish to register for BS5750. An equal number of reasons in favour and against registration were offered to respondents, and the sequence of these statements was intermingled in order to avoid reinforcing either positive or negative perceptions. Respondents using BS5750 were subsequently asked to assess the subsequent impact of registration in terms of the benefits and disadvantages experienced.

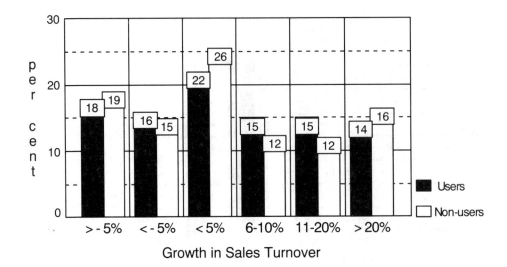

Growth in Sales Turnover

Figure 6 Business growth

Table 3: Motives for BS5750 Registration

	%
To improve quality procedures in my business	88
To win new customers and/or open new markets	84
To 'hold on' to existing customers	61
To increase profit and/or efficiency	55
To satisfy the needs of one major customer	39

Reasons for adopting BS5750 and industry sector

It has already been identified that larger firms and those in the manufacturing sector are more likely to use BS5750. Cross-tabulations were utilized to test whether the reasons for adopting this quality assurance standard differed by size of firm or the industry sector of operations. No statistically significant differences could be identified by size as measured by turnover. However, manufacturing firms were significantly ($p=.02$) more likely to agree or strongly agree with the objective 'to improve the quality procedures in my business' than firms in other sectors.

Reasons for adopting BS5750 and market dynamics

Roughly the same number of respondents identified motivations for registration relating to efficiency and profitability and marketing and competitive advantage (Table 3). Thus it appears that these are the prime reasons for adopting BS5750. Over four out of five of all BS5750 user respondents identified 'winning new customers or markets' as an important objective. Over 60% chose the more defensive goal of holding on to existing customers, whilst 39% were concerned with the needs of one major customer.

Table 4 shows that the largest benefits actually obtained ranked as 1 or 2 (on a scale of 1 to 5), related to marketing and competitive advantage, for example 'retaining business which would otherwise have been lost' (52%), 'less customer complaints' (44%) and 'broke into new markets' (38%). In addition almost 30% scored 'increased sales turnover' highly.

Table 4: Benefits of BS5750 Registration

	%
Retained business which otherwise would have been lost	52
Less customer complaint	44
Breaking into new markets	38
Increased sales turnover by customer	30
Reduction in scrap and/or waste	29
Improvement in plant and equipment utilization	20
Reduction in supervision cost	17
Reduction in training cost	14

These issues relating to the external position and perception of the business represent a mixture of positive elements (eg entering new markets) and defensive tactics (retaining customers which would otherwise be lost). It appears that the defensive goals were realized in practice more often than the creative ones. This may be a result of the presently depressed market conditions in which most firms are operating.

Interestingly the smaller firms in this sample of BS5750 users were more likely to realize their objective of 'breaking into new markets' (p=.02). However, the relatively small number of BS5750 users dealing with domestic customers were significantly more likely than other firms to face increases in labour costs (p=.02), overhead costs (p=.03) and to require a higher level of inspection and supervision (p=.00) as a result of implementing BS5750.

Reasons for adopting BS5750 and management style

Cross tabulations of the operational and managerial characteristics of registered firms versus the benefits obtained did not reveal any statistically significant differences. This is not surprising given the fact that most BS5750 users have similar organizational characteristics and motives towards BS5750 as they tend to be more sizeable organizations. Almost 88% of BS5750 users were operating with a more formal management structure which included delegation of authority.

Those BS5750 users which were less inclined to use formal management techniques were found to be significantly more likely to face increased costs in terms of labour, overheads and higher levels of inspection/supervision as a result of implementing or using BS5750. For example, those firms not utilizing planning and budgetary control were more likely to report rises in overhead costs and increased levels of inspection/supervision (p=<.05).

Measuring the impact of using BS5750

The most important 'internal' reasons why businesses register are shown in Table 3 (and in Table 7 forthcoming). BS5750 users expressed the highest level of agreement to the desire to 'improve the quality procedures in my business'. Of the other two 'internal factors' just over half the sample (55%) chose 'to increase profit or efficiency' whilst 42% expressed agreement or strong agreement to 'reduce scrap and/or waste'. Firms which were BS5750 users were asked if they had measured the resulting effect of implementing the standard and, if so, in what areas they had identified advantages or disadvantages (Table 5).

Just over half the respondents (55%) stated that they had measured the effects of introducing BS5750. The two areas of benefit identified most frequently were 'reduced scrap and downtime' (33%) and 'increased and wider sales' (30%). In addition almost one quarter (24%) identified 'other' benefits; whilst 15% reported 'increased profits'.

A smaller number of respondents recorded negative effects (n=110 compared with n=240 for the question relating to benefits of using BS5750). Adverse 'administrative' effects accounted for over half (53%) of the negative consequences with very much smaller numbers of disadvantages in the areas of productivity (13%), profitability (12%), and other (12%). Negative effects in the areas of production (8%) and sales (5%) were also identified.

Table 5: Impact of BS5750 Registration

		%
Q59: Did you measure the effects of introducing BS5750 ?	Yes	55.4
	No	44.6
(a) Q60: If 'Yes' and the effects were POSITIVE, in which areas:	Reduced scrap	33.3
	Increased/wider sales	30.0
	Other?	23.8
	Increased profit	15.0
(b) Q61: If 'Yes', and the effects were NEGATIVE, in which areas:	Administration	52.7
	Productivity	12.7
	Profitability	11.8
	Other?	12.0
	Production	8.2
	Sales	4.5

Other consequences of using BS5750

It has been previously identified that over 85% of all respondents expressed satisfaction with their existing quality systems, but that non-registered firms were managing quality in a more informal manner. This informality did not, however, appear to have any adverse impact on the market acceptance of their products/services. However, BS5750 users with more formal quality management systems reported that, as a consequence of registration, they are likely to have 'less customer complaints' (p=.00) and to 'retain business which otherwise would have been lost' (p=.02). In addition, there is a tendency for the smaller businesses to face an increased need for inspection and supervision of their products/services (p=.09).

These two interesting consequences of registration are probably indicative of the balance which most firms must achieve in deciding the appropriate level of formality to adopt. Whilst increased formality improves the 'defensive' marketing tactics for the smaller firms in the sample this is achieved at the expense of a higher cost burden.

BS5750 and risk management

It was thought that professionals might advise firms to adopt BS5750 to assist in the management of the risks associated with issues such as product liability or the need to operate documented work practices for health and safety or employers liability insurance. It is not known whether such advice was actually proffered, but very few respondents identified this as a reason for adopting the quality assurance standard. In total fewer than 3% of respondents agreed with statements indicating that they chose to implement BS5750 because 'my accountant or lawyer said that I should' or 'my insurance company said that I should'.

SURVEY RESULTS: BARRIERS TO THE USE OF BS5750 IN SMALL FIRMS

This section considers the position of firms which have decided not to register with the objective of identifying the barriers to registration which exist. Given that BS5750 appears to offer advantages at both the macro and micro level it is appropriate to ask why, at least as yet, such a small proportion of the total population of businesses in the UK has adopted the standard. There are approximately 28,000 registered firms compared with a UK population of businesses which certainly exceeds 3 million.

Profiles of firms not adopting BS5750

BS5750 is a formalized management system designed to ensure that firms produce their products, goods or services to a pre-determined and consistent level of quality. Like any other management process there are costs associated with maintaining and operating the system. These costs comprise both direct costs (for example consultants, fees and registration costs) and indirect costs (such as staff time in operating and managing the system).

From the analysis presented so far it may be concluded that the indirect costs are significantly greater than the direct costs. For smaller organizations, which tend to benefit from the flexibility and economies of the informal management structures, this cost burden appears to be disproportionately high. As a result small firms tend not to register for BS5750 (p=.00). As a consequence businesses with lower asset values, sole proprietorships and partnerships tend not to be BS5750 users. Also the fastest growing small businesses tend not to be BS5750 users, possibly because of the need to retain flexibility and because there is no apparent market pressure from customers. Evidence suggests that retailers tend not to register but there is a disproportionate number of manufacturers that are BS5750 users. These manufacturing firms are particularly keen to improve their quality management procedures (p=.01) and to satisfy the needs of one major customer (p=.00), to hold on to customers (p=.00) and to win new customers/markets (p=.00).

There is also strong evidence that the smaller firms in this sample agree or strongly agree that BS5750 'costs too much to implement' (p=.00), 'adds too much paperwork' (p=.00), 'adds too much time' (p=.00). Because of these cost barriers it appears that registration for BS5750 in its present form is not a realistic objective for the smaller firms who comprise the vast majority of the population of businesses in the UK economy.

Market structure as a barrier to using BS5750

It has been identified that small firms are more likely to cater for the needs of domestic customers, to sell to the local market (p=.00) and less likely to produce or sell a range of products (p=.00). It appears that these market characteristics influence the relationship of small firms and BS5750. As a result businesses which tend not to register for BS5750 are those with a smaller number of customers, firms who deal directly with domestic customers, have direct contact with their customers and trade 'locally'. Also firms selling to other smaller business customers are less likely to be BS5750 users (p=.00) and businesses who do not need to satisfy one major customer are less likely to be BS5750 users (p=.00).

As it was previously revealed, important marketing advantages accrue to firms that register for BS5750. However, huge proportions of the small business sector comprise retailers and firms dealing in local markets. At present BS5750 does not appeal to these important segments of the UK economy.

Management style as a barrier to using BS5750

Small businesses are predominantly owner controlled organizations with informal management systems and simple organizational structures. This contrasts with the more formal systems approach of BS5750. Non-users tend to be informally managed businesses (p=.00), small organizations with fewer levels of authority (p=.00) and, firms employing few formal management techniques (p=.05).

The systems approach to quality consistency of BS5750 presents a dilemma which requires business owners to reach careful decisions about the level of formality appropriate to their scale of operations. In its present form BS5750 conflicts with the informal management style adopted by the majority of firms in this sample. A consequence of such firms adopting the requisite level of formality is an increased cost base. For example, firms with informal management structures, low levels of delegation and few authority levels identify that BS5750 'costs too much' (p=.00), and adds 'too much paperwork and time' (p=.00). At present adopting BS5750 would raise the costs of such businesses.

Informal quality systems as a barrier to using BS5750

Given that the majority of respondents expressed satisfaction with their present quality systems and that the level of formality of such systems does not appear to affect the demand for their products or services, it is apparent that a wide range of quality management systems and standards have been flexibly adopted by smaller businesses. In these circumstances it appears that BS5750 represents an additional burden on the scarce management resources of smaller firms. As a result businesses that use their own quality standards tend not to be BS5750 users (p=.00). Similarly, those firms with fewer inspection points and non-specialist quality inspection staff tend not to use BS5750 (p=.00). Where business owners or staff supplying the goods/services are personally responsible for 'quality', firms tend to believe that registration for BS5750 would result in an unacceptable increase in their cost base. Businesses that disagree that BS5750 can help reduce scrap also tend not to use the standard (p=.00).

In addition, firms utilizing internal standards and customer specifications believe that BS5750 results in additional cost burdens (p=.00) and claim that 'better alternatives are available' (for example compliance with government regulations or trade and professional standards) (p=.00) and that BS5750 is 'not relevant to their business' (p=.00). However, those firms using customer specifications are more likely to be prepared to register in order to 'satisfy the needs of one major customer' (p=.04).

The consequences of adopting BS5750

Respondents using BS5750 were asked to score four potential handicaps of registration on a scale of 1 to 5, with one representing the most severe handicap. The potential disadvantages all related to operating efficiency and profitability (Table 6). Consistent with the observations in earlier sections of this chapter, the most highly ranked disadvantage was 'increased overhead cost' (42% of responses scored 1 or 2 out of 5). The remaining three items were each scored as 1 or 2 by 20–30% of respondents.

In addition the questionnaire asked if the implementation of BS5750 was a financial success. About half (51%) of the BS5750 users replied in the affirmative, 21% stated that it was not a financial success and 28% did not know.

Both BS5750 users and non-users were asked to score, on a scale 1 to 5, a range of commonly stated reasons for and against using BS5750. The three most important motives *for* registration were (in descending order) to improve quality, to win customers and to hold on to existing customers (Table 7).

Whereas the three most important reasons against adopting BS5750 were (in descending order) high cost, too much paperwork, too much time (Table 8).

This evidence suggests that the main reason why small businesses do not use BS5750 is because they perceive it would increase their costs in time and expenditure, without providing adequate financial reward. It may, therefore, be concluded that for BS5750 to become a practical tool for small businesses the administrative burden associated with the standard must be reduced.

Table 6: Handicaps of BS5750 Registration

	%
Increased overhead cost	42
Increased inspection/supervision	31
Reduction in flexibility	28
Increased labour cost	25

Table 7: Motives for BS5750 Registration

	Non-users %	Users %
Reduce scrap and/or waste	24	42
Improve quality procedures in the business	57	88
Satisfy the needs of one major customer	36	39
'Hold on' to existing customers	39	61
Win new customers and/or open new markets	49	84
Increase profit and/or efficiency	31	56
Follow the suggestion(s) of accountant and/or lawyer	3	2
Follow the suggestion of insurance company	3	2

Table 8: Reasons against BS5750 Registration

	Non-users %	Users %
Better alternatives available	26	9
High implementation cost	75	40
Adds too much paperwork	74	46
Time-consuming	66	34
BS5750 is a short-term wonder that will soon pass	31	16
Government regulations meet organizational needs	23	4
Trade and or Professional organization ensures quality	29	8
BS5750 is not relevant to my business	34	12

CONCLUSIONS

'BS5750 was designed by big business for big business and it has been a victim of its own success' (BSI, 1994). This quote is confirmed by the results of this large scale study which shows that the firms which adopt BS5750 tend to be:

- larger, multi-product firms in the manufacturing sector
- those who deal with customers which are larger than themselves or are government departments
- BS5750 users who employ their own sales force
- and have adopted a formal management structure.

In comparison firms which do not adopt BS5750 tend to be:

- smaller businesses
- dealing with domestic customers and selling in local markets
- over the counter or by mail order
- firms without a formal management structure, utilizing little (or no) delegation of authority
- and operating informal quality systems or utilizing a recognized trade standard.

Only a small minority of all firms in the UK have registered for this standard. However, a great majority of BS5750 users felt the advantages of using BS5750 outweigh the disadvantages. Based upon the preceding analysis it may be concluded that BS5750 provides a formal solution to the problems of quality management, and that BS5750 provides a 'badge of quality' (Batchelor, 1992) for purchasers who are either unable or unwilling to judge for themselves the quality consistency of their suppliers.

Small businesses, however, by their very nature tend to be owned and managed by individuals who have close personal involvement in every aspect of the business, including the process of manufacture and supply of their products/services. They, therefore, have an informal or 'hands-on' approach to management (Bolton, 1971). There is no evidence to suggest that such informal quality systems, based upon the personal involvement of business owners and employees with detailed knowledge of customer requirements, are in any way inferior to more formal systems.

In contrast, BS5750 approaches quality assurance though the installation of a rule based management system. The additional costs of operating such a system are modest for larger firms but can represent a significant additional burden for small businesses. In addition to this cost burden, the formality of the BS5750 systems approach to quality clashes with the culture of the informally and personally managed small firm.

In this sample, 10% of businesses were BS5750 users. Improving their quality procedures and winning new customers were expressed as the main reasons for using BS5750. Other reasons relating to internal efficiency and profitability and market advantages are important (such as holding on to existing customers and reducing scrap and waste). These conclusions are broadly consistent across all sizes of BS5750 user firms and most industry sectors.

However, manufacturing firms (who are the most likely to register) are more concerned about improving their internal quality procedures than firms in other sectors. Furthermore, the 10% of small firms who are BS5750 users derived significant benefits from adopting the standard. However, these benefits did not necessarily accord with the literature supporting BS5750. The most highly scored benefits relate to marketing and competitive issues rather than internal operational efficiency. In the present economic climate defensive reasons relating to the protection of the existing customer base were more highly ranked than pro-active business development advantages.

Thus it appears that for the minority of small firms who do use BS5750 the standard plays an important role in signalling information about a firm to the market place. This highlights a potentially important economic role for the quality standard – a role which may be of particular relevance in the small business sector. BS5750 can therefore contribute to the performance of businesses by improving operational efficiency and providing marketing and competitive advantages. It is, therefore, essential that the barriers to registration are minimized for all businesses providing goods and services to an adequate standard and consistency of quality. However, at this time BS5750 does not meet the needs of the majority of the small business community.

Failure to adapt to the needs of small businesses may lead to market distortion in the short-term (as some purchasers are erroneously persuaded that the BS5750 'badge' is the only reliable guide to quality). Eventually the entire system may fall into disrepute, as businesses learn that the information conveyed is not necessarily accurate. High quality goods, products and services may be obtained from unregistered firms. Furthermore, the evidence presented above suggests that important marketing advantages accrue to businesses registering for BS5750. However, a large proportion of the small business sector comprises retailers and firms dealing in local markets. At present BS5750 is inappropriate to the circumstances of these important elements of the UK economy.

POLICY RECOMMENDATIONS

Based on the above analysis, a number of policy recommendations are summarized below:

1. Businesses which are already achieving a high standard of quality through informal methods should not have to apply formal systems where these are not needed.
2. External evidence (eg from customers) should be acceptable as part of the BS5750 assessment and registration process.
3. The time and costs of operating BS5750 should be reduced especially for small firms.
4. It must be recognized that BS5750 is, at present, primarily seen as a marketing tool by many small businesses.
5. Adherence to other quality standards (such as trade standards and Government regulations) should be recognized as part of the BS5750 assessment and registration process.
6. No small supplier should be required to register for BS5750 if they are able to provide alternative evidence of the consistent quality of their products, goods or services.

ACKNOWLEDGEMENTS

This research was sponsored by the Small Business Research Trust (SBRT), with the support of the British Standards Institute, the Department of Trade and Industry, and National Westminster Bank. The views expressed are not necessarily those of the sponsoring organisations. The SBRT and the authors wish to thank the Forum of Private Business, the Federation of Small Businesses and the Rural Development Commission for providing access to their membership and for distributing the questionnaires.

NOTES

1. BS5750 was launched in 1987 following the adoption of the International Standard ISO9000. ISO9000 is largely based on BS5750 and has been titled EN29000 in European Union (DTI 1987)
2. A further 1700 completed questionnaires have subsequently been received, bringing the total response rate up to 18%.

REFERENCES

Bannock G (1991) BS5750: 'No Rush to Register', Small Business Perspectives, 15–16, January-February
Batchelor C (1992) 'Badge of Quality, Financial Times, 4 September.
Best M (1990) The New Competition, Polity, Oxford.
Bolton (1971) Report of the Committee of Enquiry on Small Firms, Cmnd 4811, HMSO, London.
BSI (1994) 'New Service to "Demystify" BS5750 for Small Businesses', British Standards Institute-Press Information, April.
Department of Trade and Industry (1987) BS 5750/ISO9000/EN 29000: A Positive Contribution to Better Business, The Enterprise Initiative, DTI/Pub 1180.
Gourlay R (1994a) Seeking Credibility for Quality Standards, Financial Times, 12 April.
Gourlay R (1994b) 'Quality under Fire', Financial Times, 21 June.
Halliday S (1992) ' Small Firms and BS5750', Journal of European Business Education, 2, 2, May.
North J, Curran J, and Blackburn R (1993) 'Small Firms and BS5750: A Preliminary Investigation', 16th National Small Firms Policy and Research Conference, Nottingham, November 1993.
North J, Blackburn R, and Curran J (1994) 'Maintaining Quality in Small Firms and the Role of BS5750', Small Business and BS5750 Workshop Kingston Business School, February 1994.
SEPSU (1994) UK Quality Management-Policy Options, Science and Engineering Policy Studies Unit , London.
Small Business Research Trust (1992) 'Quality Procedures: BS5750, NatWest Quarterly Survey of Small Business, 8, 3, 18–22, August.
Storey D (1994) Understanding the Small Business Sector, Routledge, London.
Woodcock C (1992) 'The Cost of Keeping up the Standard', The Guardian, 31 August.
Woodcock C (1994) 'Benefits of Quality Standard Doubted', The Guardian, 28 March.

12.

The Impact on Small Business Development of a Dedicated Intermediary Networking Resource Within TECs and Business Links

Suzan Gunn

INTRODUCTION

Are bankers, solicitors and accountants a good source of business referrals and raising awareness for TECs and emerging Business Links? Is it worth dedicating a manager and budget to develop relationships with them – and do their business customers do anything differently as a result? In 1992, Hertfordshire TEC employed a Network Manager to investigate and fully utilise this perceived communication channel. This chapter summarises what happened, with some ideas about how best to communicate with this group.

TECs are trying to communicate with a large and diverse market place – in Hertfordshire for example, the economy consists of over 30,000 businesses, 85% of whom employ fewer than 5 people. While larger companies are simple to target, owner/managers are harder to identify and different approaches are required to reach this audience. Such owner/managers already have obliged relationships with organisations such as banks, accountants and solicitors, and it therefore appears logical for the TEC to also build a relationship with these organisations, treating them as intermediaries.

This chapter analyses 133 business calls to the TEC where enquirers stated the source of referral as a bank, accountant or solicitor who was a targeted contact. It summarises three surveys examining the nature and effectiveness of the intermediary interventions, and outcomes of the intervention process in terms of perceived benefits to banks, accountants, solicitors and small businesses.

The Network Manager was largely responsible for creating awareness of Hertfordshire TEC in 90% of intermediaries. All refer customers, but bankers refer the most – 82% of all referrals were from banks, 6% and 5% respectively from accountants and solicitors. 55% of businesses referred were start-up. Opinions among intermediaries towards the TEC/Business Link differ widely between the banks and the accountants/solicitors. All intermediaries agreed the benefits customers gained, including access to information, time and advice given, and the ability to access services outside the field of the intermediary.

From the businesses' point of view, none in the survey was aware of TEC services before being told by an intermediary, but all were keen to contact the TEC/Business Link. All benefited in some way from the contact. Unexpected benefits include direct access to new customers, customer feedback, increased dialogue at regional and national level, sponsorship, and effective partnership activities. Hertfordshire TEC/Business Link is perceived by business users as very professional and the services offered are seen as useful and of a high quality.

TEC services are many and varied, and need promoting to a diverse target market. Owner/managers are harder to identify than their larger counterparts, and a separate communications strategy is required to effectively target this audience. Such businesses have obliged relationships with banks, accountants and solicitors and it therefore appears logical for the TEC to build links with them so that each becomes an intermediary. They are often a credible message source, in that advice from such an organisation is normally respected.

In 1992, Hertfordshire TEC decided to use face to face contact to communicate effectively with key business players, and a team of four Business Advisers was formed to manage relationships with larger firms. However, this did not solve the problem of how to raise awareness in the minds of smaller business owners – the majority group.

THE TASK OF THE NETWORK MANAGER

The Network Manager position was created to investigate and fully utilise this perceived communication channel, which was thought likely to be efficient and cost effective. Hertfordshire TEC was at the time unique in having resources dedicated to this task. The objectives of the role, occupied by the author, were to start, lead, and manage relationships with key county intermediaries to increase TEC awareness, and encourage them to refer small business customers to services offered by the TEC. Bankers, accountants and solicitors were picked as key contacts because they potentially offered the maximum impact, and best use of resources, as they have contact with most businesses. A period of intense activity followed during which the Network Manager made personal contact at head office, regional and local level within the banks, and targeted local firms of accountants and solicitors. Presentations, one to one meetings, and visits by the intermediaries to the TEC premises followed.

Intermediaries were also encouraged to observe and use the services. A number of special events were staged with particular relevance to an intermediary group. These included a Customer Care and Sales seminar for Barclays Business Bankers, and evening seminars on Legal Aid Franchising and The Law Society Practice Management Standards for solicitors.

By arranging joint presentations with these intermediaries to specially invited customers, the Network Manager has also contacted over 400 small businesses. A straw poll at each event consistently showed that over 80% of those attending did not know before the event what the TEC did.

The first business to be referred to the TEC services via an intermediary was in June 1993 and at the time of this research in June 1994 there were 133 in total, although not all referrals are recorded.

RESEARCH OBJECTIVES

This research has five main objectives:

1. To establish the nature of historical referrals to the Hertfordshire TEC.
2. To assess how the Network Manager has improved :
   a) intermediary awareness of the TEC,
   b) intermediary perception of the TEC,
   c) intermediary referrals to the TEC.
3. To understand better the perceived benefits to an intermediary from referring a customer/client to the TEC.
4. To identify if businesses have benefited as a result of being referred.
5. To identify policy implications and areas for improving the work of the Network Manager.

METHODOLOGY

Four surveys were conducted:

1. An analysis of historical referrals:
   Enquiry sheets containing the source of referral to the TEC are completed. Those showing the source of referral as an intermediary from the targeted list were collected over a 13 month period.
2. A survey of intermediaries:
   A randomly selected sample from the Network Managers list. This consisted of 23 intermediaries, including 10 banks, 8 accountants and 5 solicitors. Some referred regularly and were thought to be positive, others did not, and a third group had had no contact.
3. A telephone survey of businesses :
   A randomly selected sample of 13 of the 133 referrals which included 10 from a bank, two from a solicitor and one from an accountant.
4. A small survey of Midland Bank staff at Harlow branch:
   Questions were put to the bank's Business Counsellors before and after a presentation to them by the Network Manager.

Initially the Network Manager was a TEC resource dedicated to raising awareness of TEC services in small firms. During the period of the research, Hertfordshire TEC joined forces with other key business support organisations to form Business Link: a Business One Stop Shop. The Network Manager began to represent the Business Link and partners rather than simply the TEC, and it was necessary to mention both Business Link and TEC in many questions to establish which name the respondent associated with the services provided.

Throughout this report, Business Link and TEC always refer to the Hertfordshire Business Link and the Hertfordshire TEC respectively.

RESULTS: SURVEY 1: ANALYSIS OF HISTORICAL REFERRALS

There were 133 fully documented referrals of businesses which were initiated by an intermediary (Table 1). Of all referrals by an intermediary to the TEC, 82% were from a bank. Accountants and solicitors referred less frequently, with figures of 6% and 5% respectively.

Table 1: Referrals by Intermediary Type

	Actual referrals	% of total
Bank	109	82
Accountant	8	6
Solicitor	7	5
Other/unknown	9	7
Total	133	100

Table 2: Bank Referrals by Banking Organisation

	Actual referrals	% of total
Barclays	35	32
Lloyds	24	22
Midland	9	8
NatWest	30	28
Other/unknown	11	10
Total	109	100

Bank referrals by banking organisation

As banks contribute 82% of referrals, they have been segmented further to reveal activity for each bank. Table 2 shows that Barclays initiated 32% of referrals, NatWest 28% and Lloyds 22% while the Midland Bank referred 8%. The Royal Bank of Scotland and the TSB made a small number of referrals, which are included in the 'Other/unknown' classification.

Volume and spread of referrals

As would be expected, the work of the Network Manager appears to have built up momentum, resulting in an overall upward trend of referrals (Table 3).

This trend was broken in January 1994, which may simply be a reflection of seasonal factors. However, it is more likely to be down to the TEC move to Business Link. As a moving date, budgets and services were uncertain, the Network Manager did not make any presentations during January 1994. In February activity increased rapidly as the new centre and services required publicising. Large preview sessions for 300 intermediaries were held in early February, and referrals really started picking up (Table 3).

Table 3: Monthly Volume of Referrals by Intermediary Type

	Bank	Acct	Solicitor	Unknown	Total
Jun	1				1
Jul	8	1			9
Aug	3	1	1		5
Sep	8				8
Oct	8				8
Nov	7	2		2	11
Dec	7		1	2	10
Jan 94	2			2	4
Feb	11		1	1	13
Mar	10	2	1	1	14
Apr	14	1			15
May	14	1	2	1	18
Jun	16		1		17
Total	109	8	7	9	133

Trends in bank referrals

Table 4 shows that Barclays have been actively referring since the outset, with a steady increase. Referrals from Lloyds began in August 1993 but again show a regular increase, while the Midland Banks first referral occurred in November 1993. NatWest referrals have shown a large increase since March 1994 and they have been referring most since.

Barclays have one Regional office contact, and a strong relationship with the Intermediary Manager. TEC awareness is high, and moves with the staff as they change jobs within the county. The NatWest regional contact pointed out that the increase in their referrals occurred immediately after a series of presentations by the Network Manager to regional Small Business Advisers in March 1994.

Referrals by business age

Of the referrals to the TEC, 32 could not be classified according to the age of the business (Table 5). Over half of the referrals were start-ups and 45% established firms, most of which had been trading for over 18 months.

Start-up services were by far the most frequently requested, accounting for 57% of referrals (Table 6).

General information on business operations, marketing advice and expansion advice accounted for about a further 10% each. Finance advice was sought by 4% of referrals, and legal advice by 2%. Any other requests have been grouped together under the single heading 'Other'. These five referrals requested information on management buy-outs, exporting, relocation, patents and recruitment.

Table 4: The Monthly Volume of Referrals by Banks

	Barclays	Lloyds	Midland	Nat-West	Unknown	Total
Jun	1					1
Jul	2			4	2	8
Aug	1	1			1	3
Sep		1			3	8
Oct	2	3		1	2	8
Nov	3		2	1	1	7
Dec	2	2		3		7
Jan 94			1	1		2
Feb	4	4	2	1		11
Mar	3	2		5		10
Apr	3	5	1	4	1	14
May	4	3	2	4	1	14
Jun	6	3	1	6		16
Tot	35	24	9	30	11	109

Table 5: Total Referrals by the Age of the Business

	Number of referrals	% of total
Planning start-up	56	55
Less than 18 months old	7	7
More than 18 months old	38	38
Total	101	100

Table 6: Number of Referrals by the Service Required

	Number of referrals	% of total
Start-up	66	57
Expansion	15	13
General information	12	11
Marketing	10	9
Finance	5	4
Legal	2	2
Other	5	4
Total	115	100

Table 7: Referrals by Company Size

Number of employees	Number of referrals
1	59
2	12
3	7
4	7
5	3
6	2
7	1
8	3
9	2
10	2
11–49	2
50+	2
TOTAL	102

Business referrals who were actually trading when they contacted the TEC sought services on expansion, marketing or finance.

Referrals by company size

Of the 133 records, 102 could be classified according to the size of the company. Referrals at the planning start-up stage estimated the number of employees they expected to have once trading.

Table 7 shows the heavy weighting towards referrals by intermediaries of sole traders. Only 4 of the 102 referrals had 11 or more employees.

SURVEY 2: THE TELEPHONE SURVEY OF INTERMEDIARIES

The awareness and behaviour of intermediaries

If the respondent knew nothing of the TEC or Business Link, the interview was terminated, and information sent. These accounted for about 10% of those telephoned, and were generally people new to a position, or those who had not yet been contacted. The TEC or Business Link had therefore been heard of by about 90% of intermediaries contacted. Over 95% of those also knew the building was located in St. Albans, and what services the TEC/Business Link offered.

Within the banks, 70% had first heard of the TEC or Business Link at a presentation, normally by the Network Manager. This contrasts to the vast majority of accountants and solicitors who spontaneously mentioned *Pink Pages* (a Business Link newsletter) or just being aware of business issues within Hertfordshire. They had often had individual meetings with the Network Manager but appear to have forgotten them later. This method therefore seems to have less impact than presentations.

Accountants and solicitors are likely to become more heavily involved in the business environment and stay in the same position for many years, while bank staff are inclined to job rotate. They like to refer to named, established contacts in their networks. One intermediary in this group said he was 'waiting to see how long Sue Gunn stayed in post before referring'. Two years was not long enough.

Bankers who referred most admitted they had limited knowledge of business development issues, and were glad to have another organisation to call on – it was seen as adding value. Accountants and solicitors are more likely to consider that they know about most business issues, and occasionally saw the TEC/Business Link as a possible threat.

The level of referrals varied too. All bank staff surveyed had referred a customer at some point, but half of accountants and solicitors had never done so. This particular research will not uncover whether this fact is directly connected to the different communication methods mentioned in the previous paragraph. What was uncovered, however, was that throughout all intermediary types, there was a perception that a referral was more relevant if the business was small or at start-up stage. Some intermediaries did recognise that services were available for existing businesses, but a common line was that 'I don't refer because I don't deal with start-ups'. This is of further interest if the pre-visit views of business counsellors at the Midland Bank, Harlow are considered. Here too, when asked what the TEC does, the answer normally focused on start-ups.

This is understandable, as the original remit of the Network Manager was to increase awareness and take up of services among smaller businesses. Therefore these services were discussed more frequently, and individuals within intermediary organisations who were more likely to deal with this client group had been targeted.

The attitudes of intermediaries

When asked how professional the TEC/Business Link appeared, 90% of banks said very professional while accountants and solicitors were slightly less positive classifying it as quite professional. The new Business Link building, which many visited at one of three large intermediary preview sessions, was mentioned frequently. Bank staff were impressed while accountants and solicitors had various opinions. Some thought that the size and quality of the building implied that services would be very expensive, while others thought that it is the only way for Business Link to be taken seriously! They had expected a small part time office, but their perceptions were changed dramatically after a visit.

When asked how useful the TEC/Business Link was, banks viewed the services as being very useful while solicitors and accountants were evenly spread in their opinions from quite useful to slightly useful. This may be connected to their opinion that the TEC/Business Link is primarily aimed at those starting up in business. A bank is a normal starting point for this type of enquiry, hence the high level of referrals by them. The following are examples of responses to this question:

'It is a lot of use to the small guy' – Solicitor
'The start-up course is excellent' – Accountant
'I cannot be an expert on marketing, book-keeping etc. but I can direct customers to these experts through the TEC' – Banker

Because a low referral level does not necessarily mean that an intermediary holds a low opinion of the TEC/Business Link, the question was asked, How keen are you to refer customers to the Hertfordshire Business Link? The banks replied with a unanimous very keen while solicitors and accountants were far less committed in their responses ranging from very keen to I'll reserve my judgement until I know some more. It appears that solicitors and accountants are less clear on how the TEC will help their clients, and therefore how much benefit a referral will bring to themselves.

The intermediary was then asked how they saw their company benefiting from directing businesses to Business Link. Accountants liked being able to help improve the performance of their clients, and to refer businesses which were not yet likely to earn them any fees. They believed these businesses could come back stronger, more profitable, and better able to use an accountant efficiently. It saved them wasting time on unprofitable work, but left the door open for future business.

They saw little possibility of any large financial gain. Responses from accountants included 'I help from one angle, the Business Link helps from another'. Another said, 'The Business Link enhances the number of services that we can be associated with'. This was particularly useful in the very small firms.

Solicitors shared similar views with accountants with little mention of financial gain to themselves: 'I would hope for the performance of my clients to improve and to produce a more prosperous business community'. Another said, 'I see the TEC as another tool in my toolbox – a client might be pleased to be directed there'.

The banks expressed a somewhat different view of the benefits they gained. Image was an issue, as was the fact that a customer's performance had a direct impact on the performance of the bank. Indeed, this impact is far more noticeable than it would be to an accountant or a solicitor. The banks spontaneously responded more enthusiastically to this question than did accountants or solicitors. The following quotes are a representative cross section of responses.

Bank responses:

'It makes us look better – an all round package can be offered.'
'The business plan is vetted by the Business Link which helps us. We can send the dodgy cases to them and they help the customer see where they are going wrong.'
'The customer sees referral as being positive assistance.'
'If we can get better quality businesses banking with us, then our job is easier.'

Respondents were then asked how they benefited personally. Most said there was no personal benefit, but it felt good to tell customers about complimentary services that were available. Bank staff are encouraged/instructed to keep up contact with TECs and some privately told the Network Manager they get brownie points from demonstrating regular TEC contact and knowledge.

When asked how the intermediary sees the customer benefiting from the Hertfordshire Business Link, all intermediary types shared similar views:

a) the customer receives more information
b) the customer receives good, often free, advice
c) the customer receives services which that intermediary could not offer.

Many praised the start-up course and the resultant excellent business plans. Other intermediaries said marketing was an area where a business could benefit by speaking to the Business Link.

The question of drawbacks existing from directing businesses to the Business Link normally resulted in the answer 'None'. A small number wondered if they might lose a customer or client but expected the advice to be impartial.

The survey also investigated whether the customer had given feedback on what happened at the TEC/Business Link. The following quotes are from those who answered yes:

'They came back fully equipped and understood their own business plans!'
'Several customers have been through the start-up course and said it was excellent.'
'Many customers return and recount their experiences. I decide whether to keep referring based on what they tell me.'

Finally the intermediary was asked how they thought the TEC/Business Link could improve its services. The response tended to be related to the individuals specific needs and understanding, but suggestions concentrated on improving communication.

Some would prefer more written information on services available, others general information about the TEC/Link in bullet points. Posters and display stands for customers were popular.

A specifically targeted newssheet from the Network Manager would be useful, and postcards for re-ordering stationery or adding names to the TEC database were suggested. Others were concerned about customers travelling to the Business Link Centre in St. Albans for advice. It would appear that there is a lot of support for the planned branch or satellite network of offices across Hertfordshire.

SURVEY 3: THE TELEPHONE SURVEY OF BUSINESSES REFERRED TO TEC BY INTERMEDIARIES

The awareness and behaviour of referred businesses

Over 80% of businesses referred had a long standing relationship with a bank, accountant or solicitor while the 20% remaining did not normally bank at the branch which referred them (start up businesses had often had a personal account previously). One referral was initiated because Business Link was mentioned in a Barclays Bank publication.

When asked if they knew what the TEC or Business Link did before being referred, none had any idea of the services provided. A small number had heard of the TEC or Business Link but didnt know what it was. One respondent had been sent leaflets 'but never had time to read them' while two had seen the building: one of these 'thought it was a telecommunications company which linked businesses!'

The respondent was then asked how keen they were to contact the TEC or Business Link. All responses were positive with most people being very keen to make contact while some were quite keen. This reflected the reason for making contact. One respondent whose business was having problems said, 'As soon as I returned to the shop (from the bank) I phoned the TEC. It frightened me what the future had in store and once I had spoken to them I was even more frightened. But things have got better.'

At the other extreme the response was 'We didn't fall over ourselves but we phoned within a week'. Considering this was the most negative comment, there is hardly cause for concern! A common stance was that 'We wanted all the help we could get'.

When asked whether they would have contacted the TEC or Business Link had it not been for the intermediary only a couple said that they might have done. Most customers questioned how they would ever have heard of the TEC. They were impressed with the enthusiasm and genuine belief in the help available from the TEC expressed by the intermediary. They were not told about all of the services, and did not need to be, but had heard enough about similar businesses who had been helped, for them to make contact. The strongest referrals came from intermediaries who knew the Network Manager well, and who had themselves been to the building and/or tried the services.

The attitudes of businesses referred by intermediaries

Those surveyed were asked what their perception was of the TEC or Business Link in terms of how professional it is? Respondents who had only recently visited the TEC or Business Link, were asked to give views before and after visiting. In all cases the organisation was perceived as being highly professional before contact was made, with some stating that the enthusiasm for the TEC/Business Link by banks had probably helped form that opinion. In no instance did their perception fade, and in some cases it increased slightly. A selection of spontaneous quotes from respondents follows:

'A well run course and impressive building.'
'Their approach and attitude was very professional.'
'I was amazed at the size of the building. I expected a small set up.'

The overwhelming view was that the services provided were very useful, and the few who saw drawbacks still classified the services as being quite useful. The only drawback mentioned was the time between courses on the start-up programme – a maximum of two weeks. Business Advisers were seen to be particularly useful as the following selection of quotes below highlights:

'The adviser opened my eyes. It has been a long and slow process to recover but things are better'
'The adviser has been very, very good but it has taken a year to act on all the advice she gave. I now feel ready to see her again.'
'The adviser was a nice man who obviously had years of experience. He knew things that I would never have thought of and made good suggestions which I have acted upon.'
'It was nice to be able to contact somewhere when I was uncertain. Where else could I have turned to?'

When asked if they were still in contact with the TEC or Business Link there was a mixed response. Some were currently on courses, others gave responses such as, 'I keep meaning to give them a ring'. Others were not sure how to contact the organisation again: 'I am not sure who to contact, the TEC or Business Link'.

All of those surveyed clearly said that the services provided had benefited their business, whether it be at the start-up stage or at times of survival. There was never a problem in recalling the benefits that had been achieved with most respondents enthusiastically recounting short stories about their particular case. The following quotes provide a clear picture of the variety of benefits:

'It helped prevent me from making financial mistakes.'
'I have adjusted my operations and things have improved.'
'The main benefit is the business plan. It would not have been so thorough if it were not for the Business Link.'
'I realised I needed to be good at many trades but it was my marketing which needed the most improving. But all operations have benefited a bit as well.'
'They helped me develop my idea and advised on my business plan.'

When asked how they saw the intermediary benefiting from referring them to the TEC or Business Link, it was surprising how few saw any benefits until they were prompted. Most appeared to see the referral as part of the normal service provided by the intermediary. This is a useful message for the banks as those who knew about TECS were getting more accounts.

If prompted, image, account retention and charges/fees were mentioned. The following is a selection of responses given:

'They benefit by saving my business and keeping my account there. If things do get better then they won't need to pick up the pieces.'
'If we manage to stay in business for longer then he will retain a client.'
'Probably through improving their image and then through bank charges once the business is formed.'

Finally the respondent was asked 'How they thought the TEC/Business Link could improve its services?' One response was that 'I can't really fault it', and most respondents were most impressed by the service received. Most suggestions involved communications.

There was a strong feeling that the services of the TEC would never have been discovered if the particular intermediary had not mentioned them. Respondents said the services were so useful that all intermediaries should be aware. A typical statement was 'How would I have heard of the TEC/Business Link if it were not for the . . . . bank?'

Those who received communications questioned the format used. A common view is summed up in this quote : 'Information must be short and concise – I rarely have time to read it.'

SURVEY 4: A TELEPHONE SURVEY OF MIDLAND BANK STAFF, HARLOW

A practical survey was carried out on a bank which the Network Manager had not previously been in touch with, to test the research results. The Network Manager and a Business Adviser were due to give a presentation at that bank to introduce the role of the TEC and how it could help their business customers. A survey was conducted on the business counsellors at the branch before and after the presentation. This allowed changes in both behaviour and attitudes to be measured.

Harlow is situated on the Hertfordshire/Essex border, some 20 miles from St. Albans. As Hertfordshire TEC deals only with businesses in the county, this could affect the attitude of businesses and intermediaries in the referral process. Appendix 1 shows the responses to all questions before and after the visit.

Before the presentation, the TEC was seen as providing services for businesses at the start-up stage only but afterwards they recognised that advice and training related to both new and existing businesses. The TEC and Business Link were completely unknown beforehand. During the presentation Business Link was referred to as a 'gateway' to other services and this image stuck with the audience as they mentioned it in the post-visit survey. They were impressed by the size of the organisation which gave them confidence. After the presentation they knew how to refer customers and felt that customers would react positively to being referred.

When asked how they perceived the TEC, there were few opinions before the presentation. Afterwards their perceptions gave the TEC a high profile and considered it as highly professional. This perception of the TEC appears primarily based on the audience's opinion of those giving the presentation, highlighting the importance of face-to-face communication.

Expectations of the usefulness of TEC services were high and remained so after the presentation. Benefits were seen to be in improving both the bank's image and the bank's performance, with no drawbacks. The staff were not keen to refer a customer before the presentation, primarily due to a lack of knowledge. Once they understood the services on offer they were unanimously very keen to refer.

Communication improvements were suggested as being necessary to improve the work of the TEC. Before the presentation the view was that awareness needed improving. After, it was suggested that maintained communication be a priority.

CONCLUSIONS

The benefits of a dedicated Network Manager include:

1. Raised awareness of TEC/Business Link within parts of the business community which would not otherwise have been reached, leading to an increase in referrals.

2. Awareness of the Hertfordshire TEC exists at 90% of intermediaries. Assessing how much of this is attributable to the work of the Network Manager is difficult to measure accurately, but according to key contacts, it was because of this role that they first heard of the TEC. Also, if they made contact by chance, they were quickly referred within the TEC to the right person who knew how to deal with them. Both Regional contacts at NatWest and Lloyds say that they contact Herts TEC most as a direct result of this role. They have had difficulty forming such a close relationship in other TEC areas, although they cover them.

3. Close relationships at Regional level within the banking organisations, facilitating feedback, immediate response and support for particular initiatives both ways. It also allowed them to receive customer views, and improve their own services. In Hertfordshire, for example, a discussion at senior level in NatWest bank was arranged as a result of information from advisers about how Loan Guarantee Scheme applicants were dealt with. Finally, the close relationship gave the TEC access to input at policy level within the banks and audiences with national networks. The TEC Chief Executive was asked to present at Lloyds National conference because of the good local relationships.

4. Sponsorship for events, seminars, and other TEC activities. Around £40,000 over 18 months, from six banks, two accountants, and a solicitor.

5. Focused marketing. The building of a separate, and accurate database of all intermediaries facilitates perfectly targeted mailshots, and achieves an excellent response.

6. Feedback on TEC services. Bankers particularly, were very helpful in identifying gaps in provision, for example, seminars on applying for an LGS loan for businesses wishing to raise finance.

The number of referrals made to the TEC have shown a steady increase over the 13 months, particularly from the banks. As 70% of these first heard of the TEC through the work of the Network Manager, this work has quite clearly had a direct effect on the number of referrals.

Perception of the TEC is formed primarily through how professional and useful it appears. As staff were largely unaware of the TEC before being contacted by the Network Manager, their perception is first formed through the face-to-face contact, with a professional and enthusiastic manner being cited as key reasons for trusting the services. This has left a very positive image in their minds, an image reinforced in subsequent visits to the Business Link. The banks also find the TECs start-up programme of tremendous importance, both for vetting potential businesses and developing business plans. Banks consequently view the TEC services as being of great use.

The impact of the work of the Network Manager on small business development is shown in that none of those referred knew what the TEC/Business Link did before being informed by the intermediary. The majority were very keen to contact the TEC, and most doubted whether they would have ever heard of the TEC if it were not for that intermediary. All had benefited in some way and to some extent from the TEC services.

POLICY IMPLICATIONS

A key point to emerge from this research on developing business support services is that active intervention is required. Business Links must take the initiative and make personal contact with intermediaries to encourage them to refer customers on to them. Without that input, very little will happen. Moreover they need to appreciate that Business Links help established firms, not just start -ups. The intermediaries need to clearly see what is in it for them.

Both intermediaries and businesses shared the view that communication should take place in two ways:

First, face to face presentations by a lively and professional representative to explain the role of Business Link. There is still a lack of awareness, and the idea of a gateway to information and services is useful. The size of the organisation, a clear overview of all services, and a snapshot of those most relevant to the intermediary group need to be presented clearly. How to access services is essential, and a one stop phone number or pass-on leaflet are favoured methods.

A Network Manager primarily performs a public relations role. This achieves certain objectives (ie awareness and perception), but has a limited life cycle and cannot deliver all the information regularly required by intermediaries. Between presentations, a different form of communication is required that meets the complex demands of different groups of individuals within different intermediary types, including, for example, newsletters, precisely targeted.

Second, presentations are needed at roughly six monthly intervals to encourage referrals and notify staff of any changes. Within the banks it is necessary to communicate at regional, head office and local levels, providing a consistent, reliable service, and ensuring information reaches all parts of the organisations. It is important to emphasise the most important, relevant and appropriate services to meet the intermediaries' needs. Trust is a very big issue with this group; nothing must go wrong in the referral process, or intermediaries stop referring. Encouraging them to actually use the services or observe them is extremely effective at building trust and confidence.

Where premises are impressive and partners can be seen to be working together, a visit by the intermediary to the Business Link office is recommended. This works particularly well with people from the same practice or bank, as competition is not welcome. Proper resources must be allocated to these activities.

Finally a good referral tracking system is essential to identify what works well, and provide essential marketing information.

APPENDIX A: Midland Bank (Harlow) survey responses

Responses before presentation	Responses after presentation
What is the TEC and what does it do?	
· "It is the Training and Enterprise Council and it runs courses on setting up a new business"	· as left, plus "it is one department within the Business Link and offers advice, counselling and courses to new and existing businesses"
· "It provides training to those setting up in business"	· "It runs seminars, training and courses, both free and with a fee, to new and existing businesses of all types and sizes"
· "I thought it was a technical college until recently. It helps small businesses start-up and offers advice"	· <not available>
· "I knew the name but did not know what it did. I normally tell people just about the Harlow Enterprise Agency"	· "It provides advice, training and workshops, i.e. on VAT and accountancy, to new and existing businesses"
What is the Business Link and what does it do?	
· "I don't know"	· "It is the link between different organisations - a Gateway"
· "I don't know"	· "It promotes the services of a number of organisations"
· "I'm confused as to what it is and does"	· <not available>
· "Again, I had heard of it but I was not sure what it did"	· "It's a Gateway to different services"
Where is the TEC/Business Link?	
· "I don't know"	· "St. Albans"
· "I'm not sure"	· "St. Albans, Telephone 813813 !"
· "I don't know"	· <not available>
· "I don't know"	· "St. Albans"
How many customers do you direct to the TEC?	
· "None"	· "None"
· "None"	· "None"
· "None"	· <not available>
· "None"	· "None"
How do you instruct them to contact the TEC?	
· n/a	· "I would give them the phone number or a leaflet"
· n/a	· "Either with the telephone number or the leaflet"
· n/a	· <not available>
· n/a	· "With the phone number or the leaflet"
What do you expect their response would be to this suggestion?	
· n/a	· "I'm sure most would find it useful - I wouldn't expect to get sceptical responses"

· n/a	· "A very positive response"
· n/a	· < not available >
·	· "I think there would be a good response - I'm sure they'd be grateful"

What are your attitudes towards the TEC?	
· "I'm interested to know more and keen to ask questions"	· "There is a larger support system than I expected. It is better organised with more experts in individual fields"
· "I don't really have one"	· "My attitude has changed fundamentally! I am far more aware of what's available and see it as being of much higher profile"
· "I have no opinion"	· < not available >
· "I'm not really sure at the moment"	· "I'm very aware of what is on offer and see it as being very professional"

How useful do you think the TEC services are?	
· "They can only be useful"	· "It is very useful because of the 'limited' knowledge of bank staff. And it's unbiased"
· "It probably is useful but I'm not sure"	· "I see it as being very useful particularly as we are coming out of recession"
· "I think they would be useful"	· < not available >
· "I expect it to be useful"	· "The experts in different areas make it very useful"

What is your opinion on the quality of the services?	
· "I have no opinion - I can't say"	· "Very comprehensive"
· "Again I'm not sure"	· "It was a very professional presentation by Sue and Graham and I expect the same quality from the courses run"
· "I think very good, but I don't know"	· < not available >
· "I wouldn't like to say"	· "Good. Very professional"

How do you see your bank benefiting from directing businesses to the TEC?	
· "The bank has a better profile with the customers because it has a better understanding of what business needs are"	· as left, plus "It will filter out the dodgy businesses"
· "We would benefit from the success of a business, and I'm sure the customer would be impressed with us"	· "By positively helping customers become more successful"
	· < not available >
	· "The customer would return to Midland"

What drawbacks do you see from directing businesses to the TEC?	
· "None"	· "None"
· "None"	· "None"
· "The customer might look at other financial institutions"	· < not available >
· "None"	· "None"

How keen are you to direct businesses to the TEC?	
· "I could not direct a customer with confidence"	· "Very keen. The bank and the customer can only benefit from the TEC"
· "I would be keen because I think new businesses are very short of advice and training."	· "Very keen"
· "I'm not very keen because I don't know the location! I would not direct a customer to something I know nothing about."	· < not available >
· "I think I would be keen"	· "Very keen"

How could the work of the TEC be improved?	
· "By maintaining contact, having much greater awareness, giving us information and arranging a visit. It is much easier to talk about something when you have a mental picture of it."	· "As left, plus "a quarterly newsletter might help keep us informed. And I would like to visit the building."
· "The awareness of what is on offer is so low at present. Better communication is needed."	· "In communication. I knew the name but not the services it offered"
· "The TEC needs to communicate more and create greater awareness. A visit would help form a mental picture"	· < not available >
· "By telling us more about what it does"	· "By having one in Essex"

How do you see your relationship with the TEC developing in the future?	
· "A partnership. A permanent link between the three parties, passing queries backwards and forwards."	· "A strong and well maintained link"
· "Strengthening both partners because mutual benefits exist to both"	· "I see it strengthening considerably as we utilise the TECs services"
· "We must work closer to solve customer problems and improve business performance"	· < not available >
· "I would like the TEC to be the first people we recommend"	

INDEX